Three Faiths – One God

Three Faiths – One God

A Jewish, Christian, Muslim Encounter

Edited by
John Hick
Danforth Professor of the Philosophy of Religion
The Claremont Graduate School, California
and
Edmund S. Meltzer
Associate Professor and Associate Chairman
Department of Religion, The Claremont Graduate School
California

Foreword by John David Maguire
President, Claremont University Center
and Graduate School

STATE UNIVERSITY OF
NEW YORK PRESS

First published
in U.S.A. by
State University of New York Press
Albany

For information, address State University of New York Press,
State University Plaza, Albany, N.Y. 12246

Printed in the People's Republic of China

Library of Congress Cataloging-in-Publication Data
Three faiths—One God.
Includes index.
1. Judaism—Doctrines. 2. Theology, Doctrinal.
3. Islam—Doctrines. I. Hick, John. II. Meltzer,
Edmund S.
BM601.T48 1989   291.2   88–38014
ISBN 0–7914–0042–5 (hardcover)
ISBN 0–7914–0043–3 (paperback)

This book is Dedicated
to
Those of All Faiths
Who Have Pioneered
In the Struggle
for
Interfaith Understanding

'It is not your obligation to complete the task,
But you are not at liberty to desist from it.'
Mishna, *Avot* 2:16

Contents

Acknowledgements

The editors wish to express their gratitude and appreciation to the many organisations, institutions and individuals who have helped to make the Trialogue a reality, both as an event and as a book:

To The Claremont Graduate School, Claremont McKenna College, Pitzer College, Pomona College, the Pomona Valley Council of Churches, and the School of Theology at Claremont, for their generous sponsorship of the Trialogue;

To Harold Hewitt, Jr, and Joseph Lynch, for their invaluable assistance with organisation and logistics;

To *Horizons in Biblical Theology* for permission to reproduce an excerpt from 'The Task of Old Testament Theology', pp 52–3 n.1 *HBT* 6.1, June 1984;

To Frances Drake, Rebecca B. Prichard, Jackie Melvin, Linda J. 'Tess' Tessier, Maura O'Neill and Ellen Sun for the demanding tasks of typing, proofreading and editorial assistance;

To our editors at the Macmillan Press, Tim Farmiloe and Pauline Snelson, and editorial services consultants Barbara Docherty and Keith Povey, for their patience and help;

And to all of our fellow-participants in the Trialogue, who helped to make it a truly memorable interfaith encounter. A complete list of participants (including those who chaired sessions) follows overleaf:

Jewish	*Christian*	*Muslim*
Rabbi Ben Beliak	Msgr William Barry	Professor Jamal
Rabbi Elliot Dorff	Professor John B.	Badawi
Rabbi David	Cobb, Jr	Dr Ibrahim Hamdani
Ellenson	Professor Stephen	Mrs Susan Imady
Professor Amos	Davis	Professor Irfan Khan
Funkenstein	Professor Jane	Dr Abdul Mummin
Rabbi Laura Geller	Douglass	Professor Ismail
Ms Susannah	Professor Carl Ernst	Poonawala
Heschel	Professor John Hick	Professor Nazif
Rabbi Patricia Karlin	Professor John	Shahrani
Professor Fred	Hutchison	Dr Muzammil H.
Krinsky	Professor Rolf	Siddiqi
Professor Edmund S.	Knierim	
Meltzer	Father M. Francis	
Rabbi Chaim Siedler-	Meskill	
Feller	Professor John Roth	
	Professor James A.	
	Sanders	
	Mrs Heidi Singh	
	Professor Jack	
	Verheyden	

Notes on the Contributors

Jamāl A. Badawi is Professor of Management at St Mary's University in Halifax, Canada. He is the author of several articles on Islam and has lectured in many countries. His successful series 'Islam in Focus' has been distributed to thirty-five countries in video form as well as being broadcast on various television networks.

Ben Beliak is Chaplain at the Claremont Colleges in Claremont, California. He studied at Occidental College and Hebrew Union College – Jewish Institute of Religion, Cincinnati, where he received his rabbinical ordination.

John B. Cobb, Jr is Ingraham Professor of Theology and Avery Professor of Religion at The Claremont Graduate School, California. His books include *Christ in a Pluralistic Age* and *Beyond Dialogue.*

Elliot N. Dorff is Provost and Professor of Philosophy at the University of Judaism in Los Angeles. He has written three books and numerous articles on issues in Jewish law and ideology. A Conservative rabbi, he is a member of the Conservative Movement's Committee on Jewish Law and Standards and its Commission on Conservative Ideology.

David Ellenson received rabbinical ordination at the Hebrew Union College–Jewish Institute of Religion, Los Angeles in 1977, where he is Associate Professor of Jewish Religious Thought. He is the author of over thirty articles and a forthcoming book, *Continuity and Innovation: Rabbi Esriel Hildesheimer and the Creation of a Modern Jewish Orthodoxy.*

Carl W. Ernst is Associate Professor in Religion at Pomona College. He is the author of *Words of Ecstacy in Sufism* and is a specialist in Islamic Studies, particularly classical Islamic mysticism and Indo-–Muslim culture.

Ibrahim Hamdani has been Imam at the Islamic Center of Sacramento since 1975. After being brought up in a religious Syed family in Pakistan, he graduated in Islamic Studies from Panjab University and later took a Master's Degree in Education. He has studied Qur'an, Hadith and Islamic literature with a number of religious teachers.

Susannah Heschel is a doctoral candidate in the Department of Religious Studies, University of Pennsylvania, concentrating in the area of modern Jewish thought. Her dissertation is a study of perceptions of Christianity in German–Jewish thought in the early twentieth century. She is the author and editor of *On being a Jewish Feminist: a Reader*, and has written and lectured extensively on women and religion.

John Hick is the Danforth Professor of the Philosophy of Religion, Director of the Blaisdell Programs in World Religions and Cultures and Chair of the Department of Religion at The Claremont Graduate School, California. He has previously taught at Cornell University, Princeton Theological Seminary and the Unversities of Cambridge and Birmingham. He is the author of numerous books including *An Interpretation of Religion*.

John A. Hutchison is Professor emeritus of Philosophy and Religion at The Claremont Graduate School, California.

Patricia S. Karlin-Neumann was ordained as a Rabbi at Hebrew Union College–Jewish Institute of Religion, New York in 1982. She is a Hillel Rabbi at the University of California, Los Angeles, and she is interested in religious pluralism, Jewish feminism and the relationship between text and experience.

Rolf P. Knierim is Professor of the Old Testament and Professor of Religion at The Claremont Graduate School, California.

Edmund S. Meltzer is Associate Professor and Associate Chairman in the Department of Religion at The Claremont Graduate School, California. He teaches a course in ancient Near Eastern religions and the anthropology of religion and is the author and editor of numerous publications dealing with ancient Egypt and the Near East.

Father M. Francis Meskill was Roman Catholic Chaplain of the Claremont Colleges from 1971 through 1986 and is now Pastor of St Basil's Roman Catholic Church in Los Angeles. He earned his PhD in English and Education at The Claremont Graduate School.

Ismail K. Poonawala is Professor of Arabic and Chairman of Islamic studies at the University of California, Los Angeles. He has lived and travelled extensively in the Near East and has written several articles on various Islamic subjects. His recent book, *The Formation of the State: From Hunayn Expedition to the Prophet's Death*, is a translation of the last three years of the Prophet's life by al-Tabari.

James A. Sanders is Professor of Inter-testamental and Biblical Studies and Professor of Religion at The Claremont Graduate School, California. He is largely responsible for the founding of the Ancient Biblical Manuscript Centre in Claremont of which he is president. He has also served as president of the Society of Biblical Literature and currently serves on the editorial boards of several journals.

Chaim Seidler-Feller is Director of the Hillel Council at the University of California, Los Angeles. He has particular interests in the Jewish spiritual tradition and in contemporary manifestations of messianism and religious extremism.

Muzammil H. Siddiqi is Imam and Director of the Islamic Society of Orange County in California and Professor of Islamic Studies at California State University in Fullerton and Long Beach. Previously, he served as the Director of the Islamic Center of Washington, DC and was Chairman of the Muslim World League Office for North America and United Nations. He has taught courses on Islam and Comparative Religion at various universities in the USA and overseas.

Heidi Singh is Lecturer on Comparative Religion at the College of Buddhist Studies in Los Angeles. Formerly, she was a Roman Catholic laywoman and a member of Los Angeles Archdiocesan Commissions on Ecumenical and Interreligious Affairs and was a consultant on Eastern Religions. She was also the Los Angeles Director of the Youth Institute for Peace in the Middle East. Since 1982, she has been a consultant on World Religions at the annual Conference/Workshop of the Multi-Faith Resources Unit, Birmingham University.

Jack Verheyden is Professor of Theology and Professor of Religion at The Claremont Graduate School, California. He served as Chairman of the Department of Religion of The Claremont Graduate School from 1973 to 1985. He is editor of Schleiermacher's *Life of Jesus*.

Foreword

Southern California's Greater Los Angeles area includes the third largest Jewish community in the world, a large and growing Muslim population, and every variety of Christian church. It is as if every tradition had responded to the admonition to 'be fruitful and multiply!' It is thus an area in which serious conversations between people of these three great faiths can have impact locally as well as adding another small contribution to the network of worldwide interfaith discussion. It was with this understanding that the Program in Religion of the Claremont Graduate School near Los Angeles organised a Jewish–Christian–Muslim 'trialogue' in March 1985. It was attended by some forty-five scholars from these three traditions. Here all the many-sided differences of cultural background, intellectual presupposition and political viewpoint came to the surface in tension with a profound sense of common responsibility to the one God, creator of heaven and earth, who is worshipped by all three peoples of the book. These human differences, and this common awareness of the divine mandate to seek peace and justice on earth, are expressed in the papers and discussions which are here published. They seek to be a contribution to the gradual and difficult growth of Jewish–Christian–Muslim understanding in a world which cannot afford the misunderstandings and enmities of the past.

JOHN DAVID MAGUIRE
President
Claremont University Center
and Graduate School

Introduction
Edmund S. Meltzer

Though the Claremont Jewish–Christian–Muslim Trialogue owes much to all of the participants, sponsors, institutions, support personnel and others thanked in the acknowledgements, it is first and foremost the achievement of Professor John Hick, and an expression of the commitment to interreligious understanding which is one of the strongest features of his life and work. The present writer is especially grateful to Professor Hick both for the opportunity to participate in the Trialogue and for the opportunity to be closely involved in the preparation of the book.

The 1984 Trialogue, the most recent of a series of such events spearheaded by Professor Hick, is also part of the world-wide and growing network of interfaith dialogue, a dialogue which is by no means limited to the three faiths included in the present volume. A few words on the history and diversity of this dialogue are perhaps in order.

Many Christian churches and organisations have initiated dialogues and follow with other Christian denominations as well as other religions. This process was greatly accelerated by Vatican II and the increased climate of openness it fostered in interfaith and interdenominational relations, while Vatican II itself was a product of a growing climate of pluralism. This paved the way for many spinoff dialogues on the local level.

The Jewish initiative in interfaith dialogue has been somewhat different, but no less marked. The predominant thrust of Jewish concern with interfaith understanding has not been in the area of abstract theological discussion but in counteracting the dynamics of antisemitism and other prejudices. Organisations such as the Anti-Defamation League have thus emphasised social and community cooperation as a means of overcoming prejudice, and have pioneered publication, speaking and community programs to overcome stereotyping by education. Major Jewish initiatives in interfaith dialogue have sometimes been responses to antisemitism. The secondary nature of the concern with abstract dogma has something to do with

1

the Jewish conviction that 'the righteous of all nations have a share in the world to come', it not mattering as much that other faiths have different theologies; but Jewish thinkers have realised that theology is the source of much prejudice, and their role in that aspect of dialogue has expanded.

While Muslims have not had as long or as extensive an involvement in this dialogue process as Jews and Christians have – largely because of the sociology of the European/North American societies which are the main *loci* of Jewish/Christian dialogue – they have been involved in dialogue with Hindus in India, and have engaged in a vigorous campaign to increase the knowledge of Islam and overcome the negative portrayal it has had in many Western cultures. The Islamic concept of the People of the Book has provided a framework in which Muslims can enter the interfaith dialogue process. The Roman Catholic Church since Vatican II, and other Christian groups, have entered into dialogue with Muslims.

The ideals and goals of the present Trialogue are beautifully expressed in the welcoming remarks delivered by Dr Maher M. Hathout, Chairman of the Islamic Center of Southern California, at the opening dinner of the gathering:

> It has always been inspiring and a cause of happiness and satisfaction to attend such meetings where the representatives of the three major religions can get together for discussion and dialogue.
>
> I am glad that these positive feelings have been expressed with enthusiasm and optimism. However, I find myself obligated to invite the attention towards three pitfalls, represented in three attitudes that I noticed commonly in such trials and that in my judgment were always counterproductive.
>
> The first attitude I call the combative attitude: Everyone is jumping into the arena to knock down the others, to prove that he and what he stands for is right while others are wrong and need to be shown the light. It is needless to say that by adopting a faith, a person sees and is convinced that this is the right path; what he should also see is that others see things in their own way, and if he chooses this particular arena to prove them wrong, the energy, time and effort of all parties will be in vain.
>
> The second attitude is what I call the over-simplifying attitude, a tendency to claim that all the religions are the same, that the

differences are too minute to be considered. The lines of demarcation are so thin and so hazy that we can ignore them and live happily ever after.

It is needless to say that deep in our hearts we know that this is not true. We are different along very important lines and on very fundamental issues and I don't think that I need to mention examples. If we indulge in this over-simplified euphoria, we will soon discover the reality and fail the first easy test.

The challenge then is not to ignore, underestimate or deny the differences but rather to know them and accept each other in spite of them, as God-loving, decent human beings.

The third attitude is what I call the compromising attitude – i.e., the attitude that advocates trimming the different religions here and there, delete or add, acquire and modify to tailor a new religion convenient to all of us and suitable to the modern American Civilization.

Discussions of this kind usually are wasted because the participants of the dialogue, to start with, are already committed to a faith and a way of life, not searching for one.

If we take these three dangers into consideration and avoid them we ought to remember that the major achievement we can gain is that great factor cherished and advocated by the three religions – i.e., to know the truth; at least the truth about each other and what we are supposed to represent.

We have assumed both agreements and disagreements, and unfortunately assumptions in a good number of cases have been wrong. So why don't we just try to know the honest-to-God reality? We ought to remember that we live through a time when half of the world denies God, while the other half disobeys Him and it is the responsibility of those who believe in Him to show that they, while taking the different paths to Him can acknowledge each other and have a straightforward, honest, informing and fruitful dialogue together.

It will be obvious from the presentations which occupy the following pages that these ideals were often not attained, and this exemplary advice often not followed. The major reason for this is that the Trialogue represents the beginning rather than the end point of this dialogue. However, there are a number of more specific observations which can be made about the dynamics of the Trialogue, its results and the significance of those results in a broader perspective. (These comments owe much to personal retrospectives volunteered by the participants after the event, but the synthesis is that of this writer.) In discussing these aspects of the Trialogue, the writer realises the need for a detachment and objectivity which are very difficult, as he was a participant as well, but which he will strive to the utmost to maintain.

Professor Hick has stated that the Trialogue illustrated realistically the convergences and divergences of the three faiths represented. While this is essentially correct, it must be qualified with reference to the different standpoints of the delegations *vis-à-vis* their own traditions, differences which gave rise to the major areas of tension in the discussions. While the Jewish and Christian participants were overwhelmingly liberal to moderate thinkers, the Muslims were generally conservative exponents of their tradition. The effect was thus to minimise the points of contention between the Jews and Christians and see them as representatives of a common point of view over against the Muslims. This effect was intensified by the concomitant difference in academic orientation: the Jewish and Christian participants, including those who are ordained rabbis, priests and ministers, have grown up with and work within the modern Western academic tradition, and in general approached their material as scholars involved in historical–comparative studies. This approach was not only foreign to most of the Muslim participants, but perceived by them as anti-religious secularism in direct opposition to their faith commitments, which they expressed from a homiletic and apologetic standpoint. Along with these disparities, there were widely divergent presuppositions and expectations regarding the Trialogue itself – as a forum for the mutual exploration of similarities and differences on the one hand, and as a forum for faith statements on the other. It is not surprising that there were considerable difficulties in communication which themselves occupied much of the discussion. The composition of the delegations did not only serve to minimize the differences between Judaism and Christianity and overemphasise those between each and Islam, but to underestimate the diversity of all three groups. Thus, while there were three Roman Catholic participants, there were none from the Eastern Orthodox churches and none from the fundamentalist segment of the Protestant community, and the Orthodox bodies of Judaism were likewise not represented. (In point of fact, fundamentalist–evangelical Protestants were approached, but declined the invitation.)

Several aspects of the format and logistics of the Trialogue probably exacerbated these difficulties. The presence of the audience and the public nature of the event – and the 'parliamentary' rotation of speakers necessary in such an event – made real dialogue among participants difficult and helped to polarise the stances of participants. The impossibility of a seating arrangement in which all the participants faced one another was a major drawback. The lack of time for private discussion and getting acquainted inhibited not only direct dialogue but the development of trust and openness. And defensive attitudes were intensified by politically divisive issues which could not be prevented from entering into the discussion. There was a widespread feeling that much of the difficulty in communication could have been avoided had there been a preliminary in-depth discussion of hermeneutics.

The present book is not a transcription or recapitulation of the entire Trialogue. Because of space considerations, the extemporaneous discussion, all of which was taped, has had to be omitted. While we regret this, we hope that the major papers and solicited responses will indicate the positions and the main substance of the discussion. The editors can take no responsibility for any opinions or statements except those attributed to them by name in papers or introductory material. As already alluded to, our dual role as editors and participants makes this task an unusually delicate and demanding one, and we have made a consummate effort not to permit our personal points of view to make themselves felt. With the sole exception of one bibliographical note added in the interest of balance, we have refrained from the sometimes great temptation to manifest editorial omniscience and try to have the last word on this or that controversial point. As observed above, this Trialogue represents the beginning rather than the last word in Jewish–Christian–Muslim dialogue, and the proper spirit of Trialogue is epitomised by the Heavenly Voice which proclaimed to the contending schools of Hillel and Shammai, 'These and these are [both] the words of the living God'.

1 'This is my God': One Jew's Faith

Elliot N. Dorff

I THE TRADITIONAL STANCE

Judah Halevi is known as the most Jewish of Jewish philosophers. He is characterised that way because he rejected the attempts of the philosophers of his time to arrive at an understanding of God through reason. Writing in the twelfth century, he created an imaginary dialogue between a rabbi and the king of the Khazars, whose historical counterpart had converted himself and all of his realm to Judaism in the eighth century. In convincing the king of the truth of Judaism, Halevi's rabbi argues that rational speculation is subject to mistakes and often leads to doctrinal errors. Even at its best reason may inform us of an abstract, philosophic God but not the living, commanding Lord with whom the religious Jew interacts. Only revelation and God's actions in the history of Israel can provide an accurate (even if partial) description of Him, an explanation of the real grounds of the believer's belief, and an understanding of why believers are prepared to sacrifice so much for their beliefs, in sharp contrast to the theology, justifications, and resultant behaviour of the philosophers. Anticipating Pascal by five hundred years, Halevi carefully and consistently distinguishes between the God of Abraham and the God of the philosophers (which, for him, meant primarily the Aristotelians) in their differing depictions of God, the reasons for believing in Him, and the conduct that grows out of that belief.

Halevi represents both the position and the epistemology of the tradition, against which all modern Jewish philosophies must be measured. Consequently, I shall quote him at some length to set the context for our exploration of a Jewish philosophy designed for the modern age:

THE RABBI: I believe in the God of Abraham, Isaac, and Israel, who led the Israelites out of Egypt with signs and miracles; who fed them in the desert and gave them the Holy Land after having made them traverse the sea and the Jordan in a miraculous way;

7

who sent Moses with His Law, and subsequently thousands of prophets; who confirmed His Law by promises to those who observed, and threats to the disobedient. We believe in what is contained in the Torah – a very large domain.

THE KING OF THE KHAZARS: I had intended from the very beginning not to ask any Jew, because I am aware of the destruction of their books and of their narrow-minded views, their misfortunes having deprived them of all commendable qualities. Should you, O Jew, not have said that you believe in the Creator of the world, its Governor and Guide, who created and keeps you, and such attributes which serve as evidence for every believer, and for the sake of which he pursues justice in order to resemble the Creator in His wisdom and justice?

THE RABBI: That which you express is speculative and political religion, to which inquiry leads; but this is open to many doubts. Now ask the philosophers, and you will find that they do not agree on one action or on one principle, since they rely on theories; some of these can be established by arguments, some of them are only plausible, some even less capable of being proved.

THE KING OF THE KHAZARS: What you say now, O Jew, seems to me better than the beginning, and I should like to hear more.

THE RABBI: But the beginning of my speech was the very proof, yea, the evidence which makes every argument superfluous . . . The way of inference is misleading and may produce heresy and error . . . True, there are differences in the ways of demonstration; some of them are exact, others insufficient; but the most exact of all are the ways of the philosophers, and even they are led by their inferences to say that God neither benefits nor injures, nor knows anything of our prayers or offerings, our obedience or disobedience, and that the world is as eternal as He Himself! . . . There is a broad difference, indeed, between the believer in a religion and the philosopher. The believer seeks God for the sake of various benefits, apart from the benefit of knowing Him; the philosopher seeks Him only that he may be able to describe Him accurately, as he would describe the earth . . .; ignorance of God would therefore be no more injurious than ignorance concerning the earth . . .

The meaning of 'God' [*elohim*] can be grasped by way of speculation, a Guide and Manager of the world being inferred by Reason; opinions about Him differ among men according to their faculty of thought; the most evident of them is that of the philosophers. The meaning of 'The Lord' [*yhwh*], however, cannot be grasped by analogic thought, but only by that prophetic intuition by which man ascends, so to say, from his kind and joins the angels . . . Then there vanish all previous doubts of man concerning God, and he despises all these analogic proofs by means of which men endeavour to attain knowlege of His dominion and unity. Then he becomes a servant who loves his master, and is ready to perish for the sake of his love, finding the greatest sweetness in his connection with Him, the greatest sorrow in separation from Him. Otherwise the philosophers; they consider Divine worship only as refinement of conduct and confession of truth, so that they extol Him above all other beings, just as the sun is to be extolled above all other visible things, and the denial of God only as a mark of a low standard of the soul which acquiesces in untruth.

THE KING OF THE KHAZARS: Now I understand the difference between 'God' and the 'Lord', and I see how great is the difference between the God of Abraham and the God of Aristotle. To the Lord we yearn, tasting and viewing Him; to God we draw near through speculation. And this feeling invites its votaries to give their life for the love of Him and to suffer death for Him. Speculation, however, tends to veneration only as long as it entails no harm, nor causes pain for its own sake. We must not take it amiss that Aristotle thinks lightly of the observation of religious laws since he doubts whether God has any cognisance of them.

THE RABBI: Abraham, on the other hand, bore his burden honestly, in Ur Kasdim, in emigration, circumcision, removal of Ishmael, in the painful resolution to sacrifice Isaac; for he conceived the Divine power by tasting, not by speculating; he had observed that no detail of his life escaped God, that He rewarded him instantly for his piety and guided him along the best path, so that he moved forwards or backwards only according to God's will. How should he not despise his former speculations? The Sages (*Shabbat* 156a) explain the verse, 'He took Abraham outside' (*Genesis* 15:5) as meaning, 'give up your astrology.' That is to say: He commanded him to leave off his speculative researches into the stars and other matters, and to devote himself to the service of Him whom he had tasted, as it is written: 'Taste and see that the Lord is good' (*Psalms* 34:9). The Lord is therefore rightly called 'God of Israel' because this seeing is not found elsewhere, and 'God of the land' because the peculiarity of its air, soil, and heaven aids this vision, together with actions such as the cultivating and tilling of the soil for the higher prosperity of the species. All followers of the Divine law follow these 'seeing' men; they find satisfaction in the authority of their tradition, in spite of the simplicity of their speech and the clumsiness of their similes, not in the authority of philosophers, with their graphic elegance, their excellent dispositions, and their brilliant demonstrations. For all that, the masses do not follow them, as if the soul had a presentiment for truth, as it is said, 'The words of truth are recognizable' (*Sotah* 9b).[1]

II THE MODERN REALITY OF JEWISH BELIEF

Halevi's trust in God's revelation and His actions in history is difficult for contemporary Jews to accept. Their problem is not that of their medieval ancestors, who needed to explain why Judaism is to be preferred to other religions and other revelations. It is rather the question of why religion is necessary in the first place. More than contemporary Christians, and certainly more than contemporary Muslims, Jews in large numbers profess little or no belief in God, and even less in revelation. Their doubts about God are not so much the philosophic ones; in the spirit of Halevi, even the reasons for Jews' disbelief are not primarily philosophical! Some deny God because of the Holocaust, but most do so because God is not part of reality as they know it. In other words, many Jews have become thoroughly secularised. They do not actively deny God; they simply ignore the whole issue.

Revelation is even more problematic. In addition to the competing revelations that bothered the medievals so much, modern Jews sometimes know about questions raised by the modern, historical approach to the texts of revelation. Even if verbal revelation took place, we do not have a record of it. But the main problems that Jews have with revelation come from other quarters: knowlege as they know it derives from scientific method and experimentation, not revelation. They do not recognise an authoritative text or tradition.

Nevertheless most Jews are not interested in denying their Jewishness. They identify as Jews, however, for non-theological reasons.

Historical rootedness, family ties, and especially communal feelings and activity (aided by occasional flare-ups of antisemitism) motivate their identification as Jews.

That is not enough to prevent intermarriage or check assimilation, but it is enough to mark Jews off in a variety of areas as being different from non-Jews. The traditional, Jewish emphasis on education still permeates many secularised Jewish homes, so that a much higher percentage of Jews complete undergraduate and graduate degrees than the comparable percentage of the general population, and Jews become professionals (especially in medicine, law, and social work) and professors in great disproportion to their numbers. Until very recently traditional family values made the Jewish home a bastion of stability, but the divorce rate among Jews is now as high as that in society generally. Although there is now some alcoholism among Jews, the rate is still far lower than that of the general population, and I would guess that at least a part of that is the traditional acceptance of alcohol in moderation. Jewish social activism, rooted in the strong emphasis in Judaism on improving this world, is still highly evident in the Jewish community. For example, a third to a half of the Peace Corps participants have been Jewish.

Christians and Muslims rarely understand how Jews can fail to be religious and still carry on traditional values and patterns of living. The key is the strong sense of Jewish peoplehood that Jews inherit, a sense that is made all the stronger by its independence of land and governmental structure. Even so, the real question is how long such an ethnic Jewishness can last. Rabbi Robert Gordis has claimed that secular Jews are only living off the capital of their religious parents and grandparents and that that will cease to be possible once a given generation no longer even has memories of religious forbears.[2] Recent studies of young American Jews seem to support his thesis. In any case, we certainly are a far cry from Halevi's brand of Jewish identity.

And yet there are signs of a religious revival among Jews. Since my own case is typical in many respects, perhaps it will be best to begin with me, remembering the admonition of a good friend, Professor James McClendon, Jr, that theology makes no sense detached from biography.[3] Protestants will call what I am about to do 'giving my witness', but I have heard from many Protestants that have heard my story that it is a very strange form of giving witness. But its very strangeness to Protestants will help to identify what is characteristically Jewish in theology.

III MY OWN GROWTH INTO RELIGIOUS BELIEF

I grew up in a typical 'second generation' home. Although there were Jews in the United States since 1654, the vast majority of Jews came to America from Eastern Europe in the last decades of the nineteenth century and the first decades of the twentieth. The immigrants, the 'first generation', had all they could do to eke out a living, but they concentrated all their efforts in making sure that their children learned English and the skills to get by in America. Their Judaism was largely that which they brought with them from Europe.

When their children (the 'second generation' of American Jews) became adults, they carried out their parents' interest in 'making it' in America, but in their understanding that often meant giving up many of their traditions in order to become as much like white, Anglo-Saxon Protestants as possible. Consequently 'third generation' youngsters learned quickly that their parents' real interest in their Jewish education was that they fulfill whatever remaining obligation their parents felt to make sure that their children identified as Jews. The socially accepted – and, indeed, expected – manifestation of that was the Bar Mitzvah or Bat Mitzvah ceremonies. Beyond that no further learning was expected ('After all, do you want him to be a rabbi?'), and Jewish practice beyond that which the parents were doing (or even at that level) was considered to be unusually religious, bordering on the fanatic.

I grew up in just such an atmosphere. The vast majority of my contemporaries dropped out of Jewish education after their Bar or Bat Mitzvah at the age of thirteen, and they generally remember the experience of the religious school as one of boredom and meaninglessness. Those who have found meaning in Judaism as adults commonly talk about their childhood religious education in anger, questioning how the adults of that time could ever have distorted the richness of Judaism and failed to communicate its meaning so completely. Most have assimilated or intermarried, raising real questions about the survival of a viable Jewish community two or three generations hence. One of the real ironies of history is that Jews may find it more difficult to survive under conditions of freedom than they did during centuries of ghettoisation and persecution.

In my own case, the situation was very different because I attended Camp Ramah, a chain of seven camps of the Conservative Movement in the United States and Canada. I was twelve years old during my

rst summer there, and I am convinced that had I not gone there
then, I would have gone the way of all my other friends after my
Bar Mitzvah ceremony in June of the following year. It was not that
I had some kind of religious revelation at Ramah; at the beginning
it was simply a nice camping experience. Even at age twelve,
however, I was impressed by the fact that Judaism was truly a way
of life for the people at camp. It was not restricted to prayer and
study, although we did more of that than I had ever done in my life
before; it affected every aspect of life, from the bunk to the evening
activities to the sports field. I loved the singing and the dancing, the
Hebrew that I was learning to speak in classes and at the waterfront
and on the baseball diamond, and the beauty of the traditional
Sabbath observances at camp. It was all so natural and unselfcon-
scious. For the first time in my life, Judaism was a source of guidance
and joy, and not simply a burden that I carried as someone who was
not fully part of the culture in which he lived.

In order to go to Camp Ramah, however, you had to attend classes
in Jewish subjects during the course of the year for at least six
hours a week. Consequently I continued my Jewish education and
participated in Jewish youth groups throughout my teenage years
even though almost every one of my friends in high school had
dropped out long before. Through my summers at Ramah as a
camper and then, during my college years, as a counsellor, I came
to recognise the factors that were involving me more and more in
religious life. I liked the depth of the relationships that the Jewish
environment created. We were certainly not saints in any sense of
the term, but at Ramah we had a heightened awareness of moral
norms and of the need to be sensitive to other people's needs. We
were not embarrassed about talking about behaviour and helping
people with their problems; it was simply part of what was expected
of every one of us. The intellectual stimulation grew by leaps and
bounds as I grew older. Indeed, the most exciting and mind-
stretching conversations I had anywhere took place at camp. Ironically, in this religious environment, I felt much more able to raise
any questions that occurred to me, and in fact the leaders of the
camp prodded us into confronting problems with religious commitment that we either never thought of or never dared to ask in the
religious institutions in the city. There was a sense of structure, of
rootedness, and of purpose to life that was missing in the lives of all
of my non-religious friends. Consequently, when I decided to become

a rabbi, my chief aim was to reproduce the experiences that Ramah had given me, to share the spoils, as it were.

The one area where camp did not provide much help for me was in theology. We had discussions about God, but somehow they did not take hold in me. I loved all of the other aspects of being Jewish that I had been exposed to there, but I continued to feel embarrassed by the fact that ideologically it was all dependent upon certain theological propositions. I remember that even in applying to Rabbinical School I attempted to evade theological language as much as I possibly could, and my decision to major in philosophy and ultimately to complete a doctorate in it was largely motivated by the desire to try to make some sense of the theological underpinnings of the Judaism that I had found to be meaningful in so many other ways.

IV ACTION AND RELATIONSHIPS AS KEYS TO FAITH

Not all Jews benefit from the Ramah experience or its equivalent, and certainly not all become rabbis (thank God!). But my experience was typical in that relationships and actions came first and thought patterns later, and that is characteristically Jewish. It also may be the distinctively Jewish approach to religious epistemology. Halevi may be right after all!

At first it may seem strange to try to gain knowledge of God through action and communication. Discussions about our knowledge of God, in fact, commonly concentrate exclusively on the mode of gaining knowledge that we use so effectively in science – i.e., observation, experimentation, and reasoning based upon those. In light of the success that we have had with those methods in science, it is certainly understandable that we should turn immediately to them in trying to acquire knowledge about God.

Moreover, any claims to knowledge about God must be consistent with, and integrated into, our knowledge of other areas of life, and that too would argue for using scientific methods to obtain knowledge of God.

That line of reasoning, however, ignores the fact that the object of the desired knowledge is a being who is both personal and unique, for the God of the Western religions is, after all, not simply a creative force or moral principle, but a personality. That is a tenet which goes to the heart of the thought and practice of Judaism, Christianity, and Islam, and any theology which ignores the personal character of

God distorts the fundamentally theistic character of those religions. Consequently we must focus on the ways we learn about people in order to choose an appropriate method for learning about God.

When we do that, we discover both that it is difficult to learn about individuals and that scientific methods are not very helpful. That is the insight of modern existentialists like Franz Rosenzweig and Martin Buber as well as our old friend, Judah Halevi. Why is it so difficult, and why is scientific method largely ineffective in this area? In part it is because personalities are not directly observable by others, as objects are. We use bodily clues and our own experiences to guess what other people think and feel, but we never are able to observe the mind, emotions, or will of another person directly. Further to complicate matters, each of us is the product of a unique combination of factors that make up human personality, and each of us has at least a degree of free will. That makes it virtually impossible to formulate any neat, general rules about a person's behaviour in the way that science generalises the behaviour of objects. We are not totally helpless, of course: we have learned some general features of human thought, feeling, and behaviour through the work of psychologists, sociologists, and the like. We are even discovering some biological bases for human personality. But the fact remains that knowing another person is not amenable to fixed, general rules and that analogies to other people are often misleading. Even when we know a person in one context, we find that he or she may think, feel, and act very differently in other contexts. We know that from studies that have been done of mob psychology and peer pressure, and we know that more pervasively on the basis of our own experience with other people. Objects sometimes behave differently when their environment is altered, but human behaviour seems to vary with the context even more.

All of these factors make it difficult to know another person and make the methods of science only moderately helpful in that task, but probably the most significant stumbling block is the fact that knowing another person depends upon the willingness of both parties to engage in the relationship. I cannot force someone else to open himself to me; he must agree to do so. Initiating contact therefore involves a risk on my part, the risk of rejection. The other person may either ignore me or actually scorn me. And there is even a greater risk involved: to create a relationship I must also be willing to open myself to the other person. That requires self-confidence and trust in the other. Beyond that, I have to be willing to expend the physical and psychological energy needed to maintain and explore the relationship once it has been formed. These personal investments on the part of both parties make forming a relationship a hard thing to do, and yet that is the only way that we can escape our loneliness. It is also the only way that we can truly get to know another person as the individual being that he or she is.

How do we begin? We learn most about people and we foster relationships with them through doing things together and through talking with each other. Observation and cogitation have limited value in such contexts. Since God in the Jewish tradition is both personal and unique, human experience would suggest that we use common action and verbal communication in seeking knowledge about God. The Jewish tradition uses both.

V ACQUIRING KNOWLEDGE OF GOD THROUGH ACTION

An oft-quoted Rabbinic Midrash says the following:

> 'They have deserted Me and have not kept My Law' (Jeremiah 16:11). God says, 'Would that they had deserted Me and kept My Law, for if they had occupied themselves with the Law, the leaven [or, perhaps, the light] in it would have brought them back to Me.[4]

The boldness of God's willingness to be forgotten on condition that the People Israel observe His Law accounts for the renown of this passage, but that unfortunately obscures the epistemological point that the last clause makes: practice of the law can be a method of coming into contact with God. The Jewish tradition makes that point emphatically through its insistence on observing Jewish law and understanding it as God's commandments. The Law is not only a set of decrees by an absolute monarch; it is a mode of revelation of God's will and, indirectly, of God Himself.

How can action provide knowledge? Acquiring knowlege is most often conceived as a combination of verbal and mental processes, but in fact we gain knowledge from our actions too. Probably the clearest example of that is in the area of technical skills; 'book learning' is often not necessary and usually not sufficient to impart a skill. Our emotional maturity and sophistication are also dependent upon experience. 'You do not know what it feels like until you have done it' is a common remark made to people who have not done or experienced something specific, and the remark is accurate: one cannot understand the joy of having a child or the pain of a parent's death, for example, unless one has experienced those events personally, and the ability to empathise with people involved in such experiences is limited if you yourself have not had them. Jewish law gives poignant expression to this when it requires that all judges in a capital case be people who have children of their own;[6] only then does one know fully the stakes that are involved, for the defendant is, after all, somebody's child. Similar considerations apply to morality. Children learn about right and wrong through the reactions of their family and friends to their behaviour long before they are able to verbalise anything about it, and that process carries on into adulthood.

But it is not only technical, emotional, and moral knowledge that we acquire through action; we gain factual knowledge as well. I learn, for example, what happens to skin if I sit in the sun too long – however painful that lesson may be! I may learn that ahead of time (and without the pain) from books or discussions, but that detached learning is really only a substitute for my own, first-hand suffering, a substitute that is available to me because somebody was sunburned before and warned me about the consequences of too much exposure to the sun. In effect, much of our knowledge about ourselves, other people and the world around us is gained either through direct experience or vicariously through the actions and observations of others.

Learning about the nature of God through obeying the commandments is, of course, considerably more complex epistemologically. In contrast to the cases mentioned in the previous two paragraphs, such learning through action is not easily confirmable by other modes of gleaning information, such as first-hand sensory experience or the reliable reports of others. On the other hand, *all* of our modes of inquiry are the products of our terrestrial experiences, and all of them will have to be stretched if they are to enable us to deal with celestial matters. The insight of the Jewish tradition is that learning through action is, in many ways, a better method to learn about God than the usual observational and verbal alternatives.

That is true for several reasons important to the objectives of religion. Actions are concrete and more easily learned than complex theological argumentation. This type of learning is therefore available to the young and uneducated as well as to the mature and learned. Moreover, actions are repeatable, especially if they are short and specific, as many of the *Mitzvot* (commandments) of Judaism are. That is important if the knowledge gained is to become an integral part of our lives and not just a piece of our intellectual storehouse. Actions also involve the body, emotions, and will in an active way as well as the mind, and that is important if the knowledge of God is to influence our whole being and not just a part of us. Since religions aim to affect our actions as well as our thoughts, and since our cognitive knowledge all too often has little effect on our behaviour, teaching directly through rules for action is an especially appropriate form of learning about God.

Even if we restrict our attention to the cognitive claims of religion, learning through action is no more problematic as a way to God than learning through observation and thought. We do, after all, learn about the existence and nature of other people by doing things with and for them – more, probably, than we do through observing them or thinking about them. Applying that mode of learning to God clearly involves an extension of our normal experience, but it is an extension of the method by which we gain the type of knowledge in human affairs closest to the type of knowledge that we seek in regard to God, i.e., knowledge of a personal being.

VI ACQUIRING KNOWLEDGE OF GOD THROUGH WORDS: REVELATION

We also learn about other people through verbal communication. The phenomena parallel to that in the context of religion are revelation and prayer. Both are highly problematic from a philosophical point of view primarily because one of the communicators (i.e., God) is not available for direct, reciprocal communication in the same way human beings are to each other when they are having a conversation. That raises many questions. How do we know that it is indeed God communicating with us through revelation? On what basis do we accept one revelation over others, or one record of a revelation over others? When we speak to God through prayer, how can we ever be sure that God hears? Is it really communication, or only an extended monologue?

Despite these immediately apparent difficulties, there are philosophical as well as religious reasons for investigating whether revelation and prayer can serve as ways of knowing God. One of the ways we come to know other people is through speaking with them, and revelation and prayer are at bottom ways in which we hear from, and speak to, God. But if we examine verbal communication among human beings, we find that some of the same questions exist that we raised earlier in regard to God. We assume that most speakers identify themselves correctly and tell us the truth when they speak to us, but some do not. If we do not know a person through any previous contact, it is hard to determine whether the person is telling the truth about anything, even about who he is. For that reason fugitives from the law and former FBI informants can successfully assume totally new identities, sometimes for life. The new identity often includes not only a change in name, but a wholly false personal history. As a result, when it is important to ascertain that the information which a person gives is correct, we regularly check crucial aspects of the person's story by contacting former employers, friends, etc. We do not rely on the person's assertions alone.

The chances of being deceived are even greater when the verbal communication takes place over the telephone or in some other way which prevents the hearer from checking the speaker's identity and intent through seeing him or her. We learn to identify the voices and intonations of the people we know, but sometimes even they can trick us into thinking someone else is talking as part of a practical joke.

The problems grow worse still when the verbal communication is in written rather than oral form. Handwriting is an identifying mark, but even that is sometimes open to dispute. Hence the existence of contested wills and the need for notary publics. When the written words are typed or written by someone else, or when the document is unsigned, the reader's ability to identify the author and his or her intent diminishes yet further.

Even when verbal communication is articulate and accurate, we do not depend upon it alone because we recognise that it gives us only partial knowledge of the other person. So, for example, people who have been pen-pals for years may know a lot about each other, but they often feel that they do not really know each other until they communicate in non-verbal ways by seeing each other and doing things together. We are somewhat different people in writing than we are in person because writing lacks the immediacy and spontaneity of personal contact. But we learn to account for possible deceptions in verbal communication and to compensate for its insufficiencies through other means of contact, and so we do learn about each other and interact with each other through words.

When we apply these considerations to our knowledge of God, the problems that we have with revelation and prayer become less awesome and less peculiar to religion. Specifically, we do not rely exclusively on the Biblical revelations for our knowledge of God; on the contrary, those accounts have meaning for us precisely because Jews throughout the centuries have found that their own experience confirms the world-view and value system of those documents and is, in turn, illuminated by them. In fact, the very meaning of the Bible has been constantly changed through the process of *Midrash* (interpretation) – so much so that Judaism is really the religion of the Rabbis more than it is the religion of the Bible – and that process provides a formal mechanism whereby the ongoing experience of the people is invoked to confirm, disconfirm, and modify Biblical revelation. Moreover, the Rabbis themselves narrowed the domain of revelation by refusing to recognise the legitimacy of revelations much after the destruction of the First Temple, and by stressing the primacy of the revelation to Moses over the others that they did legitimate.

Problems, of course, remain – problems, for example, of learning about God second-hand through a document that is old and is the sole source of our information about crucial events like the revelation at Sinai, problems regarding the unity and authenticity of the Bible and problems of defining the nature of revelation in the first place. But these problems are mitigated by the small number of revelations to which Judaism is committed, and the problems are diminished yet further by the fact that we do not depend exclusively on revelation for our knowledge of God. The constant interaction between the Jewish community and its revelatory documents provides a solid basis for testing, confirming, modifying, and ultimately trusting what the revelation has come to mean.

Does this process reduce revelation to a wholly human phenomenon? Has it effectively become simply the record of human experience with God phrased in language which makes it seem like God talking? That depends on your view of revelation and on the source and nature of its authority.[7] The documents may be a record of God speaking, or they may be an expression of the Jewish People's experience with, and insight into, God. In either case, revelation adds to our knowledge of God by framing and informing our present experience with God through the insights and experiences of our ancestors. Neither the original revelation nor the continuing testing of that revelation with our own experience should be ignored: the key to using revelation as a source of knowledge of God is the *interaction* between the original revelation and its ongoing interpretation.

VII ACQUIRING KNOWLEDGE OF GOD THROUGH WORDS: PRAYER

The other side of learning about God through verbal communication is prayer. There is no doubt that prayer is an important vehicle for keeping the community of Israel together, for enabling it to express its joy and mourning, and for sensitising it daily to the literature and values of the Tradition, but the issue here is whether prayer has value in affording us knowledge of God. Prayer is at the heart of the religious experience, an expression of religious life in its own terms, and so we need to pay attention to its meaning and epistemological potential if we are ever to have an adequate understanding of religion itself.

When we try to detach ourselves from the world and learn what we can as dispassionate, 'objective' observers, we learn a great deal, and that knowledge has shaped virtually every aspect of our lives in this scientific twentieth century. In the realm of theology, detached reflection of that type generally leads thinkers to abstract concepts of God, making God similar in many respects to the forces and features of nature.

Our experience, however, is not limited to what we gain in our function as observers of the world. We also interact with it. At such times all of our rational, physical, emotional, moral, aesthetic, and conative powers come into play, and we become personally involved with other segments of reality. It is essential to recognise that our personal experiences are just as true and objectively verifiable as our detached, cognitive experiences. We can, do, and should learn from the latter, and theology should reflect that learning.

This consideration becomes especially important in prayer, for there the personal side of God is most in evidence. The traditional God hears our praises and appeals. People as simple as Tevye, the milkman, can talk with Him. In contrast, the detached God of power and moral principle does not hear prayer. That is a major drawback to the theologies that emerge from such thinking, for the warmth generated by one-to-one contact with a personal God is then lost. Prayer is a format by which the community is brought together for purposes of comradeship, education, celebration, mourning, sensitivity training, and moral stimulation, but if there is no personal Being to interact with us in prayer, then all of the noble functions I have just listed are not enough to sustain our interest. Without a personal God, prayer loses its soul.

Many who think theoretically feel an obligation to reconcile the results of their detached reflection with their ongoing thinking and practice. Nevertheless, even those who are led by their thought to construe God in untraditional, abstract ways commonly pray to the traditional God. They may explain this to themselves as intellectual laziness. It is easier to picture a Being in our mind's eye than to conjure up the image of a Force, a series of attributes, etc. and we come to services hoping to activate the emotional and conative parts of our nature, which usually means allowing the intellect to recede into the background. Jewish prayer does include intellectually stimulating material, but it is a *separate* part of the service, centring around the Torah reading and the attendant lesson or sermon. Even there, we expect to learn about our emotional or moral life, and we come away somewhat disappointed if we have been given an academic treatise – not that the lesson or sermon should be intellectually sloppy, but that we have very different expectations of teaching in the context of services than we do in a college lecture, or even a synagogue adult education course. Thus we pay to a personal, largely anthropomorphic God, if only because the context of prayer seems to require that we loosen up on the standards of intellectual rigour that we demand in the context of cogitation.

We are left, however, with a certain sense of discomfort about this apparent dishonesty. All of our conclusions about the nature of God that we reach through an effort of the intellect suddenly are abandoned in the context of prayer. Moreover, even if our prayer experiences are much richer when directed toward a personal God, there are real problems in ascribing personality to God.

Our problems are not those of the medieval Jewish rationalists, who were embarrassed by the depiction of God's personal traits in the Bible and Talmud because they thought that attributing elements of personality to the Deity compromised His infinity and eternity. Abraham Joshua Heschel and others have shown us that a Greek notion of perfection was behind their dilemma. Divine perfection as understood in the Jewish tradition requires personal involvement, even if God has to contract His being and His powers in order to enable that to happen, for only a God who cares and interacts manifests the personal characteristics that we know to be important in life.[8] Even the medievals who persistently maintained that 'He is not a body and has no body'[9] reserved that for their intellectual treatises; in prayer they employed the traditional anthropomorphic symbolism, including 'Open Your hand and satisfy every living thing with favour' (Ps. 145:16, used in the early part of the morning service), and 'Exalt the Lord and worship at His footstool' (Ps. 99:5, which is said when Jews take the Torah from the ark). Thus in their practice they themselves indicated the limitations of the theologies that they had created cognitively. If anything, this dissonance between their thought and their practice should be somewhat of a comfort to us moderns who find ourselves faced with the same dissonance.

The problems that moderns have in ascribing personality to God are much more directly connected to the nature of personality, for we find that many of the characteristics that we usually associate with personality do not apply to God in any direct way. We normally expect that a being with personality will speak to us, answer our questions, and communicate love, concern, and anger, but when we try to apply those attributes to God, we have great difficulty. Does God speak to us? The Rabbis of the Talmud thought that He did, although they restricted such communication to the biblical period, substituting in its stead the process of interpretation of the one authoritative communication of God, the Torah.[10] Does God answer prayers? If so, how? Clearly people become strengthened and relieved through prayer, but not by a direct, verbal response from God. To conclude that God replies through action rather than speech raises the problem of how to recognise an act that is meant to answer a prayer – especially since God can presumably say 'No!' And how does God show concern for us? We are clearly the beneficiaries of miracles each day, as the traditional prayerbook reminds us, but we are also the victims of suffering, disease, crime, natural disaster, and other evils of all sorts. Are these signs of His anger and manifestations of His kind and just discipline of us? Then we would expect a *quid pro quo* relationship between our actions and God's responses, as the Deuteronomist envisaged, and this is obviously not the case.

In the face of these difficulties, we might say that God has a personality which expresses itself in ways that are radically different from human personality. But that would be a pyrrhic victory because we are then talking about something very different from what we normally mean by 'personality'. That term in regard to God would then be a misuse of the word which is downright misleading.

Despite these difficulties we persist in ascribing personality to God for at least three reasons. One is historical. God's personal characteristics are so central to a Jewish conception of Him that one wonders if any theology that drops them can deservedly be called Jewish.

The second reason is moral. God has always functioned within Judaism as a model for human behaviour.[11] Consequently, if we deny personality to God in our conception of Him, we are in effect denying the importance of our personality and our concern and involvement with others. Judaism has always been, and must continue to be, centrally concerned with those aspects of life, especially in our largely depersonalised modern world, and so we are reluctant to let go of these aspects of God lest Judaism lose its moral meaning.[12]

The third reason is epistemological, and it goes to the heart of our philosophical discomfort with the dissonance that we have experienced between our thinking and our prayer. Our interpersonal experiences give intersubjective evidence of the reality of human personality, and our attempts to relate to God seem to follow the same pattern. Although these attempts may be a manifestation of our tendency to anthropomorphise God, many thinkers in the Western traditions have found that their relationship with God is best expressed in personal terms. Halevi was certainly correct in affirming that the religious experience is not abstract and cerebral but rather concrete and total, involving the whole of a person's personality as an individual and as a member of a group. Buber expanded on this description by pointing out that the religious person forms a bipolar relationship with God, such that God is no longer a distant, absolute Being but our partner.[13] Again, this view may be a misinterpretation or even a total delusion, but the number of people involved and the commonality of their descriptions mean that the religious experience of a personal God can and does serve as a basis for serious knowledge claims.

Oriental experiences, of course, are very different, especially in Hinduism and Hinayana Buddhism, but I would suggest that that is due to the fact that personality (especially its element of free will) is viewed as an illusion and an entrapment in the East, while it is a reality and a blessing (indeed an imprint of the Divine) in the West. This opposition results in totally different kinds of religious experience and worship: in the East religious training and practice is designed to rid us of our sense of individuality as much as possible, while in the West we are taught to relate to God in an active and intensely personal way in both word and deed. If we are to maintain the Western evaluation of personality in non-theological matters, however, then we should not be embarrassed to include it in our theology as well.

On the contrary, we should feel ourselves compelled to do so. For Halevi, the God of the philosophers and the God of Abraham were radically distinct because philosophy was understood to include only the knowledge gained in trying to *describe* experience in as detached a manner as possible. But since we learn objective facts about the world when we *interact* with it as well, it is *intellectually justifiable* to include that element of our experience in our concept of God. Moreover, it is *intellectually necessary* to do so because otherwise our image of God neglects a major part of our experience. Indeed, it may be the case that experiences of love, anger, hope, fidelity, and the like are logical prerequisites to an adequate understanding of God; it is certainly true that sensitive souls have told us as much about the nature of God as great minds have.

How, then, can we reconcile our experiences of a personal God with our doubts about such a being? Ultimately, I think, we cannot. We must affirm the personal God of prayer because to refuse to do so would be to deny the validity of such experiences, even though there is intersubjective testimony to confirm them. On the other hand, to assert the existence of the personal God of the Bible and Talmud unequivocally is to ignore crucial questions concerning His existence. Thus it seems to me to be most honest and most adequate both intellectually and religiously to express myself in personal terms in prayer and other contexts of *relating* to God while admitting openly that this personal expression represents an extension of what we learn from a detached, critical analysis. Here, as elsewhere, we have not been able to fit all of our various experiences into a neat, systematic whole, and under such circumstances I agree with the Rabbis of the Talmud in preferring truth to consistency.

The import of philosophy of religion a decade or two ago was that different activities may well call for different rules of language usage and different procedures of justification.[14] Critics of that approach noted that, after all is said and done, we are integrated human beings, and consequently there must be some connections between the various languages that we use. That is clearly correct, but it does not negate the fact that we do use language differently in different contexts.

Our case is another example of that. What we are willing to express in prayer we are not willing to assert in detached, intellectual discussions, at least not with the same degree of conviction; and what we maintain unequivocally in such discussions proves inadequate for prayer. We have different *purposes* when we engage in those varying activities, and therefore we *use language differently* in those pursuits – even to the extent of intending different meanings by the same words when we use them in both contexts. The intellect, the emotions and the will interpenetrate in different proportions in many areas of life. In theology, that difference means that the God of the philosophers is not identical with the God of Abraham, Isaac, and Jacob – which disparages neither the one nor the other. On the contrary, as I have tried to demonstrate, both are legitimate and complementary conceptions of God, and we need both to be true to the totality of our experience as human beings and as Jews.

Having said all of that, I must reiterate that, as important as the cognitive issues are, they are not the crucial challenges to Jewish identity, survival, and vitality in our day. The most significant problems have to do with the ignorance and apathy that pervades modern American Jews, and consequently Jewish educators and rabbis are correctly devoting most of their energies to the task of combatting those ills. In our day, as in times past, Jewish belief will grow out of vibrant Jewish practice and community life, rather than the other way around. Even if logic would seem to require the beliefs first,[15] here the educational and empirical order is the reverse of the logical order, as it often is.

VIII NEW ASPECTS OF JEWISH DEPICTIONS OF GOD

While Halevi's insistence on the personal God of the tradition has gained considerable support among Jewish thinkers in recent years, those same thinkers are introducing new aspects in their understanding of God, and it would not be right to leave readers with the traditional view without some mention of these new developments.

1. Gender

Jews have been affected by the developments in gender roles in our
society and thinking as most other groups have. Most of the activity
on the Jewish scene, however, has been in areas of practice rather
than theology, as one familiar with Judaism would expect. New
rituals for women have been devised (e.g., ceremonies to welcome
a newborn girl into the Covenant with the same fanfare that is
given a boy at his circumcision; feminine adaptations of male prayer
garments, etc.), and women have taken new roles in the Jewish
community such that they serve as rabbis, synagogue presidents, and
presidents and directors of communal agencies. There have been
some efforts to incorporate aspects of femininity into the predomi-
nantly male image of God within Judaism, but those are still few
and not well known or widely accepted.[16]

2. God in History: America, the Holocaust, and the State of Israel

Three events of major proportions have happened in twentieth-
century Jewish history: the establishment in America of the most
populous Jewish community in the world within two generations, the
Holocaust, and the founding of the State of Israel. Since a crucial
part of Jewish belief is that God acts in history, one would expect
Jewish theological interpretations of these events in order to explain
them and integrate them into Jewish belief.

Almost nothing of a theological nature has been written about the
establishment of the American Jewish community. Jews apparently
accept that as just another example of the wanderings to which Jews
have been subjected throughout their history.

No theology of the Holocaust was written until Richard Rubenstein's *After Auschwitz* in 1966. Time had to elapse until Jews could
break their silence of mourning and contemplate the enormity of
what had happened to them. Since them a number of Holocaust
theologies have been produced as well as a great deal of non-theological literature. Some of the responses have been quite radical in
nature, but most practising Jews are not convinced by any of the
attempts to understand that trauma and thus continue to believe in
the traditional God, albeit chastened by the Holocaust's lesson of
the depth of depravity to which human beings can sink.

The State of Israel is, of course, a new reality, and consequently one would not expect too much theology on it yet. There has been some, written by both Americans and Israelis; but much still has to be done, especially since both the religious and non-religious Zionist thinkers before 1948 were wrong in significant aspects of their predictions.

All of this means that Jews face a new theological challenge in our time – i.e. to apply the traditional doctrine of God's action in history to the events of our time or show why it should not be applied. In either case, that tenet will probably be modified in decades to come.

IX JEWS AND NON-JEWS UNDER GOD

I have not included an extensive treatment of recent, Jewish theological understandings of non-Jews because I have done so elsewhere.[17] Aside from that, this chapter is already too long! Suffice it to say that from the Talmudic period on, Jews have believed that only Jews are obligated under the Covenant. Therefore non-Jews can attain a place in the World to Come by observing 'the seven laws given to Noah' instead of the 613 given to Moses. This liberal attitude toward others was balanced with the pride that Jews felt about being in a special relationship with God due to the extra responsibilities they took on. God hopes that eventually all of His peoples will follow the dictates of Jewish law, as His model people are obligated to do now.

As Jews, Christians, and Muslims look forward to even greater interaction in the future, one hopes that all three religions will be interpreted to maximise good will and understanding among the three Western faiths. With nuclear arms a reality, there has never been a more important time for us to recognise that we are all children of God.

Notes and References

1. Judah Halevi, *The Kuzari*, Isaak Heinemann (trans.), in *Three Jewish Philosophers* (Philadelphia: Jewish Publication Society, 1960) Book I, pars 11–15, pp. 33–4, and Book IV, pars 3, 13, 15–17, pp. 113–14, 116–19.
2. Robert Gordis, *A Faith for Moderns* (New York: Bloch Publishing Co., 1960) ch. 1; cf. also ch. 13.

3. James William McClendon, Jr, *Biography as Theology* (Nashville and New York: Abingdon Press, 1974).
4. Pesikta d'Rav Kahana, ch. 15. Although the manuscripts have *se'or* (leaven), Professor Robert Gordis has pointed out that that is probably an error. 'Leaven' is not applicable to Torah, since its metaphoric use refers to sinfulness. The reading should probably be *ma'or* (light).
5. Even the Kantian category of 'practical reason' is the exercise of our rational powers in analysing our practice, not knowledge that arises from our action.
6. *Tosefta Sanhedrin* 7:3; cf. Babylonian Talmud, *Sanhedrin* 36b and Maimonides, *Mishneh Torah*, Laws of Courts (Sanhedrin) 2:3.
7. For a thorough discussion of the Rabbinic and major contemporary positions on the nature and authority of revelation, cf. my *Conservative Judaism: Our Ancestors to Our Descendants* (New York: United Synagogue Youth, 1977) ch. III, sects C and D.
8. Abraham Joshua Heschel, *Man Is Not Alone: A Philosophy of Religion* (New York: Farrar, Straus, and Young, 1951) chs 14 and 15. Cf. also Heschel, The Prophets (Philadelphia: Jewish Publication Society, 1962) chs 12, 14 and 15.
9. From the *Yigdal* prayer, which is based on Maimonides' 'Thirteen Principles of the Faith'. Cf. Philip Birnbaum (trans.), *Daily Prayer Book* (New York: Hebrew Publishing Company, 1949) pp. 11, 153 (the third of Maimonides' principles).
10. *Sanhedrin* 11a; *Bava Metzia* 59b; *Bava Batra* 12a.
11. Cf., for example, Lev. 19:2 and the *Sifra* on that verse; *Sotah* 14; *Sifre, Ekev*, 85a; *Mekhilta Shirah* 3, etc.
12. Martin Buber has stressed this point, especially in *I and Thou* (New York: Charles Scribner's Sons, 1958). Cf. also Will Herberg, *Judaism for Modern Man* (Cleveland and New York: World Publishing Company, 1951) ch. 7.
13. Buber, *I and Thou*, especially pp. 81–3; Martin Buber, *Eclipse of God* (New York: Harper, 1952, 1957) pp. 42–6.
14. Cf., for example, Ian Ramsey, *Religious Language* (London: Student Christian Movement Press, 1957); Frederick Ferre, *Language, Logic, and God* (New York: Harper and Row, 1961); James A. Martin, *The New Dialogue between Philosophy and Theology* (New York: The Seabury Press, 1966).
15. So Rabbi Reuben in the second century said: 'Nobody proceeds to commit a transgression without first having denied Him who prohibited it', *Tosefta, Shevuot*, 3:6.
16. One of the first was by Rita Gross, 'Female God Language in a Jewish Context', in C. Christ and J. Plaskow (eds), *Womanspirit Rising* (New York: Harper and Row, 1979) pp. 167–73.
17. Elliot N. Dorff, 'The Covenant: How Jews Understand Themselves and Others', *Anglican Theological Review*, 64 (4) (October 1982) pp. 481–501.

A Christian Response to Elliot Dorff: 'This is my God': One Jew's Faith

James A. Sanders

Professor Dorff begins his chapter by emphasising the value of praxis over against theory in understanding Judaism. He then ends his chapter with a statement of the mission of Judaism in God's world, namely, that of providing a model people as paradigm of what God desires to all people.

One of Abraham Heschel's last articles, 'A Time for Renewal', published in *Midstream* (May 1972), stressed the point that Torah – and, indeed, Judaism – is made up of equal parts of haggadah and halachah. In a 1975 article of mine titled 'Torah and Christ' (a sequel to my book, *Torah and Canon*), I suggested that Torah is made up basically of the two elements: muthos and ethos, gospel and law, story and ethics, identity and life style, faith and obedience, or haggadah and halachah. Incidentally, I did not see a copy of Heschel's article until after I had written 'Torah and Christ'. I say that not to deny Heschel's influence on me – but simply to say that his influence was conveyed not only in my reading Heschel but in our many, many conversations walking along Broadway or Riverside Drive between 1965 and 1972.

My hypothesis in that article was that Pharisaic–rabbinic Judaism fell heir to those in Early Judaism who had emphasised the halachic aspect of Torah, whereas Christianity fell heir to those in Early Judaism who had emphasised the haggadic aspect of Torah. The vast amount of Early Jewish literature that read and re-read Torah and the Prophets with an eye to its haggadic element – that is, as a story of what God had done, with the hope by typology of discerning what God was yet to do – is precisely that Early Jewish literature which Christianity preserved, but which Pharisaic–rabbinic Judaism sloughed off in the period between the First and Second Jewish Revolts. It was the early churches that preserved and continued to copy and read the so-called apocrypha and pseudepigrapha. Without them – and without perhaps the Dead Sea Scrolls – to remind us of their widespread importance in Early Judaism, we would know pitifully little about the great pluralism and rich diversity of Early Judaism.

Both hasidic–Pharisaic Judaism, on the one hand, and all the other denominations of Early Judaism, on the other, fully realised that Torah – both in its strict meaning and in its extended meaning – is always made up of the two basic elements, haggadah and halachah. Even works like Jubilees and the Testaments of the Patriarchs testify to the halachic readings of Torah, as do the New Testament Gospels and Epistles. Certainly 11Q Torah testifies to it even though the library at Qumran contained much non-massoretic Early Jewish literature, in many cases providing the original Hebrew or Aramaic of what the churches later preserved only in translation – such as Enoch. As Al Sundberg said in his dissertation at Harvard, the churches had simply not heard of Judaism's decisions after 70 CE to disinherit all that marvellous literature, so they went right on reading and copying it. The Ethiopian Orthodox Church even today has 81 books in its canon!

I have elsewhere argued that the instruction which Paul received in the Damascus congregation was principally a different set of hermeneutics by which to read the self-same Torah which he had earlier learned to read quite differently under Rabban Gamliel. It makes quite a bit of difference whether one understands Torah to be principally a book of laws set in a narrative framework, or a narrative with laws imbedded in it. Early Christianity, probably taking clues from those Jews of those other Early Jewish denominations who joined the churches, read the Pentateuch in the LXX primarily as a story of what God had been doing since creation, as haggadah, rather than reading it primarily as divine guidelines for obedience. It makes a difference whether one reads Torah asking of it what God has done, or reads it asking what we should do. Paul undoubtedly learned how to do the former from his early Christian instructors at Damascus and elsewhere. This could lead him eventually to ask, in Romans, in whose works does one have faith, in God's works or in our works? And it could eventually lead him to solve the problem which Pharisaic–rabbinic Judaism had solved, in an increasingly hellenised world, but in a totally different way. Pharisaic–rabbinic Judaism solved it by the concept of Torah *she bĕ 'al peh*, a dramatic shift in their understanding of the nature of Scripture, and in the hermeneutic rules by which it could be interpreted for halachah represented by the seven middot of Hillel, the thirteen of Ishmael and the 32 of later tradition. Paul solved it by saying the halachic aspect of Torah was abrogated (Romans 7:1–10) while the haggadic or gospel aspect of Torah was holy, eternal and good (Romans 7:12; 3:31).

This move on the part of Paul, which as we all know triumphed in Christianity over against Jewish Christianity and the Petrine thrust in the early church, threw the churches – in the highly eschatalogical atmosphere in which they continued for a while to exist – back against the old principle, which Professor Dorff stresses on p. 24 of his chapter, *imitatio dei*: 'God has always functioned within Judaism as a model for human behaviour'. That is absolutely correct. Note the so-called 'first *tiqqun sopherim*' in Genesis 18:22 (which turns out not to be a *tiqqun* after all but a wonderful midrash on the passage by an *'al tiqrē* reading by Shimeon bar Parzai of about 300 CE!). This was connected by Shimeon to the ancient practice of *'amîdat ha-zāqēn*, thus giving it a Scriptural base by suggesting an original reading of God's remaining standing before Abraham instead of the way the MT and all versions read of Abraham's remaining standing before God. I once set a student to work connecting the laws of the Book of the Covenant in Exodus 20–23 to acts and statements of God up to that point in Genesis and Exodus; and indeed, many of the laws there received their first illustration in a prior act of God.

In a manner of speaking therein lies the essential difference between traditional Jewish and classical Christian hermeneutics in reading Scripture and especially Torah: Traditional Judaism seeks in it what guide it gives to how to shape life in the home, in synagogue and in the world. Classical Christianity seeks in it the story of what God has done to discern what God is now doing. Again neither reads exclusively in this way. Heschel was right. But there is an option of emphasis: the Christian primarily reads Torah as the beginning of the gospel, of God's Spell, God's story; the Jew primarily reads Torah as a book of divine guidance for lifestyle. And I think Professor Dorff's chapter and statement well illustrate that point.

Dorff valorises one's personal experiences as being as valuable as the cognitive (p. 21), and he stresses the importance of understanding God as a person. Here Judaism and Christianity are in total agreement. I will be interested to learn whether Islam differs significantly or not; I do not really know. Dorff notes how belief in a personal God leads to anthropomorphising God (p. 24). He notes how Halevi and Heschel stressed the religious experience of God as being personal, involving the whole of a person's personality as an individual and as a member of his or her group. He says we should not be offended by, or shy about, anthropomorphic understandings of God. I thoroughly agree. I think I remember correctly that Heschel was writing *God in Search of Man* about the same time that Karl Barth was writing *The Humanity of God*. Christianity, in a manner of speaking, engages in the greatest anthropomorphism of all, in its belief in the incarnation of God in Christ.

I rather think that what Christians need most to learn from Judaism and from Jews is how to monotheise as a hermeneutic in reading Scripture. If the concept of the heavenly council was the biblical and Early Jewish manner of denying the possibility of a pantheon, in its efforts to monotheise in the Iron Age and Persian period, then, as Cyril Richardson pointed out in his 1958 book on the Trinity, the latter was Early Christianity's way of monotheising over against hellenistic–Roman modes of polytheism. Christianity's constant flirtations with polytheism because of misunderstandings of the trinitarian formula and its intended function, and because of hypostatising the *Satan* or the *diabolos* into almost a fourth deity, with a power and a kingdom of his own, can be checked in part by listening to Jewish theologians like Halevi, Rosenzweig, Buber and Heschel, and now Petuchowski, Dorff and others, to be reminded of how to monotheise and pursue the oneness and Integrity of Reality. I trust that we may also receive instruction in this regard from Muslim theologians.

It could be that Jews and others might be reminded by Christians on how *first* to celebrate what God has done and then contemplate what we should do – gospel and then law, haggadah and then halachah. This, as I understand it, is quite different from Dorff's statement on p. 26: 'In our day, as in times past, Jewish belief will grow out of vibrant Jewish practice and community life rather than the other way around'. I do not challenge the validity of that statement, or the wisdom of it for Judaism today. It is, as we have noted, the option of emphasis of Pharisaic–rabbinic Judaism over against Judaism's other denominations and eventually of their heir, Early Christianity. There has always been in Pharisaic–rabbinic Judaism, as Dorff advocates, an emphasis on praxis over against theory, or halachah over against haggadah. And we can rightly thank God for it. I certainly would not recommend that Jews learn from Christian praxis or *behaviour* through the centuries either toward Jews or toward Muslims. All Christians corporately have ever been able to suggest is *imitatio dei*, certainly not *imitatio hominis*; on the level of the individual we have fared better. But since the nationalisation of the church in the early fourth century CE, Christian history has been almost, *almost* a steady chronology of unethical behaviour to non-Christians who showed no inclination to convert to Christianity. Professor Dorff speaks of the difficulty of doing theology after Auschwitz. I would say that Christians must learn to monotheise. And that means minimally to understand all peoples as children of the One God of us all, and then within that overall framework to try to work out and understand what a faithful and viable mission and purpose Christianity should have in this global village on this shrinking planet over which hangs the constant threat of nuclear holocaust. We cannot go on simply as we have in the past with a distorted christocentric singularism. We must learn how to be canonically faithful monotheising pluralists.

A Muslim Response to Elliot Dorff: 'This is my God': One Jew's Faith

Ibrahim Hamdani

In the name of Allah, the Beneficent, the Merciful

I OPENING

It is fitting to open the discussion with the word of God. Allah says in the Qur'an:

> Say, O People of the Book! Come to common terms as between us and you: That we worship none but Allah; That we associate no partners with Him [in his *powers and divine attributes*]; That we erect not, from among ourselves, lords and Patrons other than Allah.

> If then they turn back, Say: Bear witness that we [at least] are Muslims [Bowing to the will of Allah] (3:64).

I would like to draw your attention to the term 'People of the Book'. It is an Islamic term, which refers to Jews and Christians. Among all the Non-Muslims, Jews and Christians are given the special status of 'People of the Book.'

Not only every Muslim believes in all the Prophets of Israel, including Moses and Christ, son of Mary (Peace and blessing of God be upon them all). In addition, we Muslims claim that we are the only people that truly love and honour all these Prophets.

II WHERE DO WE DIFFER AND AGREE?

1. *Methodology of Research*

As a Muslim, I noticed throughout the chapter of Rabbi Dorff, and
especially in 'The Traditional Stance', the absence of quotations from
Torah and Talmud.

As a Muslim, for any issue I shall first consult the Qur'an (Word
of God), then Hadith (Traditions of Prophet Mohammad, Peace be
upon Him); and then comes 'Ijtihad'[1] of early Muslim scholars.

Rabbi Dorff instead, as it appears, has based his thesis on the
views of an Early Jewish scholar (Judah Halevi). This contrasts
with the primary sources used in Islam. Another thing which draws
attention is the title, 'This is My God'. This phrase gives the
impression of exclusiveness and proprietorship. Although Muslims
also use the term 'My God', 'My Lord', meaning that we are His
creation and He our Master and Creator, it is not used to express
possession, because God is One and He is everyone's God.

2. *Reason or Revelation*

I think the main theme of Rabbi Dorff's chapter is that revelation,
not reason, is the primary source of the Jewish belief in God.

To this extent, we agree with Rabbi Dorff.

But, I think, we have a different understanding of terms like
'Revelation', 'Reason', or even 'Philosophy'.

In the Islamic view, the ultimate belief and faith in Allah comes
from revelation and not from intellect or reason. However, in the
revelation – Al-Quran – man is urged to look at his surroundings,
at himself, and use his mind to reason and deduce the inevitability
of the existence of Allah.

Reason and intellect may take a man to the doorsteps of the
domain of faith, but only revelation and the mercy of Allah will
enable him to enter it.

The concept of 'Revelation' or the 'Inspired Word of God' appears
to be different in Rabbi Dorff's dissertation from a Muslim's concept.

A revelation in the form of Al-Quran is exactly and precisely the
word of Allah.

Interpretations, explanations, historical context and so on are
always secondary and never replace the revelation (Qur'an) itself.

This has guaranteed the authenticity of revelation throughout the history of Al-Islam.

This contrasts with the Jewish/Christian way of reporting the revelation, which is not essentially in the words of God, and is subject to differences and variations along with interpretations, revisions and editing. (The emergence of the 'Non-sexist' Bible is one example of such revisions.)

It is surprising for me to know that the Bible has been constantly changed through the process of interpretation. It is even more surprising to see the acknowledgement that 'Judaism is really the religion of the Rabbis more than it is the religion of the Bible'.

To me, the main difference with Rabbi Dorff's Jewish thought is not the importance of 'Revelation'; rather, the difference is, what is the true and valid 'Revelation'?

3. *Without Role Models*

In our view, true belief is the prerequisite of good deeds. Al-Qur'an always reminds us that

> By [the token of] Time [through the ages], Verily Man is in loss, Except such as have Faith, and do righteous deeds, and [join together] in the mutual teaching of Truth, and of Patience and Constancy.

> (CIII. 1–3)

But I agree with the logic of Rabbi Dorff when he says that 'Jewish belief will grow out of vibrant Jewish practice and community life'.

Because good deeds are a living witness of sincerity and true belief, furthermore good deeds provide that suitable environment which supports, strengthens, and nourishes true belief.

I agree with Rabbi Robert Gordis that 'secular Jews are only living off the capital of their religious parents and grandparents'. I would like to add that the same is the case of secular Muslims. Jews, as a race, probably can afford to be secular, but not Muslims, because they are a nation (*Millat*) based upon a creed. Actually Islam and secularism are two opposing idelogies, and it is impossible to create any friendship between them.

Jews as a racial group are still living and may live for long, but do

these Jews have any resemblance to those believers in God who
followed Moses (Peace be upon Him)?

4. *Unique and Personal*

As you will see from the chapter of Dr Muzammil Siddiqi (Chapter
3), as far as the personal and unique aspect of God is concerned the
Islamic view is closer to the Jewish view, with the exception that
sometimes the Jewish view may get too physical, as when we see an
account of a duel between Jacob and God (Genesis 32:22–30).

Al-Qur'an speaks about God's Hearing, Seeing, Love and Anger,
but also tells us, 'Nothing is like Him' (42:11).

5. *Whose Sacrifice was Offered?*

Although the following is a minor point, I would like to mention it.

It makes no difference to Muslims, whether it was Ishmael or
Isaac whose sacrifice was offered by Abraham, because we have the
same love and respect for both of them. But the Qur'an is clear on
this point that Isaac was not even born when the sacrifice of Ishmael
was offered.

Furthermore, from the historical perspective it is interesting to see
that these are Muslims, who have kept the tradition of sacrifice alive.
For a long time, Arabs even kept the horns of the ram, which
replaced Ishmael's sacrifice.[2]

6. *Our View of History*

From a purely Islamic point of view, the historical events are either
partial reward or partial punishment for our acts and deeds, or they
are tests and trials by Allah to see if we are worthy of His blessings.

In this context, if a Holocaust was to occur upon Muslims it would
be regarded as a warning by Allah for not believing strongly in Allah
and not resisting *Zulm* (Injustice).

Notes and References

1. *Ijtihad*: In Islamic terminology it means 'trying to derive Islamic solution from the Qur'an and Hadith by using "*Qiyas*" (syllogistic argument), "*Istiqra*" (inductive argument) and "*Tamathil*" (argument by analogy)'.
2. Syed Modudee in his commentary on the Qur'an (37:112) quotes Ibna-Katheer that Ibna-Abbas and Amr Shahabi saw these horns and that they remained in the Kabbah until the time of Abdullay-ibna-Zubair. (Syed Abu-ul-ala Modudee, *Tafheem-ul-Qur'an*. (Lahore: Islamic Publications, n.d.).

2 On the Christian Doctrine of God

Jack Verheyden

'Now after John was arrested, Jesus came into Galilee, preaching the gospel of God, and saying, "The time is fulfilled, and the kingdom of God is at hand: repent, and believe in the gospel" '.[1] This passage from the New Testament represents the origin of the Christian understanding of God, for this understanding commences with Jesus of Nazareth and has its central focus in his person, teaching, and the events connected with his life and destiny. This means that Christianity brings convictions about God and a particular historical manifestation together, it unites the ultimate nature of reality and a figure of the human past. Some life orientations appear to keep such matters sharply asunder but Christianity has accentuated their union. This must ever be kept in mind.

As specific as the focus of Christian understanding of God has been, Christian thought has not confined itself to this point alone, and the sources that have informed Christian understanding are quite various. Accordingly, the subject admits of many approaches, not only because of the inexpressible greatness of the object of Christian faith, but also because of the multiplicity of traditions and experiences that have shaped Christian understanding.

Indeed, even to begin with the proclamation of Jesus himself immediately directs attention to the tradition in which He stood, the history and religious teaching of ancient Israel. The passage cited above attests this by speaking of 'the time [being] fulfilled' and 'the kingdom of God [being] at hand'. These words indicate that something is being completed, something brought to a climax, that had been going on previously, which the hearers of such words could understand. This idea of the kingdom or rule of God courses through the sayings of Jesus as their dominating subject matter. The God to which both the speaker and the listeners relate is God as manifested in the religious tradition of Israel, and because this is so the Old Testament has been foundational for the Christian doctrine of God. In the second century AD a figure arose to contest this. Marcion said that the God of the Old Testament was not the same God as

41

that of the New Testament, that the former was responsible for this world and its prevalent suffering, while the latter God came as a stranger into this place bringing kindness and love. But early Christianity rejected this teaching as heretical. It was held that 'the God and Father of our Lord Jesus Christ' was the God of the Old Testament. Something new had transpired, but it was the same old God. If a story is to have a fulfilment and/or climax, it must have a beginning and a development of the action. The New Testament presupposes the Old Testament in its view of God.

I THE OLD TESTAMENT

The Old Testament reflects the life of the people of Israel over many centuries, and it would be unrewarding to expect its statements about God to reflect a precision of identical agreement at every turn. Nevertheless, the consistency of its view of God is remarkable. The Old Testament does not attempt to give an ordered account of the nature of God, such as might be found in a treatise of theology. Rather, it speaks of God usually through what God has done and the engagement of people who have interacted with God. This active and confrontational setting of speech about God dominates the Old Testament. God has a distinguishing name, Yahweh, manifested to Israel in Yahweh's establishing them as a people claimed by Him. He is considered to be different, very different from the Gods of other peoples. Yahweh is definite and unique. Perhaps the most defining thing that can be said of Him is that, in the words of Samuel Taylor Coleridge, Yahweh is the great 'I am'. Often attempts to define the name 'Yahweh' itself have produced phrases like 'I am that I am'.[2] The word of God spoken by the prophets again and again emphasises this first-person declaration: 'and you shall know that I am Yahweh'. This insistent 'I-ness' of God that becomes present and active in the affairs of Israel is expressed in many ways, most typically by speaking to and through Abraham, Moses, the prophets, and certain others. Yahweh is contrasted – or, perhaps more accurately, contrasts Himself – with other gods and faltering human ways. Other gods shift around blurring into each other and deposing one another; and human inconstancy and fraility cannot be attributed to God: 'For I, Yahweh, do not change'.[3] Yahweh is beyond identification with the forces of the natural world and the given order of society which do characterise so many of the deities of the ancient Near East. Later, theology used the word 'transcendent' to denote this feature of the Old Testament God. The texts themselves use words like 'lifted up' and 'sits above'. For instance: 'For thus says the high and lofty One who inhabits eternity, whose name is Holy: "I dwell in the high and holy place" '.[4] Yet, this 'I' is not simply distant and away for He becomes present and near, as the text quoted above indicates by continuing: 'and also with him who is of a contrite and humble spirit'. The contrast of transcendence and immanence that is indicated by this passage is manifested in many aspects. On the one hand, Yahweh is described in ways that seem anthropomorphic; thus one hears from the text about God's hands, fingers, arms, back, eyes, nostrils, way of walking and listening and laughing, etc. Yahweh shouts aloud in His fury against his enemies, and then like a woman giving birth, 'I will gasp and pant'.[5] On the other hand, the texts say that Yahweh is not human, that He is invisible to human eyes, 'for man shall not see me and live',[6] and that the great 'I am' shall not be depicted by any graven images. Yahweh is too 'other' for pictures and statues.

Connected with this humanlike descriptive language and its severe qualification is the matter of sex. The third person pronouns that refer to Yahweh are masculine, as is evident already above. Consequently, in recent years Yahweh is referred to as a male God. But the severe qualification of otherness applies here also. In the context of the ancient Near East sexually-defined deities abounded – female and male – but historians of religion have observed that Yahweh is the only prominent deity of the ancient world who does not have a sexual consort.[7] Does this make the Holy One of Israel more masculine, or less? Given the prominence of the exaltation of the family in Israel, this lack of consort appears to point to the fact that Yahweh transcends sexual differentiation even amidst the concrete human language utilised to describe this God of the Old Testament. To group Yahweh with Zeus and Marduk and Osiris is misleading. The central pronoun is the 'I', not the 'He'.

The transcendence of Yahweh is strongly brought to the centre of the Old Testament through His election of Israel. God's initiating activity occurs in many fashions, but the choosing of the people of Israel – indeed, forming them to be a people by means of the deliverance from Egypt – is the confessional focus of the Old Testament. The active 'I am' is largely defined by what it does. Yahweh has freely sought out and established a special relationship with this people. There is nothing in them or about them which deserved being brought into this relationship. It rests in the mysterious freedom of Yahweh's choosing.

In this election, Yahweh enters into covenant with the people of Israel. Since, 'I am Yahweh, your God, who brought you out of the land of Egypt, out of the house of bondage' you, Israel, need to live accordingly.[8] Consequently, there are obligations entailed in the relationship. Yahweh provides teaching and laws as to how people are to live. Because of what has been done in creating a people, there is an unconditional obligation to respond in obedience to the covenant agreement, beginning with the Ten Commandments and extending to instruction dealing with virtually every aspect of life. Yahweh will maintain the covenant and Israel should live by the teaching provided. There were blessings if the covenant was kept, and curses if it was not.

That Yahweh was a God of covenant is displayed in more informal ways. Abraham is told that in obeying Yahweh's call He will make of Abraham a great nation and that 'by you all the families of the earth will be blessed'.[9] And before that, God covenants everlastingly with Noah and every living creature – indeed, even with the earth itself – that never again will a flood destroy everything.

As the one who deserves and requires obedience in the covenant, Yahweh is the great king. In earlier Israel, no man should be king because Yahweh is;[10] the Old Testament insists emphatically that Yahweh is the rightful ruler. The power of God was evident in the deliverance from Egypt, and asserted itself time and again. Hymns of praise recur throughout the Old Testament that no opponents can stand against Yahweh's might. The nations are as dust in relation to Him.

This seemingly unlimited exaltation of God's almightiness is pointedly reflected in the understanding of God as creator. Creation does not come about through the strife of deities and celestial powers, it is not hatched from an egg or other natural processes escalated to cosmic scope. Rather, it is simply portrayed as coming about through God's commanding word or by fiat. 'God said, "Let there be light"', and there was light', etc; and then God saw that it was good.[11] The freedom, the power, the purpose of God is depicted in this well-known passage, as is the fact that God is different from that which is created. And as ruler, Lord, Creator, there is no point of continuing to speak of other gods, beside Yahweh.[12] As the creator, there is no limitation on where God is: 'Do I not fill heaven and earth?' says Yahweh.[13] Similarly, as creator God knows without restriction, not being limited to the outward appearance, but looking into the heart and knowing the hearts of all human beings.[14] Further, there is no limit in time to God's kingly rule: 'Yahweh will reign for ever and ever.'[15]

As the Lord and ruler who maintains the covenant relationship with Israel, Yahweh possesses certain attributes of character. The characteristic that is most prominent is righteousness. As the ruler, Yahweh is the judge of his people, and does what is right. The natural setting of the word 'righteousness' is that of jurisprudence and justice, and reflects the centrality of the covenant in the Old Testament. As righteous, Yahweh does what is right and requires righteousness or being right from human beings. In reference to the God of the covenant, righteousness includes what He does to set things right and actively to pursue the course of justice. Insofar as this pursuit of righteousness protects the innocent and the goods of the covenant, the righteousness of God can be spoken of as saving in nature, but insofar as righteousness opposes the violation of the right, it will bring judgment and be punishing.[16] In the latter case, because Yahweh possesses righteousness, this will be expressed as wrath against sin and iniquity. When Israel violates the covenant, Yahweh's wrath is provoked and poured out. But its purpose usually is meant to be a refining fire that will restore harmony to human society. Originally, it is invoked against Israel, but in the later books it is expressed as much against Gentiles. God's righteous wrath in the Old Testament stands certainly as a vivid sign that Yahweh regards sin as heinous and deserving of His repudiation and judgement.

Yahweh is also prominently characterised by love, the word having various shades of meaning. Sometimes it is the love connected with Israel's being elected by God, sometimes it is the steadfast love of maintaining the covenant, sometimes the compassionate love for the poor and needy, sometimes the love that is longsuffering because of Israel's wayward behaviour. Ideas of love and grace can shade off into the mercy that overlooks people's sins in order that they may repent. And such mercy was grounded in Yahweh's faithfulness to His Promise in the covenant relationship.

There is a tension between God's mercy and God's righteous judgement in the Old Testament. A 'Day of Yahweh' in the future came to be expected in which there would be a fulfilment for Israel, but in the early prophets such a day came to be regarded as one that would involve disaster, 'a day of ruin and devastation', a time that for Israel would be darkness and not light.[17] But then, subsequently, later prophets saw that beyond the coming judgement God's ultimate activity would involve restoration, indeed that 'all the ends of the world shall see the salvation of our God'.[18] The kingship of Yahweh, recognised in Israel, extant in heaven, because of the greatness and power of the creator, will come as a future consummation for the entire earth and all peoples. Everything that resists God will be overthrown in that day resulting in a longed-for perfect Kingdom of God. In such an eschatological time there would be an outpouring of the Spirit of God which would bring higher powers to all human beings.[19] At the close of the Old Testament and later writings characterised as apocalyptic, this eschatological expectation comes to' be interpreted by some more dramatically in terms of cosmic transformation and the elimination of the conditions of the present physical world. By the resurrection of the dead not only will those living in the future participate, but those of earlier times will be awakened. The victory of God in that day will be not only over the nations of the earth, but will conquer spiritual forces of evil. But older ideas also continued, which saw the eschatological fulfilment of God's rule more politically in earthly terms and, thus, rejected resurrection.

II THE NEW TESTAMENT

That 'the time is fulfilled, and the kingdom of God is at hand' means that the New Testament begins in the context of this eschatological outlook that involves the consummation of God's reign. Jesus announces this Kingdom as having drawn so near that it has already begun to be effective in the present. His own appearance and activity manifests the power of the Kingdom. Jesus refers to God as the Lord of heaven and earth, as the Creator, as the sustainer of all by way of making His sun rise on the evil and on the good and sending the rain, as feeding the birds and clothing the grass of the field, as knowing the needs of people, etc. That is, there is considerable teaching of Jesus that does not appear inherently connected with the distinctive message of the eschatological arrival of the Kingdom of God. There is a selective reaffirmation of the Old Testament tradition, often against current practices and understandings of first-century Judaism. It is evident that God exercises a total claim on human beings according to Jesus in his summary of the Law. Nevertheless, it is the nearness and mysterious presence of the Kingdom that provides the context of his message and supplies it with the dimension that fueled controversies.

A prominent feature of his proclamation concerns the opportunity of participation in God's fulfilment by those who were not regarded as worthy to do so by the general opinion of the time. God in His inexplicable generosity was including those who had worked since dawn; and like a father who went out and welcomed back with rejoicing and full reinstatement the son who had departed from him and wasted his inheritance; and like a shepherd who refused to simply remain with the ninety-nine sheep safely in hand but went out searching for the one sheep that was lost. God is one who caringly goes out to seek the one person who is lost and seemingly undeserving and unworthy of such regard. There is a reality of God's forgiveness becoming available for those whose faith will receive it.

A striking aspect of Jesus's message is the concerted emphasis on God as 'Abba', translated by the English word Father. This Aramaic word has its setting in the intimate context of a family name, something that the English word increasingly no longer has. Jesus did not use this word, apparently, for God's relationship to human beings generally but for those who followed him and accepted the message of the Kingdom. But, even more pointedly, he used it to depict his own relationship to God as his Father. Jesus claimed the authority to act out God's seeking grace, including the right to forgive sin. Since this was considered the prerogative of God alone in first-century Judaism, it brought against him the charge of blasphemy.

There is severity also in the proclamation of Jesus. Alongside of entering into the Kingdom and being admitted to the Father's house, there is for those who reject the promise the danger of exclusion into darkness and Gehenna. God for Jesus is the future judge. He is like one who will hold a reckoning with his servants as to how they have used their talents while he was away. Jesus tells his friends properly to fear the God who requires one's soul whatever the situation may be concerning one's body and physical possessions: 'Yes, I tell you, fear him!'[20] Certain cities of his day face a judgement worse than Sodom and Gomorrah.

But for those who turn to receive the coming Kingdom, there is no need to fear, for God's fatherly care also will be there in the future. God alone is completely good and invites human trust in His power. God cares for sparrows, but even more for human beings. God is a valuer of the human person. One can look to God as the future giver of bread and the deliverer from evil. God is one who will call peacemakers His children and who will reward in heaven those who are persecuted for righteousness' sake.

Jesus presented his hearers with a decision to turn or repent. God breaks the power of Satan and this is evidenced in the healings that Jesus performs. These acts indicate the transforming power of the Kingdom already in the present as does the reality of the forgiveness of sin that Jesus makes available. For that reason God is spoken of as one who sends Jesus: 'he who receives me receives him who sent me'.[21] All of this requires decision by the hearer.

For those who do turn and receive the forgiveness of God, there is a higher righteousness called for than Jesus thinks is taught by scribes and Pharisees. Love for one's fellows without restriction of national limitation or cultic regulation is required. But more than that, Jesus indicates that God is one who enables through His forgiveness the fulfilment of the demand of love for God and neighbour that the new life requires: 'he who is forgiven little, loves little'.[22]

When Jesus's mission took him to Jerusalem, he was convicted of blasphemous messianic pretensions by the religious authorities and turned over to the Roman political administration which in turn decided to sentence him to death, apparently as a political revolutionary. His disciples deserted him. The mode of execution by means of crucifixion combined death with several hours of torture. This was carried out under the inscription: 'This is the King of the Jews'.[23] Jesus died with the words of the Twenty-second Psalm on his lips, calling to 'my God' in the experience of abandonment.

The stunning horror of this sudden end to Jesus's life – after the proclamation of the nearness and hidden presence of the Reign of God, and Jesus's own claim to authority – appears to have left his followers in despair and disarray. But this situation was reversed within a short time with the appearance of Jesus to his followers and their realisation that God had resurrected him beyond death. This was seen as an event of marvellous proportions – not first of all because it indicated that Jesus lived immortally, although that was included, but that it confirmed and validated his message and activity during his life. The resurrection of Jesus attested something about who he really was and is: 'Let all the house of Israel therefore know assuredly that God has made him both Lord and Christ'.[24]

The New Testament, then, was written from this standpoint of faith in Jesus as the present exalted Lord. It presents the history of Jesus and who He is on the basis of the truth which had now been revealed. Jesus had been the proclaimer and the bearer of the presence of the Reign of God, or of God-ruling. Now that the truth about this hidden and mysterious presence had been made explicit, the primitive church used language about Jesus to interpret what was really transpiring in the events connected with Him. Therefore, so-called Christological language replaces language about the Kingdom of God as the most prevalent expression. The very title 'Christ' or Messiah is one aspect of this change. During Jesus's ministry according to Matthew, Mark and Luke, this title is avoided because it had the connotation of a political king through whom God's rule would be fulfilled. But after the crucifixion, an occurrence as far contrasted as could be conceived from political power because it was a means of executing political criminals, this title was considered most appropriate. The Christ was a figure connected with the eschatological expectations in Israel, so to give Jesus that title meant that he was the one through whom the fulfilment was taking place.

In light of the Resurrection, the primitive church saw the crucifixion as in continuity with that unconditional forgiveness of sin of which Jesus spoke; it represented the cost in retrieving the lost so that they could be brought back to God. Thus Paul says representatively: 'For I delivered to you as of first importance what I also received, that Christ died for our sins in accordance with the scriptures'.[25] The scriptures here, of course, are what Christianity calls the Old Testament, and this points to the fact that the Hebrew Bible is drawn on extensively for the rubrics by which Jesus and his history are understood. These rubrics – the titles of Jesus and other interpretative patterns – are the means by which the New Testament church expresses understandings of God. For instance, the speech of Stephen in the Book of Acts connects the tabernacling presence of Yahweh in the midst of Israel during the journey through the wilderness with the presence of God in Jesus Christ.[26] But this is only one passing rubric among a myriad of instances. Jesus Christ is the Suffering Servant of God who suffers on behalf of and for the redemptive benefit of others. He is the Lamb of God who takes away the sin of the world. He is the High Priest who offers up himself in sacrificial love for the eternal salvation of other human beings. He is the mediator: 'For there is one God, and there is one mediator between God and men, the man Christ Jesus, who gave himself as a ransom for all'.[27] He is the Son of Man, that heavenly figure who appears at the end of the old evil age and through whom God triumphs over that which opposes Him, who opens the gate to a new age. He is the Word of God, the creative and communicative power of God in action that preexists the historical appearance of Jesus. He is the Son of God who in his life stood in intimate obedience to his Father and is His only-begotten one. He is the pioneer of salvation and of our faith. There are many more.

These Christological affirmations of the New Testament see the activity of God in various ways as operative in Jesus Christ and the new life made actual through him. As noted, the expectation of a new influx of the Spirit of God had long been present in Israel, one that would not be limited to Israel. The primitive church comes to participate in this new life-giving and energising power of God. The Holy Spirit is released in a new manner by God's work in Christ so that there is inward transformation of human beings. It is called the Spirit of adoption through which the community became children of God, heirs with Christ, and able to say to God, Abba! Father! The Holy Spirit can lead to a person's becoming a new creation because what is participated in now is the earnest or instalment of coming glory. The Spirit of God provides the bond of unity among people that can transcend other earthly affiliation and brings freedom and love. The Holy Spirit is itself the presence of God.

With this presence and the interpretative rubrics pointed to above, the declaration comes that God is one who loves. This is most powerfully expressed in the writings of Paul and John in the New Testament: 'In this the love of God was made manifest among us, that God sent his only Son into the world, so that we might live through him', and 'God shows his love toward us in that while we were yet sinners Christ died for us'.[28] The very way God is defined is through what happens in Jesus Christ. The closest analogy here – as it also is the foundation – is in the Old Testament's fashion of speaking of God as the one who brought Israel out of the Land of Egypt. God forges a new eschatological covenant in Christ according to Paul, a covenant outside the earlier covenant of the Law. The crucifixion of Christ indicates that God deals with the people of His world in a manner that cannot be encompassed by anything human beings can accomplish: 'But now the righteousness of God has been manifested apart from law, although the law and the prophets bear witness to it, the righteousness of God through faith in Jesus Christ for all who believe.'[29] The principle of faith excludes our boasting on the basis of any established custom, law or religious practice. By this appeal to the righteousness of God, Paul shows the continuity of the New Testament with the Old. God's action in setting things right in a world of ungodliness and wickedness is meant to prove at the present time that God is righteous.[30] Further word will have to wait.

God has entered into a new way with the world in Jesus Christ. It is a way that means the tearing down of the walls between Israel and the peoples of the world so that all may inherit the gift of salvation. Much of Israel itself has rejected the gospel but when the full number of the Gentiles come in then all Israel will be saved.[31] One cannot limit the new covenant for Paul because: 'God was in Christ reconciling the world to himself'.[32] There is no more central contention to the New Testament doctrine of God.

III THE INFLUENCE OF THE GREEK TRADITION

The variety of interpretation of Jesus of Nazareth and his destiny in the New Testament itself was a significant theological problem for the post-New Testament church. But there had been even more contrasting views of Jesus in primitive Christianity which were not included in the writings of the New Testament. Most basically, there appear to have been four ways to deal with the issue of Jesus of Nazareth in relation to the reality of God. First, what Jesus had to say about God and the announcement of his resurrection could be simply rejected. Second, Jesus could be incorporated into the tradition of the Old Testament and Jewish faith in God as a later teacher of the Law, or one among the series of prophets of Israel. Some groups of early so-called Jewish Christianity appear to represent this.[33] Third, the resurrected Christ could be so spiritualised that the continuity with the God of the Old Testament was simply negated. The humanity of Jesus was really eliminated by docetists and gnostics in this type, and there was no positive relationship between Jesus Christ and the Creator and Lord of the world. Fourth, the person and history of Jesus could be assimilated into the view of God itself coming from the Old Testament tradition. In this type, faith in God came to coincide in fulfilment with believing in Jesus Christ. We have inspected above some of the ways in which this is expressed.

But as the primitive church had spread beyond the confines of Palestine to the various reaches of the Mediterranean world, its members increasingly had to come to terms with a new and different manner of thinking. The dynamically active rule of God, the import-

ance of will in God and the human, the idea of a consummation of
God's reign, these and other Hebraic patterns of understanding were
remote from much of the hellenistic mind. Particularly was this
true of the intellectually advanced tradition of philosophical thought
stemming from Greece. Conceptualities had been refined in this
philosophical tradition which raised and answered different questions, and also sometimes similar questions in a different manner,
than those ingredient to the Old and New Testaments. For instance,
what is the reason for holding that God exists? The Bible does not
approach the knowledge of God in that manner. Within the context
of the tradition of Israel, God was known through the mighty acts
of revelation. But this God of the Bible was also held to be the God
of all the earth and heavens. How are the other nations able to know
that God is? As early Christianity moved into the hellenistic world,
it had to deal with such a question and many related ones.

One answer to such a question lay in the multifarious religious life
of the Mediterranean area. But this orientation was polytheistic, and
therefore similar to the gods contrasted with Yahweh already in the
Old Testament. The God of the Bible did not correspond, in Greece
for instance, with Zeus and Dionysius, etc., either singly or in
totality. Gods such as these had already been called into question
by the philosophical tradition of the Greeks. Beginning with Thales
in presocratic thought, thinkers had proved through the use of
reasoning processes for the *arché* of all that is. Turning away from
the Homeric pantheon they sought for the nature of the divine by
reasoning about the nature of this origin and sustaining principle of
the universe. The earliest answers indicated that it was water, or
earth, or fire, but eventually philosophy arrived at positions which
interpreted the basis of all that is in terms of the incorporeal reason
that is uncreated, immutable and imperishable, beautiful and good,
ineffable and simple unity, the first and final cause of all beings.

Now it is this tradition, particularly in some of its more acceptable
platonic versions, that early Christianity said corresponded with the
God of the Bible, at least to an important extent. This divine principle of all that is was monotheistic in Christian eyes and provided
common ground for understanding in the hellenistic world.[34] Further,
the anthropomorphisms of the Bible – particularly in the earlier
portions of the Old Testament – must not be understood according
to the mythological antics of the Homeric pantheon. God's otherness
from such worldly identifications was expressed in the language about
divinity of the Greek philosophical tradition, also. God as the prin-

ciple of all that is possesses a different being or substance from things of the world.

While this alliance with Greek philosophy in the doctrine of God gave expression to the universality of God throughout the creation and to the transcendence of God beyond the idols of polytheism, there were also severe difficulties inherent in utilising this form of thought. The God of the Bible manifests His will in and through events. The activity of the great 'I am' becomes confrontationally present within the world. How can language about the immutable source indicate such activity? Further, how can such a divine substance give expression to the eschatologically-consummating events involved in the reality of Jesus Christ? How can the *arché* make covenant?

To answer questions like these proved to be an exceedingly complex – and, also, a confusing – task. Each new attempt at resolution brought new problems for theological understanding Summarily, the results received by the church took the following form. The party known as Arians thought that in order to protect monotheism, Christ and the Spirit could not be said to be fully God – that Christ was the first preeminent creature who stood divinely closer to the one God than anything else. The consensus rejected this as unacceptable because it made something other than God the saviour of the world. It is the very being of God which accomplishes salvation, so that Jesus Christ is a person who unites in himself fully human and fully divine natures. God is not only the Creator and *arché* of all but also has been within the world in Jesus Christ. This came to be referred to as 'Incarnation'. This was not a New Testament word but one used to interpret phrases like 'the Word became flesh' and 'God was in Christ reconciling'. The same being of God the Father was there in the Son, Jesus Christ, and similarly with the Holy Spirit. This means that in the economy of God's redemption of the world there are distinctions within the divine being or substance. This was the 'only' way to interpret God's eschatological act in the linguistic world of substance. The expressions 'triune' and Trinity were utilised to state the activity of God in the language of substance and being. Again, 'Trinity' was not a New Testament word but was the interpretation of the God named as Father, Christ the Son, and the Holy Spirit in the text.

But a further issue came to the fore. The distinctions within the saving economy of God as Father, Son and Holy Spirit in the world were taken by some – such as Sabellius, according to his opponents

– as referring to successive manifestations of God through time so that God the Father was at the beginning, then God the Son, and finally in temporal series, the Holy Spirit. Each of these three were modes which God passed through. Again, this position was rejected. The gospel accounts of Jesus praying to God the Father militated against such successiveness. The economic Trinity of God in the world involved all three *personas* or roles simultaneously, as it were. This Trinity of revelation and salvation, however, itself raised a new problem. If the form of revelation and salvation has this triune structure, how is that related to God as the immortal being prior and beyond the world? If such distinctions apply to God's very being in relation to the world, is there any basis for saying that they do not apply to God prior and beyond the world – that is, to God's inner being? The answer that came to this question – explicitly by Origen at first – is that the distinctions of Father, Son and Holy Spirit do apply to God's inner being. This full doctrine of the Trinity therefore became prevalent in the church.

The importance of the doctrine of the Trinity in the worship of the church gave prominence to the language of the words used to describe the distinctions of the three above names. In Western Christianity, *'persona'* through the centuries shifted its meaning from a role or mask to a word indicating a centred self-consciousness and a depth of distinct spiritual being. Most modern Protestant theology thinks that such a development means that the language of 'person' should no longer be used in trinitarian characterisation.

The dialectics of this discussion concerning the distinctions pertaining to the being of God in the Mediterranean world often took place in a manner that later appeared removed from the realities of religious life. But the intention of these attempts at theological understanding was directed to the interpretation of scripture. The doctrine of God that was produced was heavily debated at every formative stage by those closely related to church life. The resulting doctrine did not have the status of scripture, but was meant as an acceptable confession that resulted from reasoning about the biblical basis. One result of this procedure is that such effort went into formulating the issues related to the being of God that explicit agreement on what God accomplished in salvation was left much more fluid and variously defined. But it is this subject which is the focus of the material in the New Testament, and which is present even when not expressed in the controversies that involved the being of God and the Person of Christ during the early centuries. The Christian doctrine of God includes what God accomplishes in and through Jesus Christ.

Space prevents even an outline of the topic here in the early church and beyond. Through Christ God breaks the power of Satan enslaving the world; in Christ God raises the nature of human being to a higher potentiality; in Christ divine teaching is provided which directs life in a holy manner; through Christ God humbles Himself and provides the medicine that can cure human self-centred pride. Later in the church the resolution of the tension – if not conflict – between God's justice and God's merciful love in the face of human sin came to be most prominent. These perspectives were not viewed as mutually exclusive, but as aspects of God's activity that overcomes sin and evil.

Modern Protestant theology often has been critical of this Patristic discussion of the doctrine of God, for more than one reason. First, the doctrine is formulated with little insight into will and freedom in the divine being. Second, speaking of Jesus Christ as having two natures brought the danger – which was not always avoided as time passed – of the divinity overwhelming the humanity, particularly in regard to Jesus's knowledge. Third, the being of God was so sharply contrasted with creaturely being that passions were considered something corporeal and animal – and, consequently, not attributable to God. Nevertheless, the accomplishments of the attempt to state the biblical God in a philosophical conceptuality were great and erected directions which have endured in several contexts even to the present. The tradition of speaking of God as the principle of being or being-itself has continued through the centuries, most prominently in the heritage of the thirteenth-century thinker, Thomas Aquinas. Whatever other criticisms some modern Protestant thought may have rightly levelled against the categories of this era, the fact that it allied itself with the Greek philosophical tradition's one divine being rather than with cultic polytheism was of inestimable importance. The universality of God achieved unmistakable affirmation there for Christian thought.

On the other hand, the universal orientation of God in Jesus Christ which was affirmed in the doctrine of the Incarnation and the work in Christ of overcoming sin and evil has been much more ambitious in modern theology. The nineteenth-century saw, in significant streams of Protestant thought, a new and deeper appreciation of the humanity of Jesus. This has been a great gain, but since 1870 much influential Protestant theology has confined the redemptive activity of God to the revelational knowledge that Jesus performs in relation to other human beings. A new condition for the human race universally through the crucifixion and resurrection thus becomes seriously muted, if not eliminated. This type of understanding limits the effect of Jesus Christ to the particular historical tradition of those who do receive what he communicates to them. But the earliest centuries of Christian thought which took place in the context of considerable religious diversity had a different vision. It is perhaps represented best in Tertullian's dictum: 'Christ called himself truth, not custom'.[35]

Notes and References

1. Mark 1:14, 15.
2. Exodus 3:14.
3. Malachi 3:6.
4. Isaiah 57:15.
5. Isaiah 42:14.
6. Exodus 33:20.
7. William F. Albright, *From the Stoneage to Christianity* (Baltimore: John Hopkins, 1946) p. 199; G. Ernest Wright, *The Old Testament Against Its Environment* (Naperville, Ill.: Alec Allenson, 1957) p. 23.
8. Exodus 20:2.
9. Genesis 12:3.
10. Judges 8:22.
11. Genesis 1:3.
12. Isaiah 45:5.
13. Jeremiah 23:24.
14. I Samuel 16:7; I Kings 8:39.
15. Exodus 15:18.
16. Cf. Robert Dentan, *The Knowledge of God in Ancient Israel* (New York: Seabury, 1968) pp. 165–72.
17. Zephaniah 1:15; Amos 5:18.
18. Isaiah 52:10.
19. Joel 2:28.
20. Luke 12:5.
21. Matthew 10:40.
22. Luke 7:47; cf. Werner Kummel, *The Theology of the New Testament*, (Nashville: Abingdon, 1973) pp. 54–5.
23. Luke 23:38.
24. Acts 2:36.
25. I Corinthians 15:3.
26. Acts 7:44f.
27. I Timothy 2:5.
28. I John 4:9; Romans 5:8.
29. Romans 3:21–2.

30. Romans 11:25.
31. Romans 3:26.
32. II Corinthians 5:19.
33. Cf. Hans-Martin Barth, *Die Christliche Gotteslehre* (Gutersloh: Gerd Mohn, 1974) pp. 14–15.
34. Cf. Wolfhart Pannenberg, 'The Appropriation of the Philosophical Concept of God as a Dogmatic Problem of Early Christian Theology', in *Basic Questions in Theology*, II (Philadelphia: Fortress, 1971) pp. 119–83.
35. *De virginibus velandis*, I, 1. Cited in Joseph Ratzinger, *Introduction to Christianity* (New York: Herder and Herder, 1970) p. 97.

A Jewish Response to Jack Verheyden: On the Christian Doctrine of God

David Ellenson

John Hick, in his work, *God Has Many Names*, has pointed out that interfaith dialogue 'takes place on various levels and in a variety of contexts'. One level, which he entitles 'discursive theological dialogue', is marked in one of its forms by what Hick labels as 'purely confessional dialogue'.[1] In defining this form for the Christian participant in interreligious discussion, Hick states the following:

> Here the Christian, in dialogue with people of other faiths, speaks from within his own conviction that God has entered decisively into history in the person of Jesus Christ, the second person of the Holy Trinity incarnate, who has revealed the divine nature and purpose for man in a unique and unsurpassable way in comparison with which all other revelations must necessarily be secondary, in the sense of being incomplete, or imperfect, or preliminary, or in some other way vitally inferior to the Christian revelation.[2]

While the person who adopts this position may be personally open and hospitable to the non-Christian, the implications of appropriating such a stance for interreligious dialogue are clear. For the non-Christian participant in such a conversation is led, naturally and inexorably, into a defensive posture *vis-à-vis* the Christian who employs such an occasion as an opportunity to bear witness to the superiority – and by extension the self-sufficiency – of Christian revelation. The non-Christian may well view the Christian's teachings as edifying, perhaps even inspirational. However, in most instances, the non-Christian will listen respectfully and tend, as a result of an almost instinctual protective reaction, to ignore even the most mild 'truth-claims' advanced by their Christian proponent. Furthermore, when the listener is a Jew, this tendency toward 'self-defence' is only intensified.

All this is said in order to provide a context for my brief response to Jack Verheyden's articulate chapter, 'On the Christian Doctrine of God'. Indeed, as a Jew, there is much I can admire about his description of a Christian conception of God. He is careful, for example, not to fall into the all-too-common trap often evidenced in meetings of this type in which an Old Testament God of wrath is pitted against a Christian God of love. For his depiction of an Old Testament God of righteousness who expresses 'wrath against sin and iniquity' is balanced by his recognition that Yahweh, the Jewish God of the Old Testament, 'is also prominently characterised by love' (p. 45). Furthermore, as Verheyden notes, Jesus in the New Testament parallels Yahweh in the Old, for Jesus is not only a Lord of 'grace', but one of 'severity'. As he states, 'Alongside of entering into the Kingdom and being admitted to the Father's house, there is for those who reject the promise the danger of exclusion into darkness and Gehenna' (p. 47). The stereotypical pitfall of 'the good and loving Jesus' versus 'the stern and wrathful Yahweh' presented in all too many Christian polemics against Judaism is thus avoided.

More importantly, in pointing out that the Christian conception of Jesus as God Incarnate embodies the same substantive dialectical conception of the deity that is revealed in the Old Testament, Verheyden makes what I consider to be the most significant point of his chapter – i.e., that the Old Testament has 'foundational' importance for the Christian doctrine of God. He not only begins his essay with this theme, but confirms it over and over again throughout his essay. Thus, in describing Paul's view concerning the righteousness of God, Verheyden claims that the source for this view is the Old Testament conception of the deity. Verheyden, commenting upon this, thus states directly, 'By this appeal to the righteousness of God, Paul shows the continuity of the New Testament with the Old' (p. 50). Again, the Christian definition of God, arrived at in the New Testament, according to Professor Verheyden, through an analysis of that which 'happens in Jesus Christ', means that Christianity follows a pattern laid down by the Old Testament in its understanding and definition of God. For the 'closest analogy' to this Christian mode of understanding and conceptualising God 'is . . . the Old Testament's fashion of speaking of God as the one who brought Israel out of the Land of Egypt' (p. 50). This observation is not surprising, as the Old Testament, in Verheyden's view, serves

as the 'foundation' of the New. Again, while I am not a scholar of
the Christian Bible, it strikes me that Verheyden, in presenting a
description of the Christian conception of God as revealed in the
New Testament, is not incorrect in rejecting the Marcion heresy and
that he is representative of most Christians in presenting the Old
Testament as the source – though certainly not the culmination or
the embodiment – of the Christian doctrine of God. New Testament
theology, presupposing as it does the Old Testament, is thus, in
Verheyden's judgement, analogous to Biblical Hebrew theology as
it is expressed in the Old.

Analogy, however, is not identity, and it is precisely this type of
parallel which, from a Jewish perspective, is so troublesome. This is
because it tends to gloss over the substantive differences which do,
in fact, exist between Jewish and Christian conceptions of God.
Furthermore, in its Christocentrism, it fails to treat Judaism as a
religion worthy of respect and possessing an integrity and history of
its own. While the Old Testament may provide 'a beginning and a
development' for a revelatory story which is yet to emerge, it does
not provide its 'fulfilment and/or climax' (p. 42). The Old Testament,
from the Christian perspective presented here, takes on significance
only insofar as it provides a background for the divine incarnation
which is about-to-be in Christ. Indeed, the very term used here to
describe Hebrew Scriptures – the Old Testament – testifies to the
anticipatory and thus, ultimately, utilitarian role biblical Judaism
occupies in the Christian conception of God. The historical development of Judaism as a religion – and the autonomy it possesses as a
religious tradition in the minds and hearts of its adherents – is thereby
ignored and consigned to irrelevancy in a Christian schema of reality.
To say, then, that the Old Testament provides a foundation for
the New Testament is equivalent, from one Jewish perspective, to
asserting that a fossil serves as a source for what will eventually
evolve into a higher life form. While, from the viewpoint of those
'higher forms', or fuller embodiments of the 'truth', this evolutionary
view may be perceived as true, this provides little solace to the
'fossil'.

Furthermore, the type of Christocentrism evidenced here – which
has the Christian identify Judaism as a preliminary – albeit vital –
step toward Christianity – causes the teachings of Judaism and its
character as an historically developing religion to be disregarded
and/or distorted. Thus, Verheyden writes, 'God has entered into a
new way with the world in Jesus Christ. It is a way that means the

tearing down of the walls between Israel and the peoples of the world so that all may inherit the gift of salvation' (p. 51). Here, then, the view of an expansive Christian universalism is presented in contrast to the caricature of what must be regarded as a mean and narrow Jewish particularism. Yet, Judaism, while holding the doctrine that the Torah contains the knowledge of God's truth, has never tied this doctrine to an eschatology of exclusive salvation.[3] As Elliot Dorff has phrased it:

> Non-Jews were never part of the Sinai Covenant, and therefore they are not obligated under it. That does not mean, though, that they are excluded from God's concern or prevented from enjoying God's favour. On the contrary, if they abide by the Seven Commandments given to Noah and seek to be righteous, they have done all God wants of them. 'The pious and virtuous of all nations participate in eternal bliss', the rabbis said (*Sifra* on *Leviticus* 19:18).[4]

Thus, to state that Christianity offered the gift of salvation to all humanity while implying that Judaism restricted it to Israel is simply wrong.

This Christocentric view of God Verheyden presents as being the 'central contention' in 'the New Testament doctrine of God' (p. 51) thus makes it difficult for Jews and Christians to dialogue on this topic in a way which would foster change and growth. For how can a Jew, with her or his conception of a 'commanding-forgiving' God who calls persons to Covenant and the performance of commandments (*mitzvot*) respond to the words, 'God forges a new eschatological covenant in Christ . . ., a covenant outside the earlier covenant of the Law' (p. 50) with sentiments other than, 'I respect, but cannot affirm, your belief'? In short, I am suggesting that for Christians to engage in a mutually enriching dialogue with Jews, the Hebrew Bible has to be seen as more than propaeudetic to the New Testament and Christianity. Instead, Judaism must be regarded as possessing an independent standing of its own. Unfortunately, for purposes of inter religious dialogue, the Christology of the New Testament as presented in this chapter appears logically to entail a supersessionist sense of triumphalism *vis-à-vis* Judaism. Of course, as my teacher Eugene Borowitz has pointed out, Christology need not lead – and, in fact, has not led – to such supersessionary teachings in the writings of many Christian theologians.[5] Indeed, Verheyden himself alludes to this at the end of his chapter. I would recommend that he expand upon these final comments, for the type of Christocentrism expressed elsewhere in his chapter rules out dialogue between Christian and Jew on anything other than an informational level.

I would emphasise, in closing, that I am not calling for a 'Christless' Christianity. Such a request on the part of a Jew would be arrogant. Furthermore, it would not be in keeping with what I perceive to be the central doctrine of Christian faith. To deny Christology for the sake of interreligious dialogue would be a negation of the integrity of Christian religion. However, in light of the vast variety of Christologies that have been articulated by believing and faithful Christians over the centuries perhaps a Christian expression of God other than the one I believe to be found in Verheyden's chapter could be put forth. In this way, it might be easier, in settings such as this, to learn more from one another.

Notes and References

1. John Hick, *God Has Many Names* (Philadelphia: The Westminster Press, 1982) p. 116.
2. Hick, *God Has Many Names*, p. 117.
3. The insight offered here is taken from Zev Garber, 'On Tolerance and Philo-Semitism', *The Jewish Spectator* (Fall 1983) p. 56.
4. Elliot Dorff, 'The Covenant: How Jews Understand Themselves and Others', *The Anglican Theological Review* LXIV (4) (October 1982) p. 483.
5. See Eugene Borowitz, *Contemporary Christologies: A Jewish Response* (New York: Paulist Press, 1980) ch. VIII.

3 God: A Muslim View
Muzammil H. Siddiqi

This chapter is written to answer briefly the questions prepared by the Claremont Trialogue Committee on the topic of God in Judaism, Christianity and Islam. An attempt is made to answer these questions basically from the Qur'an, the most important source of all Islamic beliefs and practices.

I REALITY OF GOD

1. On What Basis do we Believe in the Reality of God?

God is not a concept or a construct of individual or collective human imagination. God is the Real, the Truth (al-Ḥaqq). This is the most fundamental position of Islam. Muslim philosophers and thinkers have used all kinds of arguments to prove the existence of God, but they have always recognised that God's existence does not depend upon the cogency or strength of their arguments; in fact, the validity of everything comes from the truth and reality of God Himself.

In the Qur'an the reality of God is expressed and argued from the reality of the Cosmos. To deny God is to deny the existence of the universe, of space and time, to deny experience, matter and thinking. Islam recognises that the material world is a real world. It is not a dream, a deception or a hoax. Because we ourselves exist and the world around us is a real and concrete world, therefore there is only one explanation possible for the existence of all this: either everything came into existence by itself or it had a creator. The Qur'an asks:

> Were they created out of nothing? or are they the creators? or did they create the heavens and earth? (52:35–36)

The Qur'an holds the second position that there is a Creator, and it considers this position as the only logical and sensible one. It says:

> Is there any doubt regarding God, the Originator of the heavens and the earth? (14:10)

The reality of God is presented by the Qur'an again and again by pointing to the created order: to the sun and moon, to the heaven and earth, creation of human beings, animals, plants, oceans and many other things. To give one example out of many that can be cited from the Qur'an, consider the following passage:

> He created the heavens and the earth in truth; high be He, exalted above what they associate with Him! He created man of a sperm-drop; and, behold, he is a manifest adversary. And the cattle, He created them for you; in them is warmth, and uses various, and of them you eat, and there is beauty in them for you, when you bring them home to rest and when you drive them forth abroad to pasture; and they bear your loads unto a land that you never would reach, excepting with great distress. Surely your Lord is All-clement, All-compassionate. And horses, and mules, and asses, [he has created] for you to ride, and as an adornment; and He creates what you know not . . . It is He who sends down to you out of heavens water of which you drink, and of which plants, for you to pasture your herds, and thereby He brings forth for you crops, and olives, and palms, and vines, and all manner of fruit. Surely in that is a sign for a people who reflect. And He subjected to you the night and day, and the sun and moon; and the stars are subjected by His command. Surely in that are signs for a people who understand. And that which He has multiplied for you in the earth of diverse hues. Surely in that is a sign for a people who remember. It is He who subjected to you the sea, that you may eat of it fresh flesh, and bring forth out of it ornaments for you to wear; and thou mayest see the ships cleaving through it; and that you may seek of His bounty, and so haply you will be thankful (16:3–18).

Argument from creation is one of the most favourite arguments of the Qur'an. Its premise is this: Since the world is real, it must have a real Creator. This argument is taken further by the Qur'an by pointing to the change, movement, regularity, proportionate variations, correspondence in natural phenomena, etc. All this is an indication that the Creator of this universe is a wise, powerful and knowledgeable Creator. Such an ordinate universe cannot come into existence by the unintelligent powers or by chance. Referring to the orderly change in the daily cycle of the night and day the Qur'an points out:

Say: 'What think you? If God should make the night unceasing over you, until the Day of Resurrection, what god other than God shall bring you illumination? Will you not harken?' Say: 'What think you? If God should make the day unceasing over you, until the Day of Resurrection, what god other than God shall bring you night to repose in? Will you not see? Of His mercy He has appointed for you night and day, for you to repose in and seek after his bounty, that haply you will be thankful' (28:71–73).

God is the Ultimate Cause, the Causer of causes and Uncreated Creator of this whole natural order and this whole universe. We, however, must be careful to say that the universe is not a 'proof' of God's existence. In the Qur'anic language these are 'signs' (*ayat*) pointing to God. Just as every contingent points beyond itself, so the universe as created order points beyond itself to an Intelligent, Wise, Powerful and Kind Creator.[1] The signs pointing to the Creator also exist within human body, soul and mind. The Qur'an says:

In the earth are signs for those having sure faith; and in yourselves; what, do you not see? (51:20).

The reality of God thus permeates the whole universe and the human soul itself. There is something in our nature and the nature of the world that points to God. In the Islamic view, God's prophets come to remind, reinforce and explicate this very truth found in the cosmos. God Himself takes the initiative to unveil the truth about Himself through His chosen prophets. The prophets, according to the teachings of Islam, present the same truth that is implicitly felt and logically sensed in the universe itself. The prophets, however, inform us in a much more explicit way and in details about the nature of God and His attributes. There is no mutual contradiction between the reality of God gained through observing the cosmos and that which is received from the revelatory knowledge of the Prophets.

II NATURE OF GOD

1. *What is the Nature of God?*

The Qur'an does not want to establish only the existence of the Creator, but its aim is to establish an appropriate relationship between Him and the human beings. God is not an abstract idea but is a living and loving Person. The Qur'an, hence, devotes much space to describing God, His person, His essence and His attributes. It tells us what God is and what He is not. But the characteristic of the Qur'anic description of God is that it contains 'short negations and detailed affirmations' (*al-nafy al-mujmal wa al-ithbāt al-mufaṣṣal*).[2] Negations are necessary to emphasise the transcendence of God, but *via negativa* alone makes God remote and 'empty'. The God of the Qur'an is certainly not a remote or empty God.

The basic dictum of the Qur'an about God is that 'there is nothing like Him and He is the Hearer and the Seer' (42:11). The Qur'an emphasises God's power and majesty, His infinite compassion and love, His goodness and His perfection and many other beautiful qualities. 'To Him belong all the good names' (7:180; 17:110; 20:8; 59:24). Although the attributes of God in the Qur'an are considerably more, traditionally, however, ninety-nine Names of God are mentioned to denote the nature of His Being and Person. Allah, the proper name of God, occurs in the Qur'an more than 2500 times. The Qur'an speaks about God this way:

> God, there is no god but He, the Living, the Everlasting. Slumber seizes Him not, neither sleep; to Him belongs all that is in the heavens and the earth. Who is there that shall intercede with Him save by His leave? He knows what lies before them and what is after them, and they comprehend not anything of His knowledge save as He wills. His Throne comprises the Heavens and earth; the preserving of them oppresses Him not; He is All-high, the All-glorious (2:255).

In another place, the Qur'an describes God in this way:

> He is the God, other than Whom there is none; He is the Knower of the unseen and the seen, the Merciful, the Compassionate. He is the God other than Whom there is none, the Sovereign, the Holy, the One with peace and integrity, the Keeper of the Faith

the Protector, the Mighty, the One whose will is Power, the Most Supreme! Glory be to Him beyond what they associate with Him. He is the God, the Creator, the Maker, the Fashioner, to Whom belong beautiful names; whatever is in the heavens and the earth sings His glories, He is the Mighty One, the Wise One (59:22–24).

The Qur'an describes God in relational and personal terms. It says, 'All that dwells upon the earth is perishing, yet still abides the *Face* of thy Lord, majestic, splendid' (55:26–27). And it says, 'Both His *hands* are spread out wide in bounty' (5:64). There are references to His *eyes* (61:37; 23:37; 52:48; 54:14), His sitting upon the Throne (7:54; 10:3; 13:2; 20:5; 25:59; 32:4; 57:4), His love (3:76; 3:134; 3:146; 5:54 and many other verses), His anger (4:93; 5:60; 48:6; 58:14), His being pleased with certain acts and persons (5:119; 9:100; 48:18; 58:22; 98:8) and dislike of certain things or persons (9:46).

The question of Divine attributes led to heated discussions in early Islamic History. There were some who understood the attributes in a more or less anthropomorphic sense. The difference between God and man, according to this view, is not of kind but of degree. This view was outright condemned and rejected as idolatrous. There were others who interpreted the attributes in a metaphorical sense. According to this view, when the Qur'an speaks about God's hearing or seeing, His eyes, hands, face, His love and anger, all these and similar statements should be interpreted in a non-physical sense, because God is not a physical being. But this was not the only alternative to the anthropomorphic position, claimed the third group. They believed that attributes of God are real and the words are used in the Qur'an in their real sense. They are, however, not like the attributes of any human being or any other created thing, because God has said that 'nothing is like Him' (42:11). This last view is what is generally held by a majority of Muslims on the nature and person of God. It is this view that inspires devotion, piety, worship, awe and all other religious attitudes in Islam.

III   GENDER OF GOD

1.   *Is God Male?*

One of the chief and most important concerns of Islam is that the Divine being should not be equated or identified with anything else, be it human or non-human. Islam has never associated any gender with God.

It is true that in the Qur'an and in all Islamic literature, the pronoun 'He' (*huwa*) is always used when referring to God, but this is not sufficient to prove that God is believed to be male in Islam. It only proves that God is not believed to be a female. The masculine nouns and pronouns in Arabic, as in many other languages, denote males as well as that which includes males and females or that which transcends maleness and femaleness. The Arabic language also has no neuter pronoun, either for persons or for things or concepts. Furthermore, because in Islam God is spoken of in highly personal terms, Muslims, when using languages other than Arabic, would abhor to use a non-personal pronoun 'it' for God.

Since Muslims have never made a portrait of God and do not believe in incarnation, it cannot be claimed on the basis of the pronoun 'he' alone that God is believed as male in Islamic thought.

From the Islamic point of view, it is absurd and dangerously silly to think of God in male or female terms. The Creator of the universe is neither male nor female. He is the Creator of males and females, but He Himself transcends these limitations. It is instructive to note here that the proper name of God, Allah, is a unique noun in Arabic language. It is pairless. It has no female counterpart and it has no plural form.

The Qur'an and other Islamic sources have also avoided – and, in fact, deliberately rejected – the use of the term 'father' for God. God is neither the Father nor the Son. It is reported that when Prophet Muhammad – peace be upon Him – began preaching his message of Islam in Mecca, some Meccans came to him asking him about the God that he was preaching. They asked him, 'Tell us about the lineage of your God' (*Ansib lanā rabbaka*).[3] The answer that the Prophet gave them is in the 112th chapter of the Qur'an:

> Say: He is God, the One and Only; God, the Eternal, Absolute; He begetteth not, nor is He begotten; And there is none like unto Him (112:1–4).

Any language that would specifically describe God as male or female is unacceptable to Islam.

IV UNITY OF GOD

1. *Are Unity and Trinity incompatible?*

That God is One in His person and Unique in His attributes, is the basic assertion of Islam. Duality, Trinity, multiplicity, none of them is compatible with Divine unity. 'It is in the very nature of the case, there can be only one God, for whenever one tries to conceive of more than one, only one will be found to emerge as the First'.[4] The Qur'an says:

God has said, 'Do not take two gods [for] He is only One' (16:51). God bears witness that there is no God but He (3:18). Say: 'If there were other gods beside Him, as these people assert, they would all seek their way to the [one] Lord of the Throne' (17:42).

Recognition of Divine Oneness is called *tawḥid* in Islam. *Tawḥid* means to recognise God as One in Person and Substance and unique in His attributes. This is a basic point of difference between Islam and Christianity. From the Islamic perspective, if the Trinity means 'three persons' then it is pure and simple polytheism, though a limited one. And unity and polytheism are not compatible at all. If the Christian Trinity stands for three modes, expressions, names, attributes or whatever of God, then the Muslim sees no reason or need for limiting them to three. It is unbecoming of God that His modes, names and attributes are limited only to three. The Qur'an says:

If all the trees in the earth were pens, and the seas with seven more seas to help it [were inks], the words of God could not be exhausted. Lo! God is Mighty, Wise (31:27). Say: Though the sea become ink for the words of my Lord, verily the sea would be used up before the words of my Lord were exhausted, even though We brought the like thereof to help (18:109).

A modern Muslim critic of the Trinity says:

The Christian may not claim that the Trinity is a way of talking about God; because if the Trinity discloses the nature of God better than unity a greater plurality would do the job better.[5]

Classical Muslim writers on Christianity also refused to accept that

the Trinity could be considered as compatible with the unity of God.
They believed that the doctrine of the Trinity has no scriptural
authority, neither is it rationally valid. Ibn Taymiyah (d. 1328)
expresses the classical position of Muslim thinkers on this subject:

> The Prophets have not said any of these words [referring to the
> Trinitarian doctrines]; it is the Christian sects who have said this
> according to their opinions and they claim that they have inferred
> these from their scriptures . . . When we ask them to explain these
> to us they say, 'It is beyond reason (*fawq al-'aql*)' . . . If someone
> narrates a verse from the Torah, the Gospel, or the Qur'an or
> narrates the statements of any of the prophets, we do not demand
> him to explain its meaning to us. But if he claims that he has
> understood what the prophets have said and expresses it in another
> expression, then one has a right to demand him to explain . . .
> Now they have produced a statement and introduced some words
> and they command people to believe in them and say this is faith
> and this is monotheism. Then they say that we do not understand
> and comprehend it, then they are from amongst 'those who ascribe
> to God things which they do not know' (Qur'an 10:68).[6]

It is the basic assertion of Islam that the doctrine of Trinity is the
offence of Christianity against the transcendence of God. Christianity
has departed from its semitic roots and its prophetic truth by
compromising the unity of God with Trinity. This offence of Christianity against the transcendence became even greater when it identified one person of the Trinity with historical Jesus, who according
to Islam was only a prophet of God. The Qur'an has severely judged
both doctrines of the church: Incarnation and the Trinity. It says:

> O People of the Book! do not go to extremes in your faith and
> do not say about God except truth. The Messiah, Jesus, son of
> Mary, was but a Messenger of God and His word that He cast
> into Mary and a Spirit from Him. So believe in God and in His
> Messengers and say not, trinity, desist from this, it is better for
> you. God is but one and only God – far above be He from having
> a son; to Him belongs whatever is in the heavens and in the earth
> (4:171; cf. 5:77).

In stronger terms, the Qur'an says:

Those are infidels who say: God is the Messiah, son of Mary. Say: Who will be of any help against God, if He should want to destroy the Messiah, son of Mary, his mother and all those who live on the earth? To God belongs the kingdom of the heavens and the earth and whatever is between them; He creates whatever He wills, and God is powerful over everything (5:117).

Again:

Committed to infidelity are those who say: God is the same as the Messiah, son of Mary; . . . committed to infidelity are those who say: God is one among three – while there is no god Except One God; if they do not desist from what they say, a painful punishment will touch those of them as commit infidelity. Why do they not repent to God and seek pardon, for God is forgiving and Merciful? The Messiah, son of Mary, was but a Messenger – before had gone many messengers; his mother was a truthful one; they both used to eat food [like other men]. Just see how We make the signs clear to them and see how they are being deceived! (5:72–75).

The incompatability between the unity of God and Trinity is quite conclusive in Islamic thought. This, however, does not mean that Muslims have not seen or valued many Christian affirmations on the unity of God. About a century ago, the Persian Sufi poet Hatif Ispahani claimed that in the Trinitarian formula of Christianity there is a hidden affirmation of Divine Unity. In one of his poems he says:

In the church I said to a Christian charmer of hearts, 'O thou in whose net the heart is captured! O thou to the warp of whose girdle each hair-tip of mine is separately attached! 'How long [wilt thou continue] not to find the way to the Divine Unity? How long wilt thou impose on the One the shame of the Trinity? How can it be right to name the One True God "Father," "son," and "Holy Ghost" '? She parted her sweet lips and said to me, while with sweet laughter she poured sugar from her lips: 'If thou art aware of the secret of the Divine Unity, do not cast on us the stigma of infidelity! In three mirrors the Eternal Beauty cast a ray from His effulgent countenance' . . . While we were thus speaking, the chant rose up beside us from the church-bell: 'He is One and there is naught but He; there is no god save Him alone!'[7]

V GOD AND HISTORY

1. *How Does God Act in History?*

Islam recognises God as the Lord, Nourisher and Sustainer of the
worlds. In the very first verse of the Qur'an God is called, 'the
Sustainer and Nourisher of the worlds' (*rabb al-'alamin*).

God has created the world and has set the order of 'natural caus-
ation' but this does not mean that God has gone to sleep or rest (cf.
50:38), God is ever watching His creation and is involved with their
affairs. 'He knows what is before them and what is behind them,
while they encompass none of His knowledge, except what He
permits. His throne envelops the heavens and the earth and their
preserving fatigues Him not – He is the High, the Great' (2:255).

The Qur'an affirms that God knows everything and everything is
under His direct control. It says:

> With Him are the keys of the Unseen; none knows them but He.
> He knows what is in land and sea; not a leaf falls, but He knows
> it. Not a grain in the earth's shadows, not a thing, fresh or with-
> ered, but it is in a Book Manifest. It is He who recalls you by
> night, and He knows what you work by day (6:59–61).

God is immanent and very close to His creatures. The Qur'an says:

> And when My servants question thee concerning Me – I am near
> to answer the call of the caller, when he calls to Me (2:186).

Again the Qur'an says:

> All that is in the heavens and the earth magnifies God; He is the
> All-mighty, the All-wise. To Him belongs the Kingdom of the
> heavens and the earth; He gives life, and He makes to die, and
> He is powerful over everything. He is the First and the Last, the
> Outward and the Inward; He has knowledge of everything . . .
> He knows what penetrates into the earth, and what comes forth
> from it, what comes down from heaven, and what goes up unto
> it. He is with you wherever you are; and God sees the things you
> do (57:2–4).

It is an established belief of Islam that God acts; but we as contingent and finite beings do not know how He the Infinite Being acts. From the Islamic point of view, it is also wrong to use the phrase that God acts 'in history'. The Qur'an has not used any mystical or mythological language about God's involvement in space and time. There is no objectification of God and God's being available for the empirical eyes or hands. God acts and He acts in the real and full sense of the word; but His action is *His* own action and cannot be identified or equated with the action of ordinary historical beings. Thus Islam does not hold any doctrine of 'sacred history' (*Heilsgeschichte*). To equate God with any historical phenomenon is called *shirk* in Islamic terminology. *Shirk* means association of any thing or person with God either through identification or equation or addition or substitution. Islam abhors *shirk* in all its forms. It is considered erroneous in the realm of metaphysics and evil for ethics and morality.

There is no denying of the fact that in history many events have taken place where God in a unique way has shown His care and concern for mankind. These revelatory events are called *ayat* (signs) in the Qur'an. They point to God; they are not God Himself. The Qur'an, the word of God, came in history; but the Qur'an, in Islamic understanding, is the Word of God (*kalam Allah*) and not God. There is no analogy between the Christian concept of Christ and the Islamic concept of the Qur'an.[8]

NO?

VI RELIGION AND RELIGIONS

1. *Is There Only One Self-revelation of God, or Several?*

Revelation in Islam is neither a 'Divine self-disclosure of His Person, nor mainly the revelation of His Purpose in the form of a people whose history and experience become embodiments of the Divine to an extent that the 'Word of God' is subsumed in the 'Act of God' as articulated in the history of a specific chosen people'.[9] Revelation is called *wahy* in Islamic terminology. It denotes a mode of communication between God and man. What is communicated is knowledge about God, His creation, His will for mankind. This communication provides guidance and increases gnosis for humankind.

Islam does not claim to be a new religion. The Qur'an clearly states that God is the Universal, Just and Loving God. He cares for all people. He is not partial to one race or one group of people.

God sent His prophets and messengers among all people. God says in the Qur'an:

> We, indeed, sent among every people an apostle (16:36).

He further says:

> There was never any people without a warner having lived among them (35:24; cf. other references in the Qur'an 4:163–5; 6:130–1; 13:7; 23:44).

Since all humanity is one family and we all proceed from the same parents, God treats all with equality and justice. The Qur'an says that for every people God assigned a religious path to follow (5:48; 22:34; 22:67), and it forbids the believers to make any distinctions in the way of ascribing superiority or otherwise between the messengers of God and His prophets (2:136; 3:84; 4:152).

The Qur'an very positively accepts the fact that the faith in God and knowledge of Him are as old and universal as human history. The first man Adam was the recipient of Divine guidance (2:37–38) and, according to Islamic tradition, he was also the first prophet of God. Hence no race, tribe or nation on this earth has been religiously illiterate, and whatever any of them know about God, they know it through His own agency, that is through His own revelation. Revelation in Islam is not confined to any particular group or period.

According to Islam, revelation of God on a spiritual and experiential level (*ilqa'*; *kashf*; *ilham*) is available to all mankind at all times. The Qur'an teaches us that human beings are given an innate and pure nature called *fiṭrah*, and the knowledge of God and innate spirituality are, thus, inherent in human existence. Human beings, however, cannot rely upon this innate spirituality alone. They need explicit Divine guidance to develop their innate spiritual nature. God chose for this purpose His reliable servants the prophets to become the teachers of mankind. God revealed to them His command and His will for mankind. The revelation in this specific and explicit sense was given to prophets alone and finally to the Prophet Muhammad.

As the source of guidance is one, so the guidance itself is essentially the same. Referring to many great prophets the Qur'an says that they were all *muslims* and they preached only *islam*. So Noah (10:71–2), Abraham (2:130–2), Joseph (12:101), the prophets among the Israelites (5:44), Jesus (3:52–3) and many others are called *muslims*. The

Qur'an in this sense suggests a common level of religiousness for all mankind. All humanity in its simple and authentic religiousness is affiliated to each other. Just as there is a level of common reason and common sense, so there is also a level of common religiousness.

Among religions differences do exist, and so there are differences between Judaism and Christianity, between Judaism and Islam and between Christianity and Islam. Some of these differences are mutually contradictory and irreconcilable. What to do with these differences, especially when we meet in dialogue? Should we accept them in some kind of syncretism, ignore them, or develop a metaphysic that would relegate all these differences to a secondary position and claim for itself the supreme, elitist and higher position? Or should we explain away these differences in sociological, cultural, historical, economic, natural or psychological terms? All these approaches in the past have proved inadequate and cannot satisfy religious people in any of our traditions. I believe that the Qur'anic approach in this matter is worth serious consideration. The Qur'an says:

> Mankind was but one people, but differed [later]. Had it not been for a word that went forth from thy Lord, their differences would have been settled between them (10:19).

The 'word that went forth from thy Lord' is His decision to give freedom to all mankind to act the way they want and His non-interference in their freedom. In another place, the Qur'an says:

> If God had so willed, He would have made you a single people, but that He may test you in that which He has given you: so strive in righteous deeds. Unto God you all will return and He will, then, show you the truth of the matter in which you dispute (5:48).

We are not asked here to resign and sit back watching our differences. Dialogue we must, study we must, try to understand we must, but we must not rush to explain them away. We must continue seeking the truth that is greater than all that we know and possess, and also we must try to be honest and fair in our relations with each other.

Notes and References

1. We have used the words 'intelligent', 'wise', 'powerful', etc. to indicate that in Islamic beliefs in general, excepting the pantheistic Sufism creation is not taken as emanation but as a purposeful and intentional act of God.
2. Ibn Taymiyah's phrase as quoted by Abul Hasan Ali Nadwi in *Al-Arkān al-Arba'a* (Beirut, 1967) p. 224.
3. See a good discussion on God in the Qur'an by Fazlur Rahman, *Major Themes of the Qur'an* (Bibliotheca Islamica, Chicago, 1980) p. 4.
4. Quoted by A. A. Mawdudi, Tafhīm al-Qur'ān (Lahore, 1972) vol. 6, p. 530.
5. Ismā'īl al-Farūqī, *Tawhīd: Its Implications for Thought and Life* (Kuala Lumpur, 1982) p. 26.
6. Ibn Taymiyah, al-Jawāb al Sahīh, vol. 3, pp. 131–132, quoted in my thesis *Muslim Views of Christianity in the Middle Ages* (New York: Harvard, 1978) p. 228.
7. Translated by E. G. Browne in his *A Literary History of Persia* (Cambridge: CUP, 1930) vol. 4, pp. 293–4.

8. Professor W. C. Smith has greatly publicised this analogy in recent years and it is often quoted by many Christian writers. We, however, do not agree with it. It does not help in understanding the Islamic position of the Qur'an. The Qur'an is not worshipped in Islam, prayers are not directed to the Qur'an. A. L. Tibawi in his booklet *English Speaking Orientalists* (Geneva: Islamic Center, 1965) p. 30 says: 'We need not go to Al-Azhar to discover stronger rejection. Three so-called "Westernized" Muslims, noted for their scholarship and liberalism, were consulted separately by the present writer. Each returned the same answer even though using stronger or milder adjectives: "superficial", "impertinent" and "blasphemous" '. There is a great deal that Smith has written on Islam that could be considered useful and enlightening, but this is not one of those examples.
9. See T. B. Irving, K. Ahmad, M. M. Ahsan, *The Qur'an: Basic Teaching* (Leicester: The Islamic Foundation, 1979) pp. 22–3.

A Jewish Response to Muzammil Siddiqi: God: A Muslim View

Susannah Heschel

Dr Siddiqi's very fine chapter has presented a complex issue in clear terms, writing from inside his tradition as a believing Muslim. He shows us some of the central concerns of Islam, using the Koran as his point of departure. He offers us the orthodox, normative perspective within Islam and raises many interesting questions which we might pursue.

Of course, one of the more difficult problems facing participants in a trialogue is how to go about formulating an Islamic or Jewish or Christian position on a particular issue. Dr Siddiqi bases his chapter on the Koran, but we might ask about later developments within Islam, about varying ways of interpreting the Koran, about Sufism or Shi'ism or Kalam or about how the very Koranic passages Dr Siddiqi cites were understood on a popular level during the centuries and also today. We might ask about differences among Muslims living in various parts of the world, Arab and non-Arab, about movements considered heretical in their day and about theological issues arising from the impact of modernity.

Similar questions can be raised about a Jewish response to Dr Siddiqi's chapter. It would be reasonable to show what Judaism holds in common with Islam, to discuss shared influences or point of contact, or to follow Dr Siddiqi's model and discuss God in the Jewish Scriptures. These would all be worthy exercises.

I would like to raise two issues with the intention of expanding our presentation of our respective religions beyond our Scriptures and hope that we can engage other aspects of each others' traditions. As I read Dr Siddiqi's chapter, one of the questions that arose for me was how Islam balances its belief in God's power and majesty with a sense of God's closeness and love. A similar problem exists, of course, in Judaism. The pivot for the balance in Judaism, it seems to me, lies with the religious law, halakha, which allows the Jew to

overcome the remoteness of God and develop a sense of closeness
and intimacy without threatening the integrity of God as God. Since
Islam also possesses a religious law, I would like to ask Dr Siddiqi
whether there are any parallels in the role played by that law in
Islam to the role played by halakha in Judaism. I would like to
present a few short Jewish mystical texts that illustrate the role of
halakha in the ways Jewish theology has defined both the nature of
God and the nature of our relationship with God.

The issue of law – of the meaning of and reasons for the commandments – is central to Judaism, and a variety of approaches to the
problem have been taken by Jewish thinkers through the centuries.
At one extreme we have the approach dominating much of rabbinic
and medieval philosophical thought that there may be no reason for
particular commandments – they are to be observed simply because
they are commanded by God, and that proper performance may at
most develop the intellect or moral fibre of the individual. By
contrast, the mystical tradition sees hidden layers of meaning in each
commandment and in each performance of a commandment.

Dr Siddiqi writes that God must never be identified or equated
with any created being or object. Jews have expressed similar
concerns, but in the striving for intimacy with God, Jewish mystics
– and perhaps Sufis as well – have come very close in their experience
of God's immanence to an identification or confusion of the believer
with God. For the Jewish mystics, this world is a mirror of a world
above and whatever takes place in this earthly realm occurs also in
the realm above. Not only does God act in history, but fulfilment of
the divine commandments strengthens and influences God's actions
in this world, including hastening the redemption. 'When Israel
performs the will of God, they add strength to the heavenly power,
as it is said, "To God we render strength". When Israel does not
perform the will of God, they weaken the great power of God Which
is above'.[1]

Thus, it is through the commandments that the distance between
the Jew and God may be overcome. Religious law gains ultimate
significance because it has an effect on the divine realm; by extension
human beings have an impact on God. When the Jew abstains from
observing the religious commandments, God suffers and the balance
of order of the entire universe is upset. God is never remote, never
uninvolved. Jewish tradition speaks of an inner life of God, of
emotional states affected by the course of history; the Talmud says
that God cried as the Temple in Jerusalem went up in flames. The

transcendent, omnipotent God of the philosophers, the unmoved mover, becuases the involved, passionate God of the mystics who can be deeply moved by human beings.

This way of looking at the relationship is put even more starkly in a second midrashic text: 'Rabbi Shimon ben Yochai taught: If you are my witnesses, then I am God. And if you are not my witnesses, as it were, I am not God'.[2] Here, it is not only that God gains strength when Israel obeys the divine law, but that God is not God without the Jewish people. The reality of God comes into being through Israel's performance of the law, an understanding central to the classical period of thirteenth-century Kabbalah, but already present in its incipient form in rabbinic literature.[3]

The closeness to God which the mystics were striving to achieve led yet a step further in Hasidism. There is a statement directed to God, popularly attributed to Levi Yitzchak of Berdichev: 'This is Yom Kippur. If you forgive us our sins against you, we will forgive you your sins against us'. Not only is God strengthened, not only is God sustained in reality, but now the very distinction between the person and God becomes blurred. In Arthur Green's biography of Nachman of Bratslav, he cites this text: 'When one finally is included within God, his Torah is the Torah of God Himself and his prayer is the prayer of God Himself . . . you have to reach such a state of self-negation that you come to God's Torah and prayer and are able to say: May it be my will'.[4]

The dangers inherent in this kind of radical statement are obvious. Identifying one's own will as God's will cannot without difficulty escape charges of heresy. Yet it may also be a kind of inevitable conclusion of the mystical train of thinking which seeks to overcome any barriers between the person and God, to shake God of transcendence and develop a sense of God's immanence. But if closeness to God is the ultimate goal, why bother with the commandments at all once that closeness is achieved?

Just as the commandments lead to a greater sense of God's presence and a greater intimacy between the Jew and God, so, too, do the commandments serve as a safety-value when the immanence threatens the religion. The retreat comes from a text by Levi Yitzchak of Berdichev:

There are two ways to serve God: one is a service by means of self-sacrifice, giving up the soul, and the other is a service through commandments and good deeds. The difference between them is

this: one who serves through self-sacrifice alone, without
commandments and deeds, is literally in Nothingness, while the
one who serves by means of the commandments is serving God
through some existing thing, because the commandments are in
existence. Therefore, the one who serves by abandoning the self
in dedication is wholly within Nothingness and cannot cause divine
blessing to flow down because such a one does not exist, but is
joined to God. The one who serves through deeds, however,
serves with something, and thus can bring blessing forth and
receive it.[5]

Thus, the same law which brings the mystic to an intimacy with God
to a sense of God's immanence, and then ultimately to the verge of
negating God through an identification with God, also acts to prevent
that final step, to keep the mystic within the fold, to put a kind of
check on the potential conclusions of that train of thinking.

Clearly, Judaism, Christianity and Islam have in common normative traditions stressing God's transcendence. God is the unknowable
knower and unmoved mover. Yet it is also clear that traditions of
God's immanence and closeness exist in the three religions, and
not always as marginal phenomena. The interior experiences of the
believer, the love of and for God, all find expression. Yet within
Judaism these spiritual expressions take a particular form in
describing God's responsiveness to the commandments and God's
need for the Jewish people, what is termed Zoreh Gavoha. I would
like to ask Dr Siddiqi if there are parallel ideas within Islamic mysticism, of God's responsiveness to religious observance, what we term
Zoreh Gavoha, or a similar role for Islamic law in the understanding
of God and in our relationship with God.

There is a second issue that I want to raise briefly in response to
Dr Siddiqi's chapter that concerns the question of religious language.
Here, is it clear to me that all three faiths represented at the conference are facing the same theological dilemma in response to recent
criticisms by the social sciences regarding the relationship between
religious language and society. These wideranging criticisms are
brought into particularly sharp focus by feminist theologians.

Let me begin by quoting Dr Siddiqi's chapter on the question, Is
God Male? He writes: 'From the Islamic point of view, it is absurd
and dangerously silly to think of God in male or female terms. The
Creator of the universe is neither male nor female. He is the Creator
of males and females, but He Himself transcends these limitations'

(above, p. 68). And, a little later, 'Any language that would specifically describe God as male or female is unacceptable to Islam' (above, p. 68).

The Jewish and Christian communities have been struggling in recent years with criticisms from feminist theologians of our language and imagery describing God.[6] The criticisms focus primarily on the impact of exclusively male God language on the religious community and on individual believers. Jewish and Christian thinkers have made defences similar to the statements of Dr Siddiqi, to the effect that our language about God is not to be taken literally. Yet these statements imply a possible contradiction of other tenets within Judaism and Christianity and Islam regarding the significance and power of language. Within Judaism, language has tremendous significance: the word of God brought the world into being; God's words express the divine commandments we are to observe; our words, like our deeds, must be uttered with care, since they affect God and the cosmos and may hasten or postpone the redemption of the world.

Yet if in Judaism our language possesses so much power, then, feminists argue, our use of nearly exclusively male language and imagery about God has serious implications. Naturally, our language is rooted in our humanness and limited by it. When we speak of or to God, we are speaking in human terms. God is described according to what we know: human attributes. The social sciences argue that our language about God both expresses the ultimate values of the community and serves as a model for human behaviour and social structure. According to the feminist critique, describing God as 'He', even when insisting that He is not male, has this simultaneous dual function of expressing and impressing. To speak of God in His heaven links maleness with the ultimate reality, the greatest good. When men are the authorities of a society, we can hardly expect to find God addressed as She. And if God is He, the superior position of the males receives clear justification. When God is associated with maleness, how can maleness fail to be the norm for society? And if maleness is the norm, femaleness will be outside, Other to that norm.

The feminist critique argues that religion has a tremendous impact on us individually and as a society, making us believe that patriarchy is both natural and divinely ordained. Yet to feminists, patriarchy is neither natural nor can it represent the will of God.

I am aware that the feminist critique of theology has received far more attention in the Christian and Jewish communities than it has among Muslims, so I wonder if Dr Siddiqi has views on how Islamic theologians might respond. Given the high regard for language and for the letter in Islam, I wonder if the response to feminism would develop some of the more esoteric aspects of Islamic mysticism that do employ female language and imagery both for God and for the soul. Or would it place greater emphasis on the human element in transmitting the divine message, risking thereby re-opening the problem of whether the Koran is the uncreated or created word of God? Or, to put it another way, is there language which is necessary and intrinsic to Islam – and to Judaism and Christianity – or is language the product of social and cultural forces, and hence replaceable?

In conclusion: Judaism shares with Islam a central concern with religious law that may link us, theologically, more closely in some ways than to Christianity. I have argued that Jewish law plays an important role in our understanding of God's nature and in the relationship between the believer and God, both as a stimulus beyond conventional boundaries and as a safety-valve against heresy, and I wonder if a similar role exists for law within Islam. The question of religious language – particularly of male imagery of God – is shared by all three faiths at the conference, but I think has been explored in far greater detail by Christian theologians than by either Jewish or Muslim thinkers. I would hope that by facing contemporary theological challenges such as feminism together we might draw closer in our efforts to shape a response and thereby attain a greater mutuality.

Notes and References

1. *Pesikta Rabbati*, Buber edn XXVI, 166b.
2. *Pesikta d'Rav Kahana*, Piske XII, section 6 (Mandelbaum edn, vol. II p. 208).
3. Nahman of Bratslav, *Likkutei Maharan*, 22:10; cited by Arthur Green, *Tormented Master: A Life of Rabbi Nahman of Bratslav* (New York, Schocken Books, 1981) p. 319.
4. The development of teachings regarding God's immanence within rabbinic literature, as well as of opposing traditions, is traced in the classic two-volume study of rabbinic theology by Abraham J. Heschel, *Torah min ha-Shamayim b'Ispaklaryah shel ha-Dorot* [Hebrew] (London, Soncino Press, vol. I, 1962; vol. II, 1965).
5. Levi Yitzhak of Berdichev, *Kedushat Levi*, parshat Lech-Lecha (Jeru salem, 1958, p. 15); see discussion of this passage in an important essa

by Arthur Green, 'Hasidism: Discovery and Retreat', in Peter L. Berger (ed.), *The Other Side of God* (Garden City, New York: Anchor Press/Doubleday, 1981) pp. 104–30, which discusses precisely this problem of halakha in Hasidic thought.

6. Numerous volumes have been published by feminists addressing this problem. Some of the most important include: Mary Daly, *Beyond God the Father* (Boston: Beacon, 1973), *Gyn/Ecology* (Boston:, Beacon 1978), *Pure Lust* (Boston: Beacon, 1984); Carol Christ, *Diving Deep and Surfacing: Women Writers on Spiritual Quest* (Boston: Beacon, 1980). See also collection, Susannah Heschel (ed.), *On Being a Jewish Feminist: A Reader* (New York: Schocken Books, 1983).

A Christian Response to Muzammil Siddiqi: God: A Muslim View

M. Francis Meskill

I am reminded today of an event which took place in a town with a similar name in another time, in another place. I am referring to the Council of Clermont in south-central France which took place on 18 November 1095. There at that giant conclave, too big for the cathedral and moved to the open spaces beyond the city gates, Pope Urban I spoke not of reconciliation, not of dialogue with Islam, but made a call to war, to crusade against it.

And yet that event which mobilised the forces of Christian Europe against Islam also marked the beginning of relationship between Christianity and Islam which moved from the hostile encounter on the battlefield, through the formal negotiations for truce and the exchange of prisoners, to the creation of an atmosphere for genuine dialogue. This meeting with Islam, which took place first in Palestine and later in Sicily and Spain, had profound and lasting consequences on medieval Christianity, for it marked a discovery – the discovery of a new civilisation, a new religion, a new morality. The consequences were that the discovery caused a change of perspective, a change of focus which led eventually to an epistemological shift that broke open the enclosed world of medieval Christianity.

That homogenous world of cathedrals, pilgrimages, pardons and intense piety was 'controlled' by a Biblical dogmatism which offered a neat, naive, *a priori*, yet theologically appealing explanation for all things. It was a world which revolved around *The Book* – the Sacred Scriptures – or rather orbited around a literal understanding of what was regarded as God's word. The change, the shift, the liberation from that kind of hegemonous theology came about not by the acceptance of the Koran or the Islamic religion but by the discovery of hellenistic works which Islamic scholars passed on to the Christian world. These Islamic scholars, however, were not passive conduits of ancient thought to the west; they offered commentaries which demonstrated a methodology that relied more on experiential, *a posteriori* knowledge rather than the *a priori* methodology of Christian scholars.

Then suddenly the Islamic connection was broken. It happened through decisive victories: the Islamic recapture of the Holy Land; the Christian reconquest of Southern Italy, Sicily and Spain. Christianity and Islam thus retreated into the old isolation, an isolation and lack of formal contact which has marked their histories from that day to this. We have advanced our range of influence over vast reaches of the world since then, but except for encounters along the ragged edges of our spheres of influence we have not entered into any prolonged dialogue.

One reason for the lack of dialogue is that neither Christianity nor Islam can speak with one voice to each other, and yet our diversity may be God's gift to be exchanged between us. I say this because I find the parable which Raimundo Panikkar draws from the story of the Tower of Babel instructive. The story is found in the Book of Genesis:

Now the whole earth had one language and few words. And as people migrated from the east, they found a plain in the land of Shinar and settled there. And they said to one another, 'Come, let us make bricks, and burn them thoroughly'. And they had brick for stone, and bitumen for mortar. Then they said, 'Come let us build ourselves a name for ourselves, lest we be scattered abroad upon the face of the whole earth'. And the Lord came down to see the city and the tower, which the sons of men had built. And the Lord said, 'Behold they are one people, and they have all one language; and this is only the beginning of what they will do; and nothing that they propose to do will now be impossible for them. Come, let us go down, and there confuse their language, that they may not understand one another's speech'. So the Lord scattered them abroad over the face of all the earth, and they left off building the city. Therefore its name was called Babel, because there the Lord confused the languages of all the earth; and from there the Lord scattered them abroad over the face of all the earth. (Common Bible, Revised Standard Version, an ecumenical edn, 1973).

The moral which flows from the story is that individuals who build a unitarian tower and intend through their artifact to reach God their way, imposing their wills, their way on all and even on God himself – that idea was rejected by God, and their language confused in languages. They who could not communicate with God except in their way could no longer communicate with each other.

But the story of the Tower of Babel has been repeated in every age. Each civilisation has wished to enforce its way as the only way. There have been the Egyptians, the Babylonians, the Assyrians, Alexander the Great, the Romans, the British, the Germans, the Russians, the Americans.

But it is not only a political matter, it is also very much a religious problem, our problem. There is the imposition of my way as the only way, my religion as the only religion, my way to God as the only way to God. As long as we insist on the imperialism of our righteousness, there can be no mutual understanding, no common ground. There can only be total and unconditional surrender.

We live in a smaller world today, a world that can no longer tolerate this kind of imperialism, particularly in the matter of religion. How can we speak to a world beset with the problems of ultimate destruction, how can we speak to that world if we cannot find a common language with which to speak to each other? We can no longer quote sacred texts at each other without allowing those same texts to grapple in our own hearts with the living problems of today. Texts that cannot deal with the living problems of today are dead, museum pieces, turning the living into the petrified dead.

But the texts of our sacred books are living words, born anew in each age, giving meaning to the lives of people – not by pushing them back into the past but by making them living witnesses to the history of the present and through the wisdom of those texts giving solutions to the great difficulties of our times.

4 The Earth and Humanity: A Muslim View

Jamāl Badawi

I INTRODUCTION

It is befitting, at the outset, to have a brief word about this 'trialogue'. For the Muslim, constructive dialogue or 'trialogue' is not only permitted, it is commendable. In the Qur'an we read,

> Say, O People of the Book! [a term which particularly refers to Jews and Christians] Come to common terms as between us and you: That we worship none but Allah; That we associate no partners with Him [in His powers and divine attributes]; that we erect not, from among ourselves, lords and Patrons other than Allah.

> If then they turn back, say you Bear witness that we are [at least] Muslims [Bowing to the will of God] (3:64).

The methodology of that dialogue (or trialogue) is also explained in the Qur'an: 'invite [all] to the way of your Lord with wisdom and beautiful exhortation, and argue with them in ways that are best' (16:125).

This chapter presents a Muslim view of humanity and the earth. While the 'reality' of Islam and a 'Muslim view' may not necessarily be identical, an earnest attempt will be made to base it on the authentic teachings of Islam. The extent of such authenticity may be measured, mainly, by its conformity to the Qur'an.

As the earth is created for humanity, the main focus of this chapter will be on the former theme.

I HUMANITY

1. *Purpose of Creation*

The Qur'an summarises the purpose of creation of humanity in the following *Āyah*. 'I have only created Jinns and humankind and they may worship [serve] me' (51:56).

Worship of Allah is not mere formalism. Nor is it restricted to the performance of certain rites or other devotional acts. Rites and devotional acts do have their place. Yet, the concept of 'worship' in Islam is much more comprehensive than the common meaning attached to the term. Any act is a potential act of worship if it meets two fundamental conditions – first, to be done with 'pure' intention: second, to be done within the limits prescribed by Allah. Even customary and mundane activities, such as eating, sleeping and 'innocent' recreation, may be regarded as acts of worship if they meet the above two conditions. An extension of this broad concept of 'worship' is the absence in Islam of any artificial compartmentalisation of the various aspects of human living. Life is seen as an integrated and interrelated whole. It includes individual and collective pursuits; moral, social, economic and political. Indeed, one of the main challenges to humanity is to relate and harmonise such activities under divine guidance.

It is that challenge which qualifies the human race as the *Khalifah* (trustee) of Allah on earth. It also makes earthly life a 'test' or trial. 'He [Allah] Who Created Death and Life, that He may try which of you is best indeed and He is Exalted in Might, Oft-Forgiving' (67:2)

2. *Human Nature*

Such is He, the Knower of all things, hidden and open, the Exalted [in Power], the Merciful; He Who has made everything which He has created most good. He began the creation of the human with clay. And made his progeny from a quintessence of the nature of fluid despised. Then He fashioned him in due proportion, and breathed into him something of His Spirit. And He gave you [the faculties of] hearing, sight, and understanding [and feelings]. Little thanks do you give (32:6–9).

From this passage, the nature of the human, as a physical intellectual–spiritual being, is indicated.

The 'clay' represents the earthly or carnal element of human nature. Urges and instincts, in themselves, act as mechanisms through which the physical survival and perpetuation of the human race are ascertained.

The human is also endowed with intellect and the power of reasoning. It is true that reason alone is insufficient to understand all the mysteries of creation. Nonetheless, reason is neither irrelevant to the strengthening of one's faith nor is it the antithesis of faith. Indeed, the use of the power of intellect and reason is not only accepted, it is also urged.

Do they not reflect in their own minds? Not but for just ends and for a term appointed, did Allah create the heavens and the earth, and all between them. Yet, are there truly many among people who deny the meeting with their lord [and the resurrection]! (30:8).

Do they see nothing in the government of heavens and the earth and all that Allah has created? (7:185).

The physical component of human nature is shared by other living beings. Animals possess intelligence in varying degrees. Yet only in the case of humans does the Qur'an say that Allah breathed into him or her something of His spirit. It is that 'breath' which endows the human with the innate spiritual and moral qualities. It also establishes the unique position of the human as the crown of Allah's creation:

We have honoured the children of Adam; provided them with transport on land and sea; given them for sustenance things good and pure; and conferred on them special favours above a great part of Our Creation (17:70).

A significant symbol of this honour was the command of Allah to bow down to Adam: 'Behold! We said to the angels "bow down to Adam". They bowed down except Iblis. He was one of the Jinns, and he broke the Command of his Lord' (18:50).

This position of honour is closely tied to the fulfilment of one's role as 'trustee' of Allah and as a free agent. This responsibility is a heavy responsibility, one which requires making the 'right' choice.

Failing to make such a choice leads to the loss of that position of honour and distinction. The human may even descend to a position which is less than that of animals. These are the ones who:

> have hearts [minds] wherewith they understand not, eyes where with they see not, and ears wherewith they hear not. They are like cattle, nay more misguided; for they are heedless [of warning] (7:179).

The physical, intellectual and spiritual elements in human existence are not regarded as three different compartments. They are no necessarily irreconcilable either. The human is regarded as neither a fallen angel nor an ascending animal. The human is, rather, a responsible being with the potential of ascending to a position that is higher than angels, or descending to a position that is lower than that of animals.

The first couple's eating from the 'forbidden tree' did not endow the human with the knowledge or capacity to distinguish between right and wrong. Such capacity was already Allah-inspired and was part of Adam and Eve's initial creation: 'We showed him [the human] the way; whether he be grateful or ungrateful' (71:3). 'And [we] showed him the two paths [good and evil] (90:10).

It follows from this that eating from the 'forbidden tree' was not a cause of a fundamental change in the innate human nature of Adam and Eve. Indeed this act of disobedience was a result of the built-in human imperfections. Had Adam and Eve been initially perfect, they would have been incapable of disobedience in the first place. The apparent correspondence between this first act of disobedience and the first couple's exit from the 'garden' does not mean that there was a change in Allah's plans. Even before Adam was created, it was Allah's plan to create the humans as His trustees on earth: 'Behold, your lord said to the angels, "I will create a vicegerent [trustee] on earth" ' (2:30).

The 'forbidden tree' symbolises the universal ethical experience of every human being. It eloquently and effectively sums up the concepts of freedom of choice, temptation, decision-making, erring, realisation of error, repentence and forgiveness. It represents the main ethical challenges before humankind:

(a) Rising above the purely physical element and ruling over it instead of being ruled by it.

(b) Developing the spiritual and intellectual elements and bringing them into harmony with Divine Will through conscious and committed submission to Allah.

(c) Realising the consequences of obedience and disobedience to Allah.

(d) Striving to succeed in the 'test' of earthly life, in order not merely to return to an even greater 'garden' after physical death, but to enjoy the ultimate bliss of nearness to Allah and the company of the pure:

> All who obey Allah and the Messenger are in the company of those on whom is the Grace of Allah, of the Prophets, the sincere [Covers of Truth], the martyrs and the righteous. Ah! What a beautiful fellowship (4:69).

3. *Overcoming Human Imperfections*

It was indicated that the human has the potential to disobey Allah or to 'sin'. How is the human to cope with this tendency? How could one achieve reconciliation with Allah?

When the question of sin arises, there is a tendency to relate it to the 'original sin'. It may be helpful to clarify the Muslim position on that issue. The Qur'anic version of the experience of Adam and Eve does not imply in any way a notion of 'original sin', inheritance of sin, or the necessity for bloodshed as a prerequisite for forgiveness. The basis of this position is summarised below:

(a) Adam and Eve realised their mistake, did not insist on it, regretted it, and prayed to Allah for forgiveness. 'They said: "Our lord! We have wronged our own souls. If you forgive us not and bestow upon us your mercy, we shall certainly be lost" ' (7:23).

(b) Knowing their weakness and being pleased with their admission of guilt, Allah the Merciful forgave them. Forgiveness did not, however, change Allah's original plan to send them as the seeds of humanity which was to inhabit the earth. 'Then learned Adam from his Lord words of inspiration, and his Lord turned towards him; for He is Oft-Forgiving, Most Merciful' (2:37).

(c) Sin is not passed on to subsequent generations:

that no bearer of burdens can bear the burden of another; that the human can have nothing but what he strives for; that [the fruit of] his striving will soon come in sight; then will he be rewarded with a reward complete (53:38–41).

(d) Absolute perfection is neither expected nor is it possible. Being beyond human capacity, it is not a prerequisite for eternal bliss. It is within human capacity, however, to avoid *Kabā'ir* (major sins) and to try one's best to avoid *saghā'ir* (minor sins):

On no soul does Allah place a burden greater than it can bear (2:286).

Allah does not wish to place you in a difficulty, but to make you clean, and to complete His favour to you, that you may be grateful (5:7).

If you [but] eschew the most heinous [Kabā'ir] of the things which you are forbidden to do, We will forgive your sins and admit you to a gate of great honour (4:31).

(e) Human lapses are to be corrected through *Tawbah* (repentence) to Allah:

O you who believe! Turn to Allah with sincere repentance in the hope that your Lord will forgive your sins and admit you to gardens beneath which rivers flow (65:8).

If anyone does evil or wrongs his own soul, but afterwards seeks Allah's forgiveness, he will find Allah is Oft-Forgiving, Most Merciful (4:110).

It is true that Allah is both Merciful and Just. Yet, for those who repent, mercy takes precedence over justice:

but My Mercy extends to all things. That [Mercy] shall I ordain for those who are Allah-conscious and practice regular charity, and those who believe in Our Signs (7:156).

Whoever does good shall have ten times as much to his credit. Whoever does evil shall only be recompensed according to his evil. No wrong shall be done unto any of them (6:160).

Tawbah, however is valid only when one does not insist on evil.

> And those who, having done something abominable or wronged their own souls, earnestly bring Allah to mind, and ask for forgiveness for their sins, and who can forgive sins except Allah? And they are never obstinate in persisting knowingly in [the wrong] they have done (3:135).

The human may cease to sin, regret it, repent to Allah and resolve not to repeat the offence. Yet, due to human weakness, he may lapse or slip again. Even then, one should never despair of the Mercy of Allah, the despair which may lead him to even more sins:

> Say 'O my servants who have transgressed against their souls! Despair not of the Mercy of Allah. For Allah forgives all sins. For He is Oft-Forgiving, Most Merciful. And turn to your Lord [in repentence] and bow to his [will], before the penalty comes on you. After that you shall not be helped' (39:53–54).

> And never give up hope of Allah's soothing Mercy.

> Truly no one despairs of Allah's soothing Mercy except those who have no faith (12:87).

Tawbah is then an on-going process. The Qur'an frequently uses the term *Tawwab* to refer to Allah, a term which implies forgiving again and again. Similarly the Qur'an indicates that Allah loves *At-Tawwabeen* or those who constantly turn to Allah in repentance.

Only one sin is unforgivable, *shirk*. *Shirk* is often translated as polytheism, which is only one form of *shirk*.

In Arabic, the term *shirk* connotes sharing or association. In the religious sense, it means any form of association of others with Allah in His Divine Attributes. This includes the deification of any physical, animal or human object or the belief that any of them shares any of

the Divine Attributes. While Prophets and Messengers of Allah
especially the major ones – Noah, Abraham, Moses, Jesus and
Muhammad – are immensely respected, their 'specialness' never
conceals their true nature as humans and nothing but. Their greatest
medal of honour is that they were true servants and chosen Messen
gers of Allah to the human race:

> Allah forgives not that partners should be set up with him; but
> He forgives anything else, to whom He pleases; to set up partners
> with Allah is to devise a sin most heinous indeed (4:48).

> Being true in faith to Allah, and never assigning partners to Him
> if anyone assigns partners to Allah [in His Divine Attributes], he
> is as if he had fallen from heaven and been snatched by big birds
> or the wind had swooped [like a bird on its prey] and thrown him
> into a far distant place (22:31).

> But said the anointed [Jesus]: O children of Israel, worship Allah
> my Lord, and your Lord. Whoever joins [or associates] others
> with Allah, Allah will forbid him the gardens, and the Fire will
> be his abode. For the wrong-doers there will be no one to help
> (5:75).

The unforgivability of *shirk* applies only to those who die insisting
on it. Repentance from *shirk* (or other sins for that matter) must
precede the arrival of the 'moment of truth' – departure from this
life, when all previous illusions and wishful thinking are discovered,
perhaps too late.

> Allah accepts the repentance of those who do evil in ignorance
> and repent soon afterwards; to them will Allah turn in Mercy; for
> Allah is full of knowledge and wisdom. Of no effect is the repen-
> tance of those who continue to do evil, until death faces one of
> them, and he says 'now have I repented indeed', nor of those who
> die rejecting faith; for them have we prepared a punishment most
> grievous (4:17–18).

> And follow the best of [the courses] revealed to you from your
> Lord, before the penalty comes on you – of a sudden, while you
> perceive not – lest the soul should [then] say;
> 'Ah! Woe is me! in that I neglected [my duty] towards Allah, and
> was but among those who mocked!'

Each person's 'moment of truth' may arrive at any time, often unexpectedly. As such, one is required to be constantly on guard engaged in the on-going process of *Tawbah*.

This Qur'anic approach to sin and atonement cultivates a sense of individual responsibility, the quality of *Taqwā* (Allah-consciousness) even as it helps motivate the person in his/her moral struggle. It avoids the laxity which may result from the wishful thought that the person has already 'made it'. Meanwhile, through the continuous process of *Tawbah*, one has assumed not only acceptance but also a warm welcome. While remaining 'on guard' until the last moment, one's trust in the Justice, Mercy and Promise of Allah removes any sense of undue anxiety.

4. *Relating To Allah*

As Islam means peace through conscious submission to Allah, the Muslim's relationship with Allah is in essence a relationship of peace:

> Peace is an attribute of Allah (59:23). Remembrance of Him brings peace to the heart (13:28) and a relationship of peace with Him leads to tranquility in this life and in the hereafter (89:27–80, 6:127, and 10:25). It is the love of Allah and the pursuit of His pleasure which makes up the religious consciousness of the Muslim, for the true believers are more intense in their love of Allah (2:165).

Reward and punishment are seen as the consequences rather than the motives for righteousness or absence of it. Love of Allah, however, is not a mere utterance, ecstatic feelings or a dutiless slogan. It requires commitment and manifestation:

> Say [O Muhammad] if you love Allah, follow me: Allah will love you and forgive your sins (3:31).

> It is not righteousness that you turn your faces towards East or West; but it is righteousness to believe in Allah, the Last Day, the Angels, the Book and the Messengers; to spend of your sustenance, out of love for Him, for your Kin, orphans, the needy, the wayfarer, those who ask and for the emancipation of slaves; to be steadfast in prayer, and practice regular charity; to fulfil the

contracts which you have made; and to be firm and patient in pain
[or suffering] and adversity and throughout all periods of panic
Such are the people of truth, the Allah-conscious (2:177).

5. *Relating To Oneself*

The way the human relates to himself is the consequence of how he
relates to Allah. It is also the basis of relating to others:

> The core of one's duties to oneself is to purify oneself. By the soul
> and the proportion and order given to it; and its enlightenment as
> to its wrong and its right. Truly he succeeds that purifies it, and
> he fails that corrupts it! (91:7–10).

Self-purification does not imply renunciation of the world as there
is no monasticism or celibacy in Islam (28:77, 7:31–32, 5:90–91).

As 'trustee' of Allah on earth, one's responsibilities include also
safeguarding one's life and health and doing away with the attitude
of 'doing with my body what I want'. The human body as a 'trust'
from Allah is the ethical basis for the prohibition of suicide, eutha
nasia, abortion for convenience and intoxicants. However, when the
sacrifice of life for the sake of Allah is called for, such sacrifice
becomes an act of supreme love of Allah.

6. *Relating To Others*

Upholding *Tawheed* (the belief in the absolute Oneness and Unique
ness of Allah) and acceptance of the essential oneness of the mission
of all prophets are solid foundations for the oneness of humankind.

Variations of races, complexions, and tongues are seen as parts of
the mosaic of Allah's creation and signs of His Omnipotence and
Mercy. There is no trace in the Qur'an of any notion of deliberately
'confounding' the tongues of humans to prevent their unity, strength
or ability to do what they want. A totally different explanation is
offered in the Qur'an: 'And among His Signs is the creation of the
heavens and earth, and the variations in your languages and your
colours: Verily in that are signs for those who know' (30:22).

The same universal outlook is clearly reflected in the following
Qur'anic *Āyah*:

O humankind: we created you from a single [pair] of a male and a female, and made you into nations of tribes, that you may know each other. Verily the most honoured of you in the sight of Allah is the one who is most righteous [Allah-Conscious] of you (49:13).

From the universality of the One and Only Creator of the universe stems the universality of the basic mission of all prophets in history to the one human family. Geographic, national, linguistic, racial and sexual differences are not legitimate bases for 'superiority'. It is, rather, the objective criterion of *Taqwā* (Allah-consciousness), sound belief confirmed by good deeds.

'Let there be no compulsion in religion', teaches the Qur'an (2:256). As such, the Muslim is required to deal kindly and justly with non-Muslims who are not oppressing him. Even in legitimate defence of oneself or one's faith, transgression [excess and plunder] is forbidden (2:190).

To promote an atmosphere of justice and decency, members of society are urged to 'ordain the good and forbid evil' (3:110) in the most effective and appropriate manner on the individual, social or political events. The establishment of a just political order is a form of worship. Allah's authority and jurisdiction are not restricted to the mosque. As such, the inner ethical appeal is reinforced by political order which ensures that the rights of others are safe-guarded. One such example is the enforceable institutionalised charity (*Zakāh*) and the minimum obligation to translate human brotherhood into a concrete and responsible form. Since *Zakāh* is also an act of worship, Muslims continue to pay *Zakāh* irrespective of whether or not their governments enforce it.

II THE EARTH

The previous discussion on humanity on both micro and macro levels is closely related to the examination of earth as one thing to which humanity relates.

Acceptance of the Supremacy of Allah and realisation of dependence upon Him, and acceptance of one's role as a trustee (*Khalifah*) of Allah on earth, implies that His bounties are tools to help humankind fulfil its trust. 'And He has subjected to you, as from Him all [bounties] that are in heavens and on earth: behold in that are signs indeed for those who reflect' (45:13).

Harnessing and using these resources require knowledge, seeking of which is an ethical duty. This may explain Muslims' attitudes towards science and scientists, and the remarkable strides and achievements when they took Islam seriously and committed their lives to the realisation of its ideals.

It may be noted that the first word of the Qur'an revealed to the unlettered prophet, Muhammad [Praise be upon Him] was *IQRA'* or 'recite' (96:1). Knowledge may be a basis for the person's higher status in the sight of Allah if based on faith in Allah (58:11). Knowledge is even related to the appreciation of Allah's bounties and Omnipotence which leads to the Allah-fearing quality (35:28).

With this orientation, the Muslim does not perceive of the earth or other natural laws as an adversary to be 'conquered'. Nor is there any notion that the earth was 'cursed' as a result of the act of disobedience committed by Adam and Eve. The earth is seen as a blessing and a bounty from Allah. As a bounty, it must be used wisely so as to prevent the quality of life from deteriorating, lest future generations be deprived from partaking their shares of such blessing.

In one sense the whole earth is holy. 'To Allah belong the East and the West: wherever you turn, there is the Presence of Allah. For Allah is All-Pervading, All-Knowing' (2:115).

The Prophet Muhammad (Praise be upon Him) also indicated that 'the [whole] earth was made as a *Masjid* [place of worship] and a clean one'.

There are, however, certain spots which are specially regarded. These spots are specially blessed by Allah and are closely related to the mission of the Prophets of Allah. Such as Makkah (Mecca) and Jerusalem. There is no implication, however, that believers should reside in a given holy location. Such locations are to be respected, visited, and taken as sources of inspiration and as spiritual centres.

III CONCLUSION

This chapter focused mainly on humanity, the purpose of its creation, its nature, its constant pursuit of reconciliation with its Creator. It examined how persons should relate to the Creator, to each other, and to the earth upon which he or she is journeying towards eternity. May all those who share life on this planet come to terms with their Creator and with each other and may they strive together for a better world of peace, justice and moral excellence.

A Christian Response to Jamāl Badawi: The Earth and Humanity: A Muslim View

Carl W. Ernst

In making my remarks, I would like to speak neither as a theologian nor as a 'representative' of Christianity in any official sense, but in my professional capacity as an historian of religion. In situations of dialogue or colloquy between members of different faiths, the historian of religion can be most useful, as Wilfred Cantwell Smith put it, by serving as a 'broker', and trying to help the process of communication by pointing out areas and principles of mutual interest.[1] With this in mind, I would like to point out some aspects of the Islamic tradition that should claim the attention of Christians, make some general remarks on the progress of the colloquy so far, and discuss the topic of the trusteeship of Adam as raised in Dr Badawi's chapter. I would like to conclude with some historical observations on the tradition of spiritual exegesis of the Qur'an.

There are a number of aspects of the Islamic tradition that Christian theologians have failed to confront, issues that may be called 'theologoumena islamica', to borrow a phrase from Henry Corbin. There have been a few attempts to discuss these issues from different points of view, such as J. W. Sweetman's volumes on *Islam and Christian Theology*, and the works of the French scholars Gardet and Anawati.[2] Nonetheless, these have remained isolated and specialised efforts, which have unfortunately not come to the attention of mainstream Christian theologians. The most notable aspect of Islam to be neglected by Christians is perhaps the central religious fact for Muslims: the prophecy of Muhammad as the vehicle for divine revelation. Long centuries of polemics and distorted portrayals of Muhammad as a Christian schismatic or worse have contributed to a climate of opinion among Christians highly unfavourable to a sympathetic evaluation of Muhammad's religious experience. Yet this is the feature that distinguishes the Islamic tradition from others; no real understanding of Islam is possible without some effort to grasp Muhammad's unique position in the Islamic worldview. A valuable and sympathetic approach to this subject may be found in the work of Annemarie Schimmel; last year at Pomona College, her Clark Lectures on 'The Veneration of the Prophet Muhammad in Islam' afforded us an opportunity to see the immense range of manifestations of Islamic piety focused on the figure of Muhammad. The forthcoming publication of Professor Schimmel's work on this subject, it is to be hoped, will be a major contribution to inter-religious understanding.[3] The Qur'an itself refers to the possibility of Christians who 'are not arrogant, but when they listen to that which was revealed to the Messenger, you will see their eyes flowing with tears, from that of the truth which they know' (5:82–3). In the realm of mystical thought, a work that should be of considerable interest to Christians is Louis Massignon's lifelong work, *The Passion of Hallaj*, which is devoted to the life, teaching, and influence of the great martyr and mystic, Hallaj (d. 922).[4] Massignon's study of Hallaj was part of his intensely personal approach to the spiritual sources of the Abrahamic traditions, and it clearly played a major role in the articulation of Massignon's own Catholic Christianity. It is worth noting that Massignon's views strongly influenced the very open recognition of Islamic religious values in the Vatican II declaration on non-Christian religions.[5] One can sample the remarkable range of Islamic theologies and Christologies in Henry Corbin's provocative article, 'Theologoumena Iranics'.[6] Here is displayed the Shi'i mystical Neoplatonism of the seventeenth century, as it was cultivated in the academy of Isfahan; this prolific school, still almost unknown in Western academic circles, included towering philosophical figures such as Mulla Sadra (d. 1640), whose works cry out for recognition by Western scholars. In short, there is a great deal to be learned from the study of Islamic religious thought, which can not only shed light on the cultural background of present-day Islamic societies, but may also serve as a creative stimulus for Christian theology.

Before turning to Dr Badawi's chapter, 'The Earth and Humanity', I would like first to make some observations about its function with regard to the ongoing discussion. In general his chapter will be informative to non-Muslims, in particular because of the explanation of Qur'anic accounts of the role of humanity on earth, and the discreet references to the way these differ from the Biblical versions of such stories as the garden of Eden and the tower of Babel. At this point, let me recall a Qur'anic verse that has been quoted in part on more than one occasion during this conference. The complete *ayah* reads, 'To every [people] have We set forth a path [*shir'ah*] and a way [*minhaj*]. Had God wished, He would have made you a single people, [but He did not,] so He may test you in that which He gave you: therefore excel in doing good. For all of you, refuge is in God' (5:48). Here, it seems to me, we have a scriptural recognition of religious diversity, which calls upon us not to gloss over any differences, but to live up to the highest standards of our own religious tradition. Since, moreover, the Qur'an goes on to say that 'He will inform you regarding that in which you differ', it is not incumbent on any human contentiously to point out errors in any other individual or group; this may be regarded as one of the Qur'anic precedents (the like of which may be found in the New Testament) for rejecting group solidarity or fanaticism (*'asabiyah*) in inter-religious discussion. Glancing at the subsequent *ayah*, however, one might suppose that discussion with Christians and Jews was one of the very dangers that the Qur'an warns against: 'And that you [Muhammad] judge between them by that which God revealed, and do not follow their desires, but beware of them, lest they seduce you from part of that which God revealed to you' (5:49). Yet it is clear from the context that this refers only to those of Muhammad's opponents who tried to tempt him to abandon the distinctive aspects of the Qur'anic revelation. Although an indefatigable literalism might still construe this as a warrant for criticising all Jews and Christians, it is my feeling that none of the Qur'anic strictures against heeding Jews and Christians applies to the present discussion. I say with all sincerity, and I think I can speak for most of the conference participants, that no one has any thought of subverting genuinely Islamic principles; it is therefore not appropriate for anyone to feel defensive in this discussion. Let me make this a plea for anyone who has had such feelings to put them away, as unworthy of the traditions that we severally subscribe to.

Of the many points raised by Dr Badawi in his chapter, there is one – the trusteeship of humanity – that I would like to make the focus of my direct response. The position of humanity is, according to the Qur'an, one of trusteeship or vicegerency (*khilafah*) over the earth; God has given this trust for humanity to bear, which even the angels refused. The practical and historical elaboration of this concept in the Islamic tradition has come to be equated with the search for religious leadership (*imamah*) and just rule (*imarah*) over the earth. In classical Islamic political theory, the only government that ever adhered to the ideal standard laid down in the Qur'an was the Muslim polity under the Prophet Muhammad. This was, in effect, a theocracy in the technical sense of the word: direct rule by God through revelation. Under the immediate successors or *khalifahs* of Muhammad, this constant access to divine revelation was no longer available, though the Qur'an remained as the total record of the revelations given to Muhammad. Most legal theorists agreed, however, that the first four successors to Muhammad were rightly guided, but that after the death of 'Ali in 656, the institution of the caliphate (*khilafah*) became transformed into kingship (*mulk*).[7] Muhammad's polity nonetheless served as the examplar (*sunnah*) for Islamic law, and was also an important source for Islamic political philosophy in its Platonic–Aristotelian form. I would like briefly to review the concept of *khilafah* in Islamic political philosophy in order to answer the question: What are the possible implications of the classical Islamic concept of *khilafah* for the modern world?

The first theoretical discussion of the nature of the ideal world state may well have been a letter of Aristotle to Alexander the Great, which survives only in Arabic. Though the argument surrounding the authenticity of this letter may not be settled, that is irrelevant to the significance of this document in medieval times. In this letter, Aristotle speaks of the time when humanity will agree on a single government that will end war and allow all to seek their proper vocation and welfare. Medieval Jewish thinkers observed that this is possible only in the messianic age, which, they insisted, is only properly described by the prophets, such as Isaiah and Micah.[8] Whether or not a peaceful world under a single government is possible only in the messianic age, the concept of such a state as the true *khilafah* was one that Islamic philosophers continually returned to. Al-Farabi (d. 950) saw the *khalifah* and *imam* as a divinely-inspired lawgiver ultimately identical with Plato's philosopher-king.[9] A similar line of thinking was followed by the Andalusian Peripatetic, Ibn Rushd (Averroes, d. 1220).[10] The Latin Averroists subscribed to the same kind of political philosophy, and one of the primary literary evidences of this thinking is Dante Alighieri's political treatise *De Monarchia*. Dante maintains that the world-state must be based on the secular Roman imperium rather than on the Catholic Church, since the Church should not attempt to govern a worldly kingdom.[11] Later Islamic political theorists used the terms *khalifah* and *imam* to designate any just ruler who upheld the system of Islamic law; these titles were thus adopted by the Ottoman and Mughul emperors. It is difficult, however, to see any direct political applicability of these concepts in the modern world. The last veritable *khalifah* of the house of 'Abbas was killed by the Mongols in 1256, and although the fiction of an 'Abbasid caliphate was maintained for centuries thereafter, the dreams of reviving its authority over Islamic nations were destroyed when Mustafa Kemal abolished the caliphate in 1924. I must admit, though, that I was fascinated by the nomination of the Aga Khan for the Secretary-Generalship of the United Nations several years ago. The Aga Khan is the *imam* of the Isma'ilis, and as such is the successor of the Fatimids, who boldly challenged the 'Abbasids by claiming the caliphate a thousand years ago as the true successors of the Prophet. It was interesting to speculate on the theoretical implications of a claimant to the *khilafah* gaining the only office with any similarity to that of the world-ruler. His campaign was vetoed, however, by the People's Republic of China, so we never had to deal with that eventuality.

If I may be allowed to philosophise for a moment, I would like to suggest that a realistic Islamic political theory will have to recognise a plurality of centres of authority, and a plurality of religious and legal systems. Dante's insistence on the secular basis of world-government is relevant here, though we are in no position to predict a single rule over the world. As al-Farabi himself pointed out, 'there may be a number of virtuous nations and virtuous cities whose religions are different, even though they all pursue the very same kind of happiness'.[12] It is no longer possible to advocate an Islamic domination of the world, any more than it is possible to advocate a Christian one. The fantasies of universal empire are the obsessions of Caesars, but the philosopher will do better to be concerned with the natural unit of civilisation, the just city and its order. On the basis of the tradition of Greek philosophy, a common inheritance shared by all the Abrahamic faiths, it may be possible for us to come to a recognition of each other that is not tyrannical or unjust. Then we may all claim to be a part of humanity's trusteeship over the earth.

Finally, I would like to discuss the issue of exegesis of scripture, which has come up several times during the conference. Speaking strictly as an historian of religion, I can say that there is an Islamic tradition of spiritual interpretation. One of the earliest of Qur'anic commentators, Muqatil ibn Sulayman (d. 767), made it a principle of his exegesis that the terms in the Qur'an have different 'aspects' (*wujuh*) that he glossed with interpretive equivalents. It is perhaps significant that Muqatil is supposed to have consulted with Jews and Christians about the meaning of certain Qur'anic passages, a practice that is recommended in the Qur'an itself. As the late Paul Nwyia has pointed out, Muqatil was but one of a number of classical commentators who saw different possibilities of meaning in the divine word.[13] The early Mu'tazili theologians made original contributions in this line, and the *imams* of the Shi'ah, especially Ja'far al-Sadiq (d. 765), have left some remarkably sophisticated commentaries.

A number of thinkers find an explicit justification of the theory of levels of meaning in an alternate reading of (3:7). In the customary punctuation, this passage reads as follows: 'And those with error in their hearts follow the symbolic part, desiring dissension and desiring its exegesis [*ta'wil*], but none knows the exegesis of it save God. And those who are firmly rooted in knowledge say, "We have faith in it" '. This would suggest that only God knows the meaning of the obscure or anthropomorphic expressions of the Qur'an, so that humans must only accept them on faith. Yet the early Qur'an scholar Mujahid (d. 722) read the verse with a different punctuation, so that it went 'but none knows the exegesis of it save God *and* those who are firmly rooted in knowledge. [Others] say, "We have faith in it" '.[14] This reading, which is well known among Sufis, philosophers, and Isma'ilis, clearly implies that there are some who have the special knowledge necessary for exegesis.[15] Those who are not qualified must accept the literal meaning without question. This view distinguishes between the elite who possess knowledge and the masses who know God only through faith. It suggests the possibility of a theory of 'two truths' that was often imputed to the Latin Averroists, but a closer examination reveals that this was not the case. Even the most extreme of the Averroists maintained only that truth is one, though it may be expressed in different ways.[16] Thus the Sufi commentator al-Sulami distinguished four levels of exegesis of scripture in his great commentary *Haga'iq al-Tafsir*. Henry Corbin has made some extremely suggestive remarks about the nature of such a spiritual exegesis in his study of the philosopher Ibn Sina.[17] Naturally, moderate scholars insisted that exegesis must be based on some kind of reasonable principles, to distinguish random allegory from legitimate interpretation. Therefore al-Ghazali (d. 1111), a widely-ranging genius who sampled philosophy and Isma'ili doctrine before settling on a legally rigorous Sufism, wrote a handy little treatise on the rules governing permissible exegesis.[18] In short, there is no reason to deny that there is a tradition of spiritual exegesis in Islam, although there are some dogmatic positions that reject the legitimacy of such attempts. This Islamic exegetical tradition parallels the great allegorical and mystical systems found in Jewish and Christian interpretations of the word of God, and it is a subject which surely deserves attention from future researchers.

I would like to summarise these remarks by saying that the spiritual heritage of Islam offers a profound set of resources for all those who wish to make use of them, whether they be Muslim, Jewish, Christian, or whatever. Closed and exclusive frameworks of interpretation, regardless of their origin, obscure the universal aspects of the Qur'anic revelation. All of us should ponder the true meaning of *islam*, submission to God. As Goethe put it, 'Wenn *Islam* Gott ergeben heisst, / In Islam leben und sterben wir alle'.[19]

Notes and References

1. Wilfred Cantwell Smith, 'Comparative Religion: Whither – and Why?' in Mircea Eliade and Joseph Kitagawa (eds), *The History of Religions, Essays in Methodology* (Chicago: University of Chicago Press, 1959; reprint edn, 1974) p. 51.

2. J. W. Sweetman, *Islam and Christian Theology*, 2 vols in 4 parts (London: Lutterworth, 1945–67); Louis Gardet and M. M. Anawati, *Introduction à la théologie musulmane, Essai de theologie comparée*, Études de philosophie médiévale, XXXVII (Paris: Librairie Philosophique J. Vrin, 1948); Louis Gardet, *Dieu et la destinée de l'homme, Les grands problèmes de la théologie musulmane, Essai de theologie comparée*, Études musulmanes, IX (Paris: Librairie Philosophique J. Vrin, 1967).

3. For a briefer presentation, see Annemarie Schimmel, 'The Prophet Muhammad as a Centre of Muslim Life and Thought', in Annemarie Schimmel and Abdoldjavad Falatūri (eds), *We Believe in One God: The Experience of God in Christianity and Islam* (New York: The Seabury Press, 1979) pp. 35–62.

4. Louis Massignon, *The Passion of Hallaj*, Harold W. Mason, (trans), 4 vols (Princeton: Princeton University Press, 1982).

5. Cf. *The Documents of Vatican II*, Walter M. Abbott (ed.) (New York: Guild Press, 1966) pp. 656–68, especially p. 663. See also Bassetti-Sani's biographical work, *Louis Massignon: Christian Orientalist*).

6. Henry Corbin, 'Theologoumena Iranica,' *Studia Islamica*, 5 (1976) pp. 225–35.

7. Ibn Khaldun, *The Muqaddimah, An Introduction to History*, Franz

Rosenthal (trans.) N. J. Dawood (ed.) (Princeton: Princeton University Press, 1967) ch. 3, especially pp. 160ff.

8. S. M. Stern, *Aristotle on the World State* (Columbia: University of South Carolina Press, 1970) especially pp. 3–8, 78–84.

9. Alfarabi (*sic*), 'The Political Regime', Fauzi M. Najjar (trans.), in *Medi eval Political Philosophy: A Sourcebook*, Ralph Lerner and Muhsir Mahdi (eds) (Ithaca: Cornell University Press, 1963; reprint edn, 1978 pp. 31–57.

10. Ralph Lerner (trans.), *Averroes on Plato's 'Republic'* (Ithaca: Cornel University Press, 1974) pp. 71ff.

11. Dante Alighieri, *On World-Government or De Monarchia*, Herbert W Schneider, (trans.), A Liberal Arts Press Book (Indianapolis Bobbs–Merrill, 1949; reprint edn, 1957).

12. Alfarabi, p. 41. 'The Political Regimé, p. 41.

13. Paul Nwyia, *Exégèse coranique et langage mystique, Nouvel essai sur le lexique techniques des mystiques musulmans* (Beirut: Dar el-Machrec Editeurs, 1970).

14. Abdullah Yusuf Ali (trans.), *The Glorious Qur'an* (The Muslin Students' Association of the United States and Canada, 1395/1975 p. 123, n. 348, emphasis mine. The present-day system of punctuatior of the Qur'an is relatively recent. Today there are seven different recen sions of the Qur'an, differing in very slight details of word-formatior and punctuation, and at one time there were more; for details, see W Montgomery Watt, *Bell's Introduction to the Qur'an*, Islamic Surveys (Edinburgh: University of Edinburgh Press, 1970) pp. 47–50.

15. Ruzbihan Baqli Shirazi, *Sharh-i Shathiyat* (ed.), Henry Corbin, Bibli othèque Iranienne 12 (Tehran: Department d'iranologie de l'Institu franco-iranien, 1966) pp. 57–8; George F. Hourani (trans.), *Averroe. on the Harmony of Religion and Philosophy*, 'E. J. W. Gibb Memorial Series, n.s. XXII (London: Luzac & Co., 1961) pp. 22–8 ('Allegorica interpretation of Scripture'); Edward E. Salisbury, 'Translation of Two Unpublished Arabic Documents Relating to the Doctrines of the Isma'ilis and Other Batinian Sects', *Journal of the American Oriental Society* II (1851) p. 310.

16. Martin Pine, 'Double Truth', *Dictionary of the History of Ideas*, II 31–7.

17. Henry Corbin, *Avicenna and the Visionary Recital*, Willard Trask (trans.) (New York: Pantheon Books, 1960), index, s.v. '*ta'wil*'.

18. Richard Joseph McCarthy (trans.), *Freedom and Fulfillment* (Boston Twayne Publishers, 1980) Appendix I, 'Faysal al-Tafriqa bayn al-Islam wa l-Zandaqa' (*sic*) pp. 145–74.

19. Johann Wolfgang von Goethe, *West-Östlicher Divan*, Goldmanns Gelbe Taschenbücher, Band 487 (Munich: Wilhelm Goldmann Verlag, 1958 p. 56 ('If *islam* means submitting to God, in islam we all live and die')

A Jewish Response to Jamāl Badawi: The Earth and Humanity: A Muslim View

Patricia S. Karlin-Neumann

I thank and congratulate Professor Badawi on an excellent chapter to which I have the good fortune of being a respondent. I do so with some discomfort, not only because I know little more about Islamic theology than your comprehensive chapter provided, but also because several of my teachers are present today. It is my hope that we will teach one another and continue to learn about one another's traditions.

The paper offered a familiar road, for to base theological assertions on sacred texts is an enterprise common to both Islam and Judaism. Indeed, it is the text – in my tradition, the Torah – which provides the keys for exploring and deepening one's relationship with the Holy One. In the discussion of the earth and humanity the keys Professor Badawi offers occasioned the following reflections on my part. The relationship between humanity and the earth as it is reflected within the Jewish tradition is one of interdependence. In a rabbinic comment on the second story of human creation, the rabbis suggest this weaving: 'For the Lord God had not sent rain upon the earth and there was no human to till the ground'. Understanding the first part of the phrase – the absence of rain on the earth, to be caused by the second part – there was no human to till the ground, Rabbi Simeon bar Yohai said, 'Three things are equal in importance: earth, humanity and rain'. R. Levi ben Hiyyata said, 'and these three each consist of three letters, to teach that without earth there would be no rain, and without rain earth could not endure; while without either, humans could not exist' (Genesis Rabbah 13:3). Humans are dependent upon the earth, we know this from their very creation. For in Hebrew *Adam*, the name of Adam, the name from which comes the Hebrew for humanity (*Benai Adam*, 'Adam's children'), is the same root as ground (*Adama*). Adam (humanity) is masculine, *Adama* (earth, ground) is feminine. Even those who focus on the second creation story, suggesting that woman comes from man, should note that the creation of man is from the feminine *Adama*. We allude to this when we call the earth mother 'earth' or 'mother nature'. The earth in this perspective is the provider – she provides the matter with which Holy One creates human beings. Here again the Hebrew word play gives us a clue, for the root Aleph-Dalet-Mem appears to be related to the Assyrian *adâmu*: to make *Adam* – that which has been made – from *Adama*, from the earth. The rabbis, recognising that the 'stuff' of which Adam was made significantly determines who he is, add the following insight. Commenting on the verse, 'Then the Lord God formed Adam from the dust (*afar*) of the earth (*Adama*)', R. Huna said, 'Dust (afar) is masculine while ground (*Adama*) is feminine: a potter takes male dust (coarse earth) and female earth (soft clay) in order that his vessels may be sound' (Genesis Rabbah 14:7).

In the first creation story male and female are created together, 'male and female God created them' (Genesis 1:27). Yet according to this tradition, even in the second creation story, the 'rib' story, there is an awareness that masculine and feminine must be combined in order to make a sound vessel.

Knowing the kind of earth from which man is created is not sufficient. The rabbis inquire about where the earth is from. Several answers are offered in the tradition:

> Why [did God gather man's dust] from the four corners of the world? Thus spake the Holy one. If a man should come from the east to the west, or from the west to the east, and his time comes to depart from the world, then the earth shall not say, 'The dust of thy body is not mine, return to the place whence thou wast created'. But [this circumstance] teaches you that in every place where a man goes or comes, and his end approaches when he must depart from the world, there is the dust of his body, and there it returns to the dust, as it is said, 'For dust thou art, and unto dust shalt thou return' (Genesis 3:19) (Pirke de Rabbi Eliezer 11).

Inherent in this rendering of Adam's creation is the awareness that, the promise of the garden notwithstanding, Adam would die. Thus, the Holy One attempted to make any place on earth a resting place for the one who comes from the earth.

Another suggestion for the location of the earth from which Adam was made is contained in the following midrash:

'Of the Ground' – R. Berekiah and R. Helbo in the name of Samuel the Elder said: He was created from the place of his atonement, as you read, 'An altar of *Adama*, you shall make unto me' (Exodus 20:21). The Holy One said: 'Behold, I will create him from the place of his atonement and may he endure' (Genesis Rabbah 14:8); and similarly, 'With the best dust of the earth God created him, from the fine grains of the earth God created him, from the place of worship God created him, from the place of atonement, God created him, and where is this? Mt Moriah, from the place of the altar God created him, as it is written "dust from the earth" (*Adama*) and "altar of the earth" (*Adama*), from a place pure and holy' (Midrash Hagadol Genesis 7:3).

In rabbinic thought, the concept of God providing a cure before an illness appears is commonplace. That is, according to the rabbis, the concept of repentence or return (*Teshuva*) was created before the world was created. Here, as well, we find God serving as an advocate for Adam. According to the rabbis, knowing that this human will be fallible, God creates him from the earth closest to the Holy One – the earth of worship at the Holy temple, the earth of the Holy place of atonements. In short, God creates Adam in a place of *Teshuva*, of repentance. And so, human beings can return to that place, not simply in death, as in the previous passage, but in life. Human beings can return to the earth which connects the Divine and the human.

Thus by combining these two passages, we have some insight into a rabbinic conception of human essence. First, the notion of worshipping God is inherent in human creation, for Adam was created at the central place of Jewish worship. Adam was also created at the point of 'return' – the place of *Teshuva* – ensuring that the human who sins can always return to the Creator. Finally Adam is created from earth spanning the length and breadth of the world – perhaps to be at home in the far-flung places of Jewish exile, certainly to be safely buried in all the earth.

Yet this fallible, mortal Adam who needs the earth in order to exist is not ruled by the earth; rather Adam rules the earth. In the first creation story God blesses an androgynous *Adam* and says, 'Be

fertile and increase, fill the earth and master it; and rule the fish o:
the sea, the birds of the sky and all the living things that creep or
the earth' (Genesis 1:28). According to the midrash:

> The Holy One decided to cause Adam to rule over God's earth
> and to make him rule over all of God's creatures. Said the Holy
> One, 'I am Ruler in the heavenly realms, and Adam is ruler in
> the earthly realms' (Pesikta Rabbati).

This view of Adam is reinforced by his role in the Garden of Eden:
to keep and to till it, and by this task, even after being banished
from the garden: to toil in the earth. In one case the kingdom is a
delight; in the other it needs to be put in order. Yet even when the
ground is cursed, to which Professord Badawi refers, it is cursed
Baavorecha, 'on your [Adam's] account'. The kingdom reflects the
triumphs and failures of the king. Both in the prophets (Isaiah 24:5,
6) and in the Siddur, the Jewish prayerbook, we read of fertility of
the earth as a reflection of the behaviour of human beings. Yet the
earth's curse manifested in Adam's day is alleviated in Noah's, 'Who
will provide us relief from our work and from the toil of our hands,
out of the soil which the Lord placed under a curse' (Genesis 5:29).
Rashi, the eminent commentator, understands this to mean that
Noah invented some agricultural tools to relieve their toil, and so
Adam's children are able to rule the earth by using knowledge.

The earth, which truly belongs to the Holy one – 'The earth is the
Lord's and the fullness thereof' (Ps. 24:1), God gives to humanity
to rule (Ps. 115:16) – 'The earth God has given to the children of
Adam'. The king, Adam, is dependent upon the subject-earth, and
the earth is never fully out of God's domain. For when Israel sins,
God calls to the heavens and earth to witness against Israel. And so
we return to the question which began Professor Badawi's chapter.
If human beings make so much trouble, why did God create us? The
ministering angels ask God the same question.

> What is man that you are mindful of him and human beings that
> you think of them? (Ps. 8:5). What do you seek from this Adam?
> The Holy One said, 'It is written in the Torah, "when a man dies
> in a tent" (Numbers 19:14), and there is no death among you; it
> is written in the Torah, "If a woman deliver and bear a son"
> (Leviticus 12:2), and there is no childbirth among you; it is written
> in the Torah, "These you may eat" (Leviticus 11:21), and there

is no eating among you. Therefore the Torah cannot go forth through you, as it is said: (Job 28:13) "It is not found in the land of the living (i.e., eternal living)"; but when the Holy One said to Israel that they should make a Tabernacle for God and they made it, they began making an altar for burnt offering, an altar of incense and they sacrificed upon it. The Holy One began to give them some commandments, commanding them on each and everything and they did them' (Tarhuma Buber Vayikra 112).

Thus the rabbinic notion is that the Holy One made human beings who would fulfil God's Torah, but, as well, humans who would eat, have children, live and die. Humans exist to bring God delight. May our lives and our study be sources of God's delight. May we recognise our responsibility toward the earth and toward God as recipients of the gift of life.

5 The Earth and Humanity: A Christian View
John B. Cobb, Jr

In interfaith dialogue one feels an obligation somehow to speak for one's whole faith community. Yet we all know this is impossible. I cannot speak for Orthodox and Catholic Christians, or even for Protestants in general.

I feel an additional problem with respect to my assignment. I have strong convictions on this topic, and I recognise that these are not shared by the majority of Christians. I think I must say something about this difference and give some justification for claiming my own views as a Christian. Fortunately, I am asked to present 'a Christian view'.

In a formal way, I suggest that a Christian view is one that is rooted in the whole Bible as that is read in light of the story of Jesus and the apostolic witness to him found in what we Christians call the 'New Testament'. The great majority of us understand our beliefs to be of this character. Debates as to what Christians should believe normally refer to this source for their most basic authority, although in some traditions later decisions by church leaders have equal, or nearly equal, authority.

Inevitably, just as all Christians see the Jewish scriptures through the New Testament, so also Christians of the several Christian traditions see the New Testament through later developments in their separate histories. Protestants, for example, read Paul through the eyes of Luther and Calvin. Whether, and to what extent, this is distorting is still debated. If further developments lead Protestants to conclude that Paul's meaning is in opposition to the interpretation of Luther and Calvin, in faithfulness to Luther and Calvin we will be inclined to turn away from them to Paul as our point of reference. For us the apostolic witness remains primary, however deeply we are informed by our subsequent history. But we know that every reading of that witness, however scholarly, will always be shaped by the tradition of thought in which it stands. We cannot return to the position of the apostles.

113

I   THE EARTH AND HUMANITY AS CREATION

This account of what it means for a position to be Christian is important with respect to the topic at hand. There can be no doubt that for many generations, the finest Protestant theology has seen the scriptures as radically anthropocentric. Human history and individual human existence have been viewed as the loci of God's concern and action. Scholars and theologians have known that the Bible also speaks of the creation of the natural world, but they have understood this to be a secondary interest, an unnecessary extension of thinking from the centre, which is the historical covenant of the people of Israel with God. God's dealing with the world is for the sake of the redemption of human beings. From their point of view references to the non-human world as praising God or participating in redemption reflect the continuing influence of Baal cults. What is distinctive of Israel is its orientation to history.

This remains the predominant position in Protestant circles. It comes to expression in preaching, in the topics discussed by Christian ethicists, and in the actions of ecumenical gatherings, as well as in scholarly exegesis and professional theology.

In historical terms, this view is rather recent. In the eighteenth century the orderliness of the non-human creation provided arguments for the existence and goodness of God. In more recent times as well there have been dissident voices who believed that the natural world bore evidence of divine care, and that human beings should not suppose themselves to be so separated from the remainder of the creation. Joseph Sittler attracted some attention to this concern in an important address to the New Delhi assembly of the World Council of Churches. In the English-speaking world there was an effort to understand God's role in the evolutionary process culminating in human beings. In the form given this vision by Teilhard de Chardin it found resonance in many people. But until widespread attention was called to the global crisis resulting from Western industrialisation of the planet, the basic anthropocentric habit of mind was not seriously challenged. Since then there has been a steady flow of books and articles calling for revision in the established view. These often seem temporarily and locally successful in altering perceptions. But as soon as the pressure to rethink these questions is relaxed, the dominant attitudes reassert themselves.

An example can be found in the World Council of Churches. The Church and Society unit led international Christian reflection throughout the 1970s on the question of concern for the environment in relation to the existing commitments to justice and participation. Many resisted the addition of this new emphasis, but gradually a consensus was shaped among the discussants that the Christian must be committed to a just, participatory and sustainable society. This consensus was sanctioned at the Nairobi Assembly. This definition of the Christian goal did not directly challenge anthropocentrism, but it did indicate that Christians were ready to consider that their behaviour in relation to the natural environment was important.

These efforts of the Church and Society unit culminated in a major conference held at MIT in the summer of 1979. Most of the sections at that conference dealt with practical issues of education, technology, energy, economics, etc. in relation to the ideal of a just, participatory and sustainable society. But there were also more theoretical discussions. The statement of the section on 'Humanity, Nature and God' included the following:

> The crisis in our scientific and technological world, seen in the light of the Bible, calls for a holistic approach in which the relationship between God, humanity and nature is developed in relation to contemporary problems . . . Science and technology, by reducing nonhuman nature to the status of a mere object, have denied the intrinsic value that inheres in every creature because it comes from the hand of God. Modern Western Christian theology put up little resistance to this development. Indeed, it undergirded the opposition between nature and humanity by making the uniqueness of humanity the predominant theme in its doctrine of creation . . .

> Western theology has introduced the above-mentioned opposition even into the interpretation of the Bible: creation and salvation have been separated; either the theology of salvation swallowed up the theology of creation, or creation was treated in isolation from it. Today, by contrast, we need to point out the numerous ways in which the Bible connects creation and salvation in Christ, eschatological hope and obedience, and justice and sustainability . . .

> What needs to be emphasised today, therefore, is the *relatedness* between God and his creation rather than their *separateness*. The dignity of nature as creation needs to be stressed and humanity's *dominium* must be bound up with our responsibility for the preser-

vation of life. Humanity is part of nature yet at the same time transcends it.[1]

It seemed to participants in that conference that some breakthrough of traditional anthropocentrism had been attained, at least within the World Council of Churches. There was hope that these gains would be consolidated at the Vancouver Assembly in 1983.

These hopes were doomed to disappointment. The planners of this assembly felt that the primary need was for the gathering to be as representative as possible of the diverse peoples who make up the churches that are members of the Council. The result was that 80 per cent of the delegates were attending their first World Council meeting. The materials prepared for study were consciously written to invite participation of people not familiar with traditional theological issues or language. There was little effort to feed into the Assembly the results of more specialised discussions that had taken place under WCC auspices. As a result, the MIT documents were neither affirmed nor repudiated. They were simply ignored.

My point here, however, is not that these documents were ignored but that Christians who had not given attention to these documents simply did not raise the questions to which they were directed. Insofar as there was a great issue before the Assembly, it was how to reconcile the commitment to peace and nuclear disarmament that dominated the concern to the First World with the issues of economic justice that remained paramount in the Third World. The effects of human action in the destruction of the environment, the need for sustainable ways of life and – most of all – the question of whether the natural world is of importance in itself, and to God, simply were not discussed. Partly because they gave little attention to theology, Christians returned to the topics to which their established theology has directed them for centuries. These questions of peace and justice are certainly important ones, deserving of all the attention they received. But so is sustainability. The evidence is that, if we are to speak of *the* Christian understanding of earth and humanity, the earth is viewed as the taken-for-granted stage on which the human drama is played out.

Many of us are convinced, however, that this dominant view reflects more the history of modern Western thought than the Biblical sources, that it is not *the* Christian view, and that more careful attention to scripture and its message to us will erode its power. We believe that a quite different understanding of the earth and humanity is more truly Christian than the prevailing one.

Superficially, the case I want to make is almost self-evident. The Bible opens with the story of creation. Beginning with the third day at each stage of creation God sees that what has come to be is good. There is no suggestion that its goodness is only for the sake of the human beings who have not yet been created. The Psalms pick up the theme of the goodness of creation and how the heavens declare the glory of God. Prior to the rise of critical scholarship, Genesis and the Psalms were among the most influential portions of the Bible in shaping basic Christian habits of mind. No one thought to question that God's creative purposes were manifest in all things. The primary distinction was between God and the created world. Within creation one could distinguish angels, human beings, other living things and the inanimate order. These distinctions were important but secondary.

Modern critical scholarship changed this. That scholarship has tried, rightly I think, to sort out the strands of tradition that have been woven together in the Bible. It has tried to learn how they are related, what their respective sources are, which represent pagan influence, and which carry the distinctively Yahwistic tradition. It was in this process that covenant was contrasted with creation, history with nature. And when these contrasts were made, creation and nature were downgraded as peripheral concerns for Yahwism.

How can one who supports the critical approach to scripture but who disagrees with basic elements in its outcome maintain a consistent position? The answer, I think, is not difficult when one reflects on the history of scholarship. It is quite apparent that this scholarship is always deeply informed by the cultural and intellectual perspectives that are brought to bear. The scholarly products are not simply a function of these perspectives. They are shaped also by the texts that are studied, and some consensus can emerge that transcends the perspectives through which the texts are viewed. Hence there are no grounds for complete cynicism about critical scholarship. But there are grounds for suspicion when, generation after generation, the deepest meaning found in the texts turns out to be identical with the changing convictions of the scholars, especially when these convictions are manifestly culturally determined.

The sharp juxtaposition of humanity and the rest of the natural world has been strongest in Protestant continental Europe. It has been Protestant continental Europe that has led the world in Biblical scholarship. It is not surprising that the nature/history distinction, never explicit in the Bible, is surely legitimate for those who do not subscribe to the German idealist tradition to question whether the understanding of the earth that follows from it is truly Biblical.

This move is fairly easy to make. But when one rejects the idealist component in Biblical scholarship, one is all too likely to fall back, consciously or unconsciously, on other currents in the modern Western tradition. There are materialism, Cartesian dualism, and an empiricism which easily becomes phenomenalist. None of these provide a satisfactory context for recovering a Biblical vision of the world. Christian theology formulated in their terms has been only a little more attentive to the co-creatureliness of humans and other beings than that formulated in the sphere of idealist influence.

For some time Catholic thought retained some sense of the positive reality and value of the non-human world through its continuity with medieval modes of understanding, especially the system of St Thomas Aquinas. But since the late nineteenth century it has been moving away from this. Thomism, in its most influential representatives, has become 'transcendental', in other words, Kantian. J. B. Metz has argued explicitly that St Thomas himself was in fact anthropocentric, and on this basis he calls for contemporary Thomists to follow in that direction. To find Christian thinking that has not been deeply informed or infected by modern Western thought one must turn to Eastern Orthodoxy. There the whole of the created world has a sacramental quality.

My argument thus far is a simple one. The Christian view to which I suscribe and which I am convinced is Biblical sees human beings as a part of God's creation, creatures alongside other creatures. All of this creation has value in itself and is recognised as valuable by God. God's concern for the creation is for all of the creation and for its inclusive redemption. The narrowing of the understanding of God's concern to human beings alone and the denial of intrinsic reality and value to the rest of the world is the result of the modern Western intellectual tradition, not the Bible. The fact that it is now dominant in Christendom does not establish it as *the* Christian view.

II   HUMANITY AS THE CORRUPTED IMAGE OF GOD

Among those who have rejected the dominant anthropocentrism of modern Western thought, many also reject any gradations of value and importance among the several species of creatures. They argue that any judgement that some creatures are of more worth than others can only express the biases of the human species, that we humans set ourselves up as supremely valuable and appraise others either in terms of their resemblance to us or in terms of their attractiveness to us. What is needed, they argue, is the impartial acceptance of differences as differences, the abandonment of the habit of evaluation and the development of a style of life that affirms one's own species while respecting others.

This view is not possible for a Christian. The Biblical account focuses upon human beings. Whereas other creatures are recognised by God as good, it is only after the appearance of human beings that the creation is *very* good. Only human beings are created in 'the image of God'. Also, they are given dominion over others. In Paul's vision, the whole creation is to be redeemed, but the redemption of human beings is the critical event which makes that possible.

Especially in light of the way that human dominion has been exercised, it is quite possible to deplore it. We may wish that human beings had remained one species struggling for survival alongside others. Much is to be said for that wish when we recognise that the abuse of human dominion may soon lead to the extinction of all life on this planet. Nevertheless, it is the Bible that is realistic. Human beings *do* have dominion. This is far more true today than when the idea of dominion was first propounded. To call on us wholly to abandon our dominion, as some anti-anthropocentric writers do, is theoretically fascinating but practically meaningless. Our decisions will determine the fate of our co-creatures. We will not cease to make decisions. What is important is to make them in the light of an understanding of their ramifications and with a deep respect for the other creatures that are affected.

The issue is not whether we exercise dominion, but how we exercise it. Here it is important to acknowledge a sinful habit of mind pervasive of much of Christian history. We have supposed that to exercise dominion over the other creatures is to exploit them ruthlessly for our own sake. To soften this tendency, we have sometimes introduced the word 'stewardship'. This makes more immediately apparent that the earth is God's and that we are to treat it as such. But even stewardship fails to carry the notion that the earth has value in and of itself, that the creatures with which we share it are to be respected.

The irony is that there is much in the Bible that protests against the exploitative and egocentric notion of dominion. There were, certainly, theories of dominion in surrounding countries which justified the ruler in treating the ruled as simply possessions to be used as he desired. But Israel resisted this view. The good king ruled for the sake of the ruled. His dominion was granted by God because of the needs of the people, not to satisfy his personal needs for wealth, power and glory. This point, pervasive of the Jewish scriptures, should have been even more clear to those who understood the true Lord as one who gave his life for others.

That we exercise dominion is connected to our special similarity to God, our being created in God's image. Much attention has been paid in Christian history to the question: in what does that image consist? In modern secular discussion, much the same issue is raised in the question of what distinguishes human beings most fundamentally from other species. 'Reason' is often used in formulating the answer in both contexts. In recent times, attention often focuses on language. Against the view that reason or language totally distinguishes human beings from other creatures there is evidence that we do not have as strict a monopoly as we had supposed. The Bible is wise not to try to identify some one human faculty that is wholly lacking in other animals. But there can be little doubt that human beings share with God in determining the destiny of the earth in a way that no other species does.

The recognition by God that the creation is good has nothing to do with its moral virtue. This is clearly true of human beings. We are creatures of great value. Whether we suffer or rejoice, serve God or evil, create or destroy, is very important. What we are, and what others become because of us, matters greatly. It matters to us and it matters to God. The fact that we are created in God's image, able to participate in shaping the destiny of the world, makes the question of our moral virtue very important. It does not insure that virtue.

The actual situation we find is one in which sin pervades the whole of human life. This does not mean that the average person is engaged most of the time in crudely anti-social behaviour. If that were the case, society could not survive at all. But it does mean that every society is replete with injustice and misery, that human self-centredness and insensitivity are always factors contributing to this injustice and misery, and that all of us discover this self-centredness and insensitivity in ourselves. It is our clinging to middleclass life-styles that justifies policies on the part of the United States which contribute to continued oppression and starvation in much of the world. This level of sin is compounded by denial and rationalisation and the demonisation of others as justification for our opposition to their aspirations. The familiar story of sin goes on. The sin does not disappear when we try to order our lives under rules of virtue. There is instead the danger that it is worsened because our obedience to such rules may enable us to suppose ourselves virtuous and justified in thinking of ourselves as better than those who do not follow them. At best, our motives for obedience are inevitably tainted by the desire for the good opinion of others and for the feeling that we are ourselves righteous. When we measure ourselves against the yard-stick of true love for God and neighbour, we can only acknowledge that all have sinned and fallen short of the glory of God.

Christians have associated this pervasive sinfulness with the Genesis story of the sin of Adam. Certainly that story indicates that the Biblical writers also saw sin as beginning with the first human beings. They carefully distinguished creation and fall, however, so as to show that we are not created sinners. We are created in the image of God, and it is for that reason that we are capable of sin. Once the actuality of sin gained a foothold in human history, it seems that we have become incapable of freeing ourselves from its power. We see that we have plunged the whole of the created order into disruption through that sin. For Christians the deepest truth about us is thus our need for forgiveness and redemption, which we can receive only as a gift from God. We scan history seeking signs of God's grace, and we find these centrally and decisively in the story of Jesus. It has become for us the clue to everything else.

We understand that the Christian life is not one of moral righteous-ness to which we can attain by an effort of the will. It is fundamentally one of openness to God's forgiving and redemptive grace. But the fact of God's undeserved grace arouses gratitude, and gratitude to God arouses the desire to serve God through service of God's crea-tures. This does not overcome the power of sin in our lives. But we do believe that despite our continuing sinfulness God can use us in the realisation of divine purposes.

I have elaborated briefly the Christian understanding of sin and redemption. It highlights the point of this section that human beings have a special place in the Biblical vision. We were created very good. We have sinned and we continue to sin, and our sin has involved the devastation of the earth. We live from divine grace and by grace we hope that our realisation of the destruction we have

wrought may enable us to repent, to turn around. Only through such
repentance can there be a renewal and replenishment of the earth.

III OUR PROPER DOMINION

The implications of the Biblical view of the earth and humanity for
human use of other creatures have been made quite explicit in the
accounts above. Nevertheless, it will be worthwhile to summarise
and expand.

Those who have dominion have the right to share in the wealth
over which they rule. Human use of other creatures for the sake of
human life, health and comfort is to be affirmed. Where the wealth
suffices, there is no reason for human beings not to live well, even
affluently. Christianity does not favour asceticism for its own sake.

However, when wealth is limited and the use of that wealth for
the sake of the ruler impoverishes the ruled, there are clear Biblical
reasons for restraint. Feasting in the king's house is wrong when it
is at the expense of hunger in the peasant's hut. Similarly the quest
for more and more luxury and waste on the part of human beings
at the price of the wholesale destruction of other species is a total
distortion of the Biblical norm of dominion. Ours is a world which
can be described well in the words of Mahatma Gandhi: 'There is
enough in the world for everyone's need but not enough for everyone's greed'. We in the affluent world have redefined 'need' to
include much that belongs truly to greed.

There are reasons for restraint even when human self-interest
alone is considered. If whole species of whales are destroyed now,
there will be none to be hunted in the future. To allow whale
populations to rise and ensure the survival of the several species will
in the long run make more whales available for human use. The
ruler who destroys the realm impoverishes himself.

But the Biblical vision is not simply anthropocentric in this way.
Whales were created before human beings. They had value in themselves for God. That value would have continued whether human
beings had been created or not. Human beings have dominion over
whales, but that does not mean that they have the right to do with
whales simply as they choose. There is no true dominion apart from
respect for those ruled. We owe respect to non-human creatures.
When they are abundant and our needs are pressing, that respect
does not forbid the killing of some for our use. But it does forbid

the killing of any for trivial purposes. It emphatically does not give us the right to impoverish the totality of creation by destroying whole species. Even if it were in the interest of human beings to destroy whales, failure to respect the whales and their interests would be a violation of the Biblical understanding of dominion.

Human dominion expresses itself more and more today in terms of 'management'. In addition to the species of animals that we have domesticated, we now manage many others. To some extent, this is the only way that these species can survive in the diminished habitat we have allotted them. It is better that they survive in this semi-domesticated form than that they be lost altogether. In other instances, we are capturing a few members of now rare species with the hope that we can preserve them in zoos. This, too, may be better than the alternative.

But all of these acts reflect a basic failure in our task of dominion. Instead of exercising proper lordship in the biosphere, treating all species justly, we have expropriated their land and destroyed their habitat. Indeed, we are now doing this on a larger scale than ever before. We make it impossible for other creatures to fulfil the divine command to be fruitful and multiply. This cannot be the intention of the commandment that we should subdue the earth.

The exercise of proper dominion does not have to do only with respect for the other species of living things over whom the dominion is exercised. It has to do also with the use of the soil, water, air, minerals and fossil fuels. These, too, are God's creation, and in relation to them the image of stewardship is particularly appropriate. We have them in trust.

If a king used up the resources of his land, leaving a desert for his successor, no one would suppose that he had exercised a proper dominion. The land is not given to us for destruction, but for tending. In traditional societies where the land passes from generation to generation within the family, the good farmer tries to leave it at least as productive as he receives it. Not to do so is to have failed and to have cut off the source of life for one's descendants. Not only the Bible, but all traditional wisdom, calls for sustainable use of the land. That there are in many parts of the world huge man-made deserts indicates not the effective dominion of human beings but our collective ignorance and sin. Proper dominion requires careful replenishment in the context of a sustainable economy.

The theoretical problem is more difficult when we deal with those resources which are virtually irreplaceable, such as the mineral wealth of the planet. In Biblical times, this issue was not clearly posed, for the use of these resources was trivial in comparison with their quantity. Today, this is no longer true. At present rates of consumption readily accessible sources of many minerals will be gone within a hundred to a thousand years. If we project continuing increases of consumption at rates that have characterised the past ten to twenty years, exhaustion times are much shorter. Our dominion gives us the right of *use*, but surely it cannot encourage us to *use up* these resources recklessly.

Sooner or later most of the stock of minerals available will be that which is already mined. Recycling this stock will be the only practical solution. Looking ahead to this situation, responsible dominion entails maximum movement now toward that recycling so as to stretch out the time before we are wholly dependent upon it, and so as to ease the transition.

With fossil fuels, on the other hand, the situation is different. They can be used only once. Here our changes must be away from using them when renewable sources would serve, along with the gradual development of alternatives.

Unfortunately even these moderate suggestions cut against deeply entrenched habits. Especially in the United States – but increasingly elsewhere as well – we are habituated to think in terms of short-term growth and development rather than sustainable economies. There is a blind faith that rapid use of available resources now will set the stage for the discovery of more resources later, or that technology will allow the endless substitution of new resources for old. This mindset does not have Biblical support. It is an unintended by-product of certain theories of modern economics encouraged by the modern anthropocentric worldview.

While we collectively resist even these adjustments, we must remind ourselves that they are not enough. Sustainability of resource use will not suffice. The way we produce and use resources today poisons and pollutes the earth. Also patterns that are now sustainable quickly become unsustainable or insufficiently productive as global population growth continues. Unless we make more drastic changes in the way we live and in population policies, we are on a collision course with disaster.

The point about population policies is today the most controversial among Christians. There is no doubt that throughout Biblical times human fruitfulness was prized. Although overpopulation may have been more of a problem at certain times and places in the ancient world than was then realised, it was trivial in comparison with our problem today. People were understandably more concerned that plagues, famines and wars might wipe out their progeny than that there be too many descendants.

The resulting affirmation of human fruitfulness came to be combined in post-Biblical Christianity with negative attitudes toward sexuality in general. Sexual activity could be justified, for many Christians, only by its function in generating offspring. This meant that any separation of sexual intercourse from the effort to conceive rendered that intercourse sinful. This profoundly unbiblical notion continues to shape the attitudes of some Christians and the official teaching of some churches to this day. It means that in a time when responsible dominion requires great restraint on giving birth to more people, much of Christian teaching rails against the instruments of that restraint. Responsible Christian dominion will have to work against a long tradition of Christian teaching.

I have provided only the sketchiest indication of what dominion entails when it is understood in the Biblical context of rule for the sake of the ruled and as stewardship of what belongs to God. The practice of Western Christians – and increasingly the global practice – repudiates dominion for tyranny. Sometimes it tries to justify this tyranny by appeal to the Bible. What is most noteworthy, what must be repented, is the silence of Christian teaching in the face of this massive abuse. Even today the Christian community does not provide its due share of leadership in opposing the tyrannical exploitation of the earth for short-term gain on the part of the more powerful members of the human community.

Sometimes this violation of the biblical injunction to exercise dominion is justified as necessary for the sake of human beings. It is argued that interest in other creatures is the luxury of the comfortable who then want to restrain the poor from gaining a livelihood. But it is becoming increasingly clear that this is profoundly fallacious. Those who exercise tyranny over other creatures are rarely much less tyrannical in their exploitation of the poor. A recent statement by a citizens' group in India makes the point clearly:

In a country like India, with a high population density and high level of poverty, virtually every ecological niche is occupied by some occupational or cultural human group for its sustenance. Each time an ecological niche is degraded or its resources appropriated by the more powerful in society, the deprived, weaker

sections become further impoverished. For instance, the steady
destruction of our natural forests, pasture lands and inland and
coastal water bodies has not only meant increased poverty for
millions of tribals, nomads and traditional fisherfolk, but also a
slow cultural and social death: a dismal change from rugged self
sufficient human beings to abjectly dependent landless labourers
and squalor-stricken urban migrants. Current development can, in
fact, be described as the process by which the rich and most
powerful reallocate the nation's natural resources in their favour
and modern technology is the tool that subserves this process.[2]

IV THE HOLY LAND

It is possible to speak of the earth as holy in the sense that it is
pervaded with the presence of the One who alone is Holy. But the
dominant emphasis must be that indeed only God is holy. Creatures
are holy only derivatively, and by virtue of God's presence in them.
To view anything creaturely as intrinsically holy is idolatrous.

This basic Biblical teaching has been in tension with other tend
encies in Christianity. Among Protestants the Bible, especially, is
declared a holy book. Catholics have often thought of the church as
holy, and they refer to the papal office as the holy see. Christians
have also spoken of Sunday as a holy day and of churches as holy
places. In a similar way we can speak of Israel as the Holy Land.
Indeed almost any place, time, person or activity closely associated
with Christian practice or Christian memory can take on an aura of
holiness.

To speak of times and places and persons as holy need not be
idolatrous. It can mean simply that they are especially associated by
the community with acts of God and human response to these. But
the danger of idolatry lies near at hand. The Protestant talk of the
Holy Bible often leads to an idolatrous view of the Bible. Its words
are supposed to be free from the limitations of all creaturely things.
The Catholic talk of the church and the papacy as holy often leads
to idolatrous views of these as well. The doctrine of papal infallibility
however carefully it is qualified, suggests a freedom from the
constraints of finitude that is hardly less dangerous than biblicism.
Talk of the Holy Land inspired the fanaticism of the holy wars, the
Crusades. The idea that the saints, as holy men and women, could
transmit their holiness to relics led to a vast growth of superstition.

It is far better to stress either that nothing is holy except God or else that all times and places are holy because God is present there. It would be better to use some other language to identify those times and places that are set aside for the worship of God or are of special interest to Christians because of their association with events in our past that we wish to remember. But since the word 'holy' is used in this latter way, I will comment briefly on the special status of the Holy Land in the imagination and thought of many Christians.

People are constituted by their histories, by the stories from which they live. To say who one is it is not sufficient to locate oneself in a variety of categories such as 'US citizen', 'professor', 'theologian', 'Methodist', 'husband', 'father', etc. If one is seriously questioned one must tell one's story, and if that is done with any fullness it goes far beyond one's private story to the story of one's people. One understands oneself as one understands this story. In the quest for self-understanding, we need to know about our ancestors.

The ancestors who are most important to us are not always our biological ancestors. The children and grandchildren of immigrants to this country already read the story of the Pilgrim Fathers and George Washington as part of their story. Americans visit Plymouth and Mount Vernon not only out of curiosity, but as a part of the clarification and deepening of their identity. We use the word 'shrine' to name places associated with major figures in our national heritage.

More important to the Christian than national identity is identity as a Christian. We Gentile Christians from Germanic tribes pay little attention to our ethnic history. What is important to us is that we are engrafted into the history of Israel through Jesus and the apostolic witness to him. The events surrounding Jesus, as well as those constituting the earlier history which is now ours, are far more important to us than our national heritage. Hence the tendencies to holiness surrounding even the national shrines are far stronger when we come to the places associated with the history of Israel, and especially the life of Jesus. To retrace the footsteps of Jesus brings the memory alive with new vividness. It has, in this way, real spiritual importance. To be cut off from the possibility of visiting the land to which we trace our roots would be a serious loss for us.

It is important, however, not to overstate this. Our identity is constituted by the story, not by physical presence at the site of the story. The physical site is so transformed since Biblical times that the gain to our imagination in being there is limited. The Crusaders' horror that the Holy Land was in the hands of 'infidels' was quite inappropriate at the time, and is irrelevant today. Christians make no claim to the land. We request and expect the right to visit, and would resent its denial. But our faith, our salvation and our future are in no way bound up with that right.

Perhaps, despite the dangers, Christians need to recover the sense, not of the Holy Land as one place alongside others, but of the holiness of the earth. We have prided ourselves as sharing with the other biblical faiths in freeing the earth from the dreadful and restricting sense of its sacredness by affirming that only the transcendent One is truly holy. But as we see the evils to which this has led, we must pause to consider how we can recall ourselves from self-destructive tyranny to proper dominion. Perhaps we must renew the sense that the breath of life in all living beings is the divine Spirit or Word, that what we do to even the least of God's creatures we do, at the same time, to God. If we can say this best by asserting that all things are holy because God is in them and they are in God, then let us use that language, remembering at the same time that the creatures, including us human creatures, are not God.

Notes and References

1. *Faith and Science in an Unjust World: Report of the World Council of Churches' Conference on Faith Science and the Future, 2, Reports and Recommendations*, Paul Abrecht (ed.) (Geneva: World Council of Churches, 1980) pp. 28–33.
2. 'A Statement of Shared Concern', from 'The State of India's Environment 1982 – A Citizens' Report' (New Delhi: Centre for Science and Environment) published in *Anticipation* (July 1983) p. 33.

A Jewish Response to John Cobb: The Earth and Humanity: A Christian View

Ben Beliak

I

It is interesting that in establishing the topics for this conference a central triad of Judaism is seemingly restated by the terms God, Earth and Humanity. Having been involved in the planning I can assure all of you that *this* 'trinity' was entirely unconscious. Restated in our trialogue's language, God, Earth and Humanity are not only theological abstractions but living realities for each of our particular peoples. The Jewish people has one word for itself, its piece of earth – and, for that matter, its divine–human relationship – that word is Israel. Respectively, this word Israel means: (1) God wrestlers; (2) the piece of earth, Israel (politically ill-defined but not undefined); and (3) the people, Israel. All three are inextricably bound up with one another. While this may seem to unsympathetic ears a reductionism or a simple rhetorical gambit, it is for me the way into an empathetic reading of Mr Cobb's chapter.

Let me begin with Mr Cobb's last point first: 'Creatures are holy only derivatively, and by virtue of God's presence in them. To view anything creaturely as intrinsically holy is idolatrous'. Later on he states:

Perhaps we must renew the sense that the breath of life in all living beings is the divine Spirit or Word, that what we do to even the least of God's creatures we do, at the same time, to God. If we can say this best by asserting that all things are holy because God is in them and they are in God, then let us use that language,

129

remembering at the same time, that the creatures, including us human creatures, are not God.

I note the tension created by these almost exclusive statements. Does the process known as demythologising of the Book (the Bible) and the City, *à la* Harvey Cox, create new tensions? How to reintroduce the category of the holy? Is holiness imputed or shared by things only at the risk of misuse? Mr Cobb recognises the abuses and the usefulness of the category of the holy. Overdoing or overstating sacredness has, on the one hand, the danger of lending *things* the masks of power that might be arrogantly worn; and, on the other hand, desacralisation carries with it the danger of an undervaluing linked to the lack of regard: a philosophy that objectifies the preciousness of the earth, its resources and non-human life. While understand something of Mr Cobb's tension, I must reassert what believe is a more active and everyday sense, at least for Judaism that there is a path to the holy and the sacred that collects the spark of *mitzvot* (commandments) that in turn lead to holiness.

Reference has been made several times to action as a way to holiness. The Jewish people are called to be and to recognise the holy in every moment in every act. We assert the notion of holy people, holy time and holy action. These are goals to be striven for to be achieved in the pathway of mitzvot.

Judaism insists upon the single deed as the instrument . . . in dealing with evil. At the end of days, evil will be conquered by the One; in historic time evils must be conquered one by one. The task is not to abandon the natural order of creation but to purify it; to humanise the sacred; to sanctify the secular (Heschel, *The Echo of Eternity*).

With regard to the Holy Land, I want to thank Mr Cobb for his disavowal of any terrestrial claims to it. Hillel ben-Sasson describing the perspective of medieval Jewry – the onlookers and oftentimes victims of the crusades – remarked that most of them viewed Esau (Christianity) and Ishmael (Moslems) as fighting over something neither had a right to claim (Ho. 1 and 2).

I welcome Mr Cobb's grappling with this issue precisely because it is not an easy one. It is the fact of conflicting claims, in particular cases, that should be our catalyst for open and frank talk.

Mr Cobb states that 'our faith, our salvation and our future are in no way bound up with that right (to the Holy Land)'. Unlike Cobb, my faith, salvation and future as a Jew are indeed bound up, in large measure, with the existence and survival of the Jews and the Jewish state on a portion of the Holy Land. It is only an earthly and mortal instrument but nevertheless it is real – real as a haven, real as a vibrant example of the Jewish return to history, and real as one particular expression of Judaism, and Jews trying to grapple in day-to-day terms with modernity.

For me this too must take place in the context of striving for holiness. At this time, 'normality' and holiness are in tension. As a Jew, born to parents who survived the concentration camps of Hitler, I'm afraid I am all too well versed in the perils of absolute powerlessness. I do not wish to return to that situation.

II

I wish to affirm Cobb's view that human beings are a part of the created order alongside other creatures. In his recent writings he has given eloquent testimony and teaching to this awareness (see *The Liberation of Life*). I find it helpful to acknowledge a Biblical view of humanity's place *vis-à-vis* the rest of the created order. In other places in the Torah many concepts are developed by Rabbinic traditions to teach about the care of the earth, for example, *bal tashchit*, which originates as a prohibition against cutting down fruit trees, even in war, for the 'voice of their [the trees'] pain is heard throughout the world'. By extension, this came to include the prohibition of destruction and disregard for other parts of nature, even down to destroying a garment needlessly (Rambam, Sefer Ha-Mitzvot). Further to parallel Mr Cobb's statements: 'Feasting in the king's house is wrong when it is at the expense of hunger in the peasant's hut'. The principle of *bal tashchit* may extend to one who can get along on barley but insists on eating wheat (the latter was less plentiful) (T. B. Shabbat 140b).

Creation is understood to be an ongoing event or process, and human beings were at all times God's partners in safeguarding its potential. Which is to say that needless and frivolous use cannot and should not be sustained on a global basis.

The biblical wisdom implied in the Sabbatical and Jubilee years is another way of speaking about caring for land and its resources. Arthur Waskow has suggested that the rhythmic seasonal, yearly and generational cycles that are associated with an awareness of our relationship to the world may help us to experience the interconnectedness of creation. Perhaps in order to be better managers we need skills not only in mastery and responsible dominion but also in regaining a sense of wonder and mystery. The critical analysis of economic and social injustice should talk about *all* that Cobb mentions, such as the use by the wealthy of technology and natural resources to render superfluous millions of poor and formerly self-sufficient people. But in addition, the experience of Shabbat writ small (weekly) and large (Sabbatical and Jubilee years) has something to teach us about repose and renewal, political renewal, ecological respect and face-to-face communities. The pause for spiritual refocusing must be woven together with our learning about the deeper ecological balance. Laws and traditions for this are still being developed. The love and respect that the land of Israel represents in Jewish tradition serves as a paradigm to be extended to the world.

Since ways of understanding dominion and its responsible exercise have been woefully inadequate, we must seek to be conscious of our commitments to as yet unborn generations who will need this planet earth.

Mr Cobb emphasised that human beings *do* have dominion. This dominion is very different. Today human beings will decide the fate of the world in a way that was not conceivable by a prior, relatively puny, human-kind. This new dominion means we have the potential to destroy all life.

III

On another subject discussed the world has a problem of overpopulation and concommitant scarcity of resources; the Jewish people has a problem of underpopulation and deteriorating familial resources. We have given our young men and women the most powerful contraceptive, a college education and all that goes with it. This is one area where we may have to demur from general trends and encourage population growth; not only for survivalist reasons (there are only 12 million Jews in the world) but also for the positive sense of affirmation that family life gives to a traumatised people. This must be done as the shared task of men and women.

IV

The nature of this kind of enterprise does not allow one to say everything that one has to say, or to say anything as fully as one would like. I do understand that Mr Cobb is also limited by this constraint in his chapter. This leads me to ask questions. Jesus seems to be almost absent from his Christianity, especially as a focus or grounding. Cobb has written elsewhere about this, but perhaps he will share a bit of what he believes on this subject?

Mr Cobb's metaphor for an unredeemed world speaks in the most Christian terms of this chapter:

> Christians have associated . . . pervasive sinfulness with the Genesis story of the sin of Adam. Certainly that story indicates that the Biblical writers also saw sin as beginning with the first human beings. They carefully distinguished creation and fall, however, so as to show that we are not created sinners. We are created in the image of God, and it is for that reason that we are capable of sin . . . For Christians the deepest truth about us is thus our need for forgiveness and redemption, which we can receive only as a gift from God. We scan history seeking signs of God's grace, and we find these centrally and decisively in the story of Jesus. It has become for us the clue to everything else.

While I cannot, obviously, affirm even this version of the fall, I note with interest what I never heard before, what for me is a new distinction. Creation of humanity is affirmed as good but separate from subsequent events. This seems to be a new emphasis.

This allows me to take note of a distinctive midrashic process that I have noticed. Whereas Judaism has spoken of the seven Noahide commandments as basic to all humanity – a kind of natural law – it seems that there is room for a more expanded conception of the Rabbinic half-positive position on gentiles. The tradition always understood the Genesis material from Adam up to Abraham as a prolegomenon to the focus on the history of the people Israel. Yet I believe we can now say that each episode comes to teach paradigmatically about our own present-day problems – the problems that face all humanity. I see these as: (1) the creation story: our relatedness to our fellow creatures; (2) the garden of Eden: human sexuality and the hubris of intellect; (3) Cain and Abel: the devastating effects of the first genocide and each subsequent loss of a single life; (4) the Flood: the potential for world destruction through a decreation or unravelling of the world, a portent of the all-burning nuclear fire; (5) the post-flood covenant of Noah: concern for the carnivorous pre-messianic person; (6) the Tower of Babel: the dangers of totalitarian and utopian schemes. All of a sudden, the midrashic process speaks volumes. All these actual and potential problems and catastrophes allow us to focus the story of humanity as bound to a potential common fate – let me add, God forbid. All of this affects earth and humanity. The metaphor may be the fall for some. For me, the need to mend and renew our shattered world will remain the image to express what comes before and after the caesura.

The thumbnail exegesis that I just mentioned may serve Jews at least to articulate a theologically-coherent introduction to pluralistic Messianism. David Hartman ('Immanuel') has written: 'It would be "bad faith" to advocate tolerance and pluralism in unredeemed history, yet maintain a triumphant monolithic universalism with regard to the end of days.'

The outbreaks of messianic fervour among Muslim and Christian communities have often led to epidemics of killing, celebrating with dubious glee the end of days. This scheme provides for a theology of the sanctity of life not limited to any race, colour, nationality or creed. The creation story of Genesis in a more universalised casting provides for the sanctity of life. As the Mishna Sanhedrin 4:5 reminds us: 'Why was the Adam created as a single person? To teach us that one who destroys one life is to be regarded as if s/he destroyed an entire world, and one who saves one life as if s/he saved an entire world'. The principle of creation goes beyond the particular community to encompass humanity.

Cobb's collapsing of creation and history might not allow for this scheme. 'The passion of commitment to the particular revelations wherein the individual community serves God in the manner mediated by its memories will remain'. The problem arises when competition between faith traditions fuels universalising dimensions and ascribes them to historical revelation. Those who aspire to a universal community of the faithful are driven toward a universalism of the sword. The dream of a universal community under the kingdom of God should be divorced from history; it becomes terribly dangerous when it is made the historical goal of a particular faith. Cobb asks 'in what does the image consist? . . . what distinguishes human beings most fundamentally from other species'. Cobb reports two possibilities, (1) the use of reason and (2) the use of language.

I'll settle for much less – much less abstraction. I'm not sure what the image is, but give me time to study – for one who mars the image of humanity mars the image of God.

Cobb is troubled about the proper hermeneutics to approach scripture. This is an important point. Cobb recognises 'grounds for suspicion when, generation after generation, the deepest meaning found in the texts turns out to be identical with the changing convictions of the scholars, especially when these convictions are manifestly culturally determined'. I share Cobb's concern about the cultural blinders, but despair of anything but trying to become conscious of them. Mr Funkenstein has already reminded us about *scriptura humane loquitur* 'scripture [Torah] speaks the language of human beings'. I would add an additional rabbinic dictum: each and every generation brings its own explanation. A remark in Susan Handelman's *The Slayers of Moses* (1980) is helpful here. Ms Handelman is speaking about the late Gershom Scholem's perspective, but it might apply to a request, almost an imploring, of liberal Protestants, Mr Cobb most especially. Scholem argued: 'that the continuity of tradition of interpretive history gains the freedom and legitimacy to creatively interpret'. For Scholem (for moderns) there is no singular authority in the tradition but rather many centres, many contradictory voices. God, so to speak, has left His text to its interpreters, *The Slayers of Moses*, p. 207).

Another way to assert my point of the relationship between liberal theologians and received texts is to ask a 'political' question. Given the enormous respect and legitimacy attained by being 'Bible-based' or 'Bible-informed', call it what you will, where is the Christian '*midrash*'?

Another way to ask this question is to wonder if 'higher criticism' becomes the end, finish of Biblical relatedness? A tangential Biblical relationship to the issue of 'the whole' of the created world is also in such Western Christian thinkers as Meister Eckhart or Bonaventura.

Yet another and final way to ask this question is, can Protestant thought reclaim its Catholic forebears?

Finally a word of admiration and thanks to Professor Cobb for his kind and gentle rigour.

6 The Land of Israel: Sanctified Matter or Mythic Space?

Chaim Seidler-Feller

The central issue to be faced as we confront the doctrine of the Land in Jewish tradition is that we have been led to believe that as an historical religion Judaism manifests a marked preference for sacred time over sacred space. Having been nurtured by A. J. Heschel's lyrical prose that declares unequivocally, 'Judaism is a *religion of time* aiming at the *sanctification of time* . . . to the Bible it is *holiness in time*, the Sabbath, which comes first . . . The sanctity of the time came first, the sanctity of man came second, and the sanctity of space last. Time was hallowed by God; space, the Tabernacle, was consecrated by Moses',[1] we are astonished by the realisation that space occupies a far more prominent place in our theology than we were, heretofore, prone to admit. One must wonder aloud as to whether Heschel himself conceded this point by devoting one of his last books, *Israel: An Echo of Eternity*, to the Land. Beyond this concern with holy territory, we, children of modernity, are offended and alienated by the 'scandal of particularity' that emanates from the twin concepts of Jewish peoplehood and nationhood. Finally, our Christian brethren have, over the years, viewed the land-centredness of 'Israel of the flesh' with some considerable scepticism, especially when juxtaposed with the immaterial sanctity of 'Israel of the spirit'.

It is with these observations as well as with the reality of the reborn State of Israel in mind that this chapter attempts to clarify and elaborate the notion of land as it is refracted through the lens of Jewish sources.

I

Jewish literature is decidedly unambiguous in its proclamation of the centrality of *Eretz Yisrael*, the Holy Land. The history of Israel begins with God's promise to Abraham that his descendants will inherit the land:

> And God said to Abram:
> Know well that your offspring shall be strangers in a land not theirs, and they shall be enslaved and oppressed four hundred years; . . . And they shall return here in the fourth generation . . .
>
> To your offspring I give this land, from the river of Egypt to the great river, the river Euphrates: the land of the Kenites, the Kenizzites, the Kudmonites, the Hittites, the Perizzites, the Rephaim, the Amorites, the Canaanites, the Girgashites and the Jebusites (Genesis 15:13–19).

The promise is repeated to Isaac (Genesis 26:2–5) and to Jacob (Genesis 28:13–15). In fact, the main theme of the book of Genesis is the convenantal guarantee, and unconditional Divine commitment, that Abraham's offspring will settle the land and possess it. Von Rad has written that 'The chief purpose of this work is to present in all its biblical and theological significance this one leading conception [the fulfilment of the Abrahamic promise] in relation to which all other conceptions of the Hexateuch assume an ancillary role'.[2] Others have noted that the entire *T'nak* (Hebrew Bible) may be seen as a complex creation myth concerning the establishment of this land in which Israel can be truly human and at home.[3] And all are familiar with the romantic Biblical description of a land 'flowing with milk and honey' and with the Psalmodic portrayal of Jerusalem as 'the perfection of beauty' and as 'the joy of all the earth'.

Rabbinic literature, the creation of the Jewish spirit during a period when we were, for the most part, deterritorialised, further exaggerates the determinative status of the Land. Behind statements such as 'S/He who resides in the Land of Israel is the one who has a God, but s/he who resides outside of the Land of Israel is like one who has no God'[4] and 'Ten measures of beauty were bestowed upon the world of which Jerusalem received nine and the rest of the world one',[5] we hear the echo of a bereaved people, torn from its home, yearning for a return. Our longing for the Land and its comforting beauty continues to be expressed in the liturgical corpus fashioned by the *Amida*, the fourteenth blessing of which reads:

> Return in Mercy to Jerusalem Your city and dwell therein as You have promised; speedily establish therein the throne of David Your servant, and rebuild it, soon in our days, as an everlasting edifice. You abound in blessings O God, who rebuilds Jerusalem.

After each meal, a lengthy prayer of thanks is recited that includes numerous references to the blessed Land and its restoration. Blessing two begins: 'We offer thanks to You, our ruling God, for having given as a heritage to our ancestors a precious good and spacious land', and ends: 'You abound in blessings O God, for the land and for sustenance'. Each and every holiday and new moon we give voice to our distress by declaring, 'Because of our sins, we were exiled from our land and driven far away from our soil'. For three weeks of sorrow, ending on the ninth of Ab which is entirely given over to fasting, Jews annually recall the devastation of their land and of Jerusalem. On the fifteenth of Shevat which falls during the North American winter Jews worldwide celebrate the 'New Year for Trees' because on that day the sap begins to rise in the trees of *Eretz Yisrael*. During the Fall Succot festival we pray that a proper rain shower the Land. And there is a distinctive blessing that is recited only after eating the seven fruits of the Land of Israel.

These are but a small sampling of the means employed by the liturgical and seasonal cycles indelibly to impress upon the Jewish psyche its enduring relationship with the Land of Israel. Our collective memories are constantly bombarded by impulses that trigger nostalgic recollections of our glorious past and that stimulate imaginative constructions of a redeemed future – in the Land. As a result, the Jewish reality has always been bound up in the Land of Israel even when – or especially when – we lived elsewhere. Attempting to overcome our perceived homelessness we linked ourselves to our beloved Israel and displayed a greater familiarity with her terrain than with that of our native countries. Along with Yehuda Halevi (eleventh-century Spanish poet and physician) we dreamt of Zion's roads and rivers, sniffed her roses and spices and sang:

> My heart is in the east, and I am in the uttermost west – How can I find savour in food? How shall it be sweet to me?

Persecuted and oppressed, landless and exiled, Jews became obsessed with their birthplace and talked incessantly of a return.

What could have very easily deteriorated into a dysfunctional state of mind had a positive effect on Jewish life. By focusing our attention on a distant geographic locale we were able to transcend the temporal misery that surrounded us and forge a national community that generated a unique identity. The ties to the Land of Israel furnished the Jewish people with a concrete base through which to express itself. Besides this salutary psychological consequence, land-centredness was also theologically fruitful. For if the land was invested with sanctity that meant that holiness was grounded in physicality. In other words, rather than accept the traditional dichotomy between matter and spirit, Judaism defined and evaluated created matter as a container for holiness that can itself be transformed into a sacred vessel. As the anonymous mystical author of the medieval *Holy Letter* asserts:

> We the possessors of the Holy Torah believe that God, may God be praised, created all as God's wisdom decreed and did not create anything ugly or shameful . . .

> The matter is not as Maimonides said in his *Guide for the Perplexed* (2:36). He was incorrect in praising Aristotle for stating that the sense of touch is shameful for us. Heaven forbid! The matter is not like the Greek said. It smacks of imperceptible heresy, because if the accursed Greek believed the world was created purposely he would not have said it.[6]

Creation implies God's involvement. Therefore, all of creation is touched by a dimension of godliness. The Israelite–Judaic concept of Holy Land is the quintessential expression of this interpenetration of matter with spirit, since land and earth, constituting the very essence of matter, are symbolic of the material universe.

Some further implications of the holiness of matter, as well as reflections on the complex doctrine of exile will be presented below.

II

The traditions regarding the Land flow from two discrete conceptual frameworks. One approach shall be termed the mythic and the other the *halachic* (legal, *halacha* = the way, the law). One viewpoint is metahistoric and mystically messianic, the other is historical and firmly grounded in this-worldly actualities. The rhetoric of one outlook is fuelled by romantic utopianism while the pronouncements of the other are couched in terms of the norms of universal *morality*.

The most articulate representative of the mythic school is Richard Rubenstein, who utilises the language developed by history of religions and modern psychology to present this convincing, albeit pagan, argument.[7] What is fascinating is that Rubenstein draws on the rather fashionable and scholarly categories illuminated by Mircea Eliade's research to legitimate a frankly primitive position. In their traditional religious formulation as represented in Talmudic and medieval rabbinic sources these ideas have a certain universal appeal, and those who are wary of the dangers of incipient messianism ought to reconsider their desire to discover the religious meaning of the Land. That is, one might learn from Judaism that the so-called secular impulses that fostered Zionist thought are more consistent with the ethics of rabbinic religious teachings than the radically religious reconstructions of Rubenstein and of messianic Zionists in Israel today. I suspect that those who claim that Zionism and Judaism are distinct entities are engaging in a subliminal conflict with a rabbinic Judaism that they either do not understand or to which they are not yet reconciled. Such people would much prefer to deal with Biblical Israel and the familiar typologies of classical religion, but do not realise that – at least as far as the Jewish religion is concerned – sole reliance on biblical sources and worldview yields a distorted, extremist, aberrant portrait of Judaism and spawns a chauvinistic, self-absorbed Judaic ideology. These critics might be surprised to learn that their real partners are the *Gush Emunim* and Rabbi Kahane.

Sacred land from the perspective of history of religions is the space that has been founded: it has been (a) given by the deity; (b) won by conquest; (c) established and constantly renewed through rituals; and (d) created by and exclusively for a particular people.[8] *Eretz Yisrael* fulfils all of these criteria. It was promised and given by God (Genesis 15:7) who led the Israelite forces in their battles of conquest (Joshua 23:35). The mighty deeds of old and the shared history of the people are constantly recalled in cultic recitations and in festive celebrations. And the *midrash* suggests that the land was pre-existent, created by the deity for Israel before anything was brought into being.[9]

The conquest is itself of great consequence. The rabbis teach that it was by virtue of Joshua's victories that the Land was sanctified. So compelling is conquest as a force for identification with the land that the *Tosephta* states that 'as long as they dwelled therein it wa as if it were conquered'.[11] It is not enough to merely live on th land, you must have sacrificed for it and fertilised the land with you blood spilled in combat; that constitutes genuine sanctification. On hears this theme adumbrated in the moving accounts of Israel soldiers and their parents, all of whom feel viscerally connected t a land for which they fought and in whose conquest many sons wer lost. These sacrifices, these Isaacs, are presented as a justification for maintaining control over every inch of conquered territory. A additional application of the conquest motif is in the service o historical analogy. Rabbi Israel Shzipanski avers that our days shoul be understood in the light of the experience of the Exodus from Egypt and the conquest by Joshua, for then too the times of redemp tions were inaugurated through victorious warfare.[12]

It would follow from the above that conquest-*kibbush* should b considered a *mitzvah*, one of the 613 commandments incumben upon all Jews. Indeed that is precisely the opinion of Rabbi Mose ben Nachman (Nachmanides or RaMBaN, 1194–1270, the mystica Talmudist of Gerona who, in 1267, went to live in *Eretz Yisrael*) i his *Commentary on the Torah*[13] and in his strictures on Maimonides *Book of the Commandments*.[14] In the latter work, he writes:

We are commanded to take possession of the land . . . We shoul not leave it in the hands of any other people or allow it to la waste as it says, 'And you shall take possession of the land an settle in it, for I have given the land to you to possess it' (Number 33:53) . . . The proof that this is a *mitzvah* follows: Regarding th spies Moses commented 'See, the Lord your God, has placed th land at your disposal. Go up *take possession*, as the Lord, the Go of your ancestor, promised you. Fear not and be not dismayed (Deuteronomy 1:21) . . . But regarding their failure to go u Moses says, 'you flouted the *command* of the Lord your God; yo did not put your trust in God and did not obey God' (Deut eronomy 9:23), proving that it is a *mitzvah* [to take possession o the land through conquest] and not a promised destiny. This i what the sages call a war of religious obligation. Behold conques is a commandment for all *generations*. And I say that the *mitzval* upon which our sages heaped abundant praise is settling the Lan of Israel. So much so, that they taught, 'whoever leaves and dwells outside of the Land should be considered an idolater', as it says, 'For they have driven me out today so that I cannot have a share in the Lord's possession, but am told,[15] "Go and worship other gods" ' (I Samuel 26:19). Many more statements of exaggerated praise were taught with regard to settling the Land. [In his Torah commentary Nachmanides refers to the ruling that a woman who does not want to emigrate with her husband to live in the Land of Israel is considered a 'rebellious wife', and likewise the man.[16]] All are derived from this positive commandment to conquer the Land and to settle in it. If so, this positive commandment for all generations is incumbent upon every individual even during the period of exile as is evident from the Talmud in many places.[17]

This is a most fascinating and revealing passage cited as a binding normative authority in many studies, sermons and treatises, including the Israeli Independence Day prayer book.[18] In it not only does Nachmanides develop the overriding significance of *kibbush* but he even subsumes under it the *mitzvah* of settling the land. When we recall the fact that Maimonides omits both commandments (a matter to be discussed below), and that Nachmanides is the sole legal decisor to declare settlement (*yishuv*) to be a *mitzvah*, our interest is further piqued. For Nachmanides holds that the only legitimate form of settlement is to rehearse the experience of our ancestors – i.e., to conquer the Land once again. So that even if one settles peacefully it is to be designated a conquest. Here the mythic notion emerges dressed in *halachic*-legal garb. Here a primitive idea is given the sanction and force of practical law. These teachings, by the way, form the bedrock of a particular tendency that is popular in Israel today.

An understanding of Nachmanides's unique doctrine of settlement comes to light when it is viewed against the background of his rather intricate presentation of the sacred import of *Eretz Yisrael*. In a lengthy comment on Leviticus 18:25 he writes, *inter alia*:

It is on the basis of this matter that the rabbis have said in the *Sifre* (Eikev, 43) 'and you will soon perish from the good land that the Lord is giving you. Therefore impress these My words upon your very heart: bind them as a sign on your hand and let them serve as a symbol on your forehead' (Deuteronomy 11:17–18). Although I banish you from the Land to outside the Land, Make yourselves distinctive by the commandments, so that when you return they shall not be novelties to you . . . And so did the prophet Jeremiah say to the people in exile in Babylon 'Set up signposts' (Jeremiah 31:21) – these are the commandments by which Israel is made distinctive'. Now the verses which state 'and you will soon perish . . . therefore impress these My words', etc. only make obligatory in the exile the observance of those commandments affecting personal conduct (*chovot haguf*), such as the wearing of *tefillin* and placing of *mezuzot* [these being specifically mentioned in the following phrases], and concerning them the rabbis in the *Sifre* explained that we must observe them so that they shall not be novelties to us when we return to the Land, *for the main fulfilment of the commandments is to be kept when dwelling in the Land of God*. Therefore, the rabbis have said in the *Sifre* (R'eih, 80) . . . ' "When you have occupied it and are settled in it, take care to observe all the laws and rules that I have set before you this day" (Deuteronomy 11:31–2). *Dwelling in the Land of Israel is of equal importance to all the commandments of the Torah*'.[19]

Nachmanides holds to the astounding opinion that not only are the specific land-based commandments binding only in the Land but that even personal commandments are essentially linked to *Eretz Yisrael*. And they are to be observed outside of the Land so that one should not grow 'rusty' in one's observance and so that when one is redeemed and comes to dwell in Israel he/she will still be acquainted with the *mitzvot*. Is it any wonder then that Nachmanides argues that settlement is a great *mitzvah* and that it is equal in importance 'to all the commandments of the Torah!'? Clearly one cannot be wholly observant unless one dwells in the Land. The fulfilment of Torah is itself dependent on the settlement. And the *Land is the determining factor*. A mysterious sanctity seems to inhere in it that lends the Land overwhelming power. Nachmanides does unabashedly state elsewhere, 'But there is in this *midrash* (the *Sifre* quoted above) a profound secret (*sod*)'.[20] Here the mythic blends with the mystic to produce an extraordinary religious dogma.

What Nachmanides does not realise is that this very tenet that he triumphally quotes equating settlement with all the commandments, can be used to justify a position diametrically opposite his own. For if mere settlement is equivalent to all *mitzvot*, why do any of the *mitzvot* at all? Living in Israel, on the soil that embodies our sacred history is enough! This contention is quite often voiced by 'secular' Israelis who maintain that religious ritual is only a necessity for diaspora Jews (just the opposite of RaMBaN) whose religiosity provides a focus for their Jewish identity. Their identity, on the other hand, is sustained by contact with the Land. The Land is, for them, an enclave, a homeland and the focal point that gives meaning to their lives. In other words the Land functions as a sacred centre! As such, the Jewish people are not much different from other ancient and modern nations who linked their innate qualities to a particular locale. The very word 'China' means centre of the universe.[21] The Iranian King was called 'Axis of the World' or the 'World's Pole'. And the city of Angkor in Cambodia with its walls and moats represents the world surrounded by its chains of mountains and by the mythical oceans.[22] The most poignant and frequently cited Judaic formulation of the centre idea is to be found in *Midrash Tahuma*, (*Kedoshim* 10) where we read:

> Just as the navel is found at the center of a human being, so the land of Israel is the navel of the world as it says, 'living at the center [navel] of the earth' (Ezekiel 38:12), the Land of Israel is found at the center of the earth. Jerusalem is at the center of the Land of Israel, the Temple is at the center of Jerusalem, the Holy of Holies is at the center of the Temple, the Ark is at the Center of the Holy of Holies and the *Foundation Stone (even shetiyyah)* is in front of the Ark, which spot is the foundation of the world.[23]

Another text amplifying this theme suggests that the Foundation Stone was none other than Jacob's pillar:

> And Jacob returned to gather the stones and he found them all turned into one stone and he set it up for a pillar in the midst of the place, and oil descended for him from heaven and he poured it hereon, as it is said, 'And he poured oil upon the top of it' (Genesis 28:18). What did the Holy One Do? God placed God's right foot thereon and sank the stone to the bottom of the depths, and God made it the keystone of the earth . . . therefore, it is called the Foundation Stone, for there is the navel of the earth and therefrom was all the earth evolved and upon it the sanctuary of God stands, as it is said, 'And this stone which I have set up for a pillar shall be God's house' (Genesis 28:22).[24]

For the Jew who journeys 'up to Jerusalem' s/he is undergoing what must be described as a mystical ascent. S/He is ascending to the centre, to that one place on earth which is closest to heaven, to that place which is horizontally the exact centre of the geographical world and vertically the exact midpoint between the upper and lower world. It is the very crucible of creation, the womb of everything, which exhibits a superabundance of reality and flows with blessing.[25] As a result, the Land emanates holiness and purity. Its atmosphere makes people wise.[26] Its earth is the centre of fertility and fecundity. At this centre, rabbinic tradition and mythology merge as the rabbis of antiquity frame their version of an age-old legend. And at this centre Richard Rubenstein, the pagan rabbi, sacrifices 2000 years of rabbinic Judaism!

Rubenstein, in a striking essay entitled 'The Cave, The Rock and the Tent: The Meaning of Place',[27] suggests that the Jewish people has become accustomed to wandering in the desert where Jews became masters of sacred time but where they were alienated from sacred space. 'The sacred is home and home is strange and alien to a society largely dominated by wandering nomadic professionals skilled in the capacity rationally to exploit an unloved natural environment'.[28] It is our destiny to dwell in tents. Happily, Zionist renewal has breathed new life into the Israelite 'Tent of Meeting' (*Ohel Moed* literally means the Tent of Designated *Time*). In a piece that appeared as part of the *After Auschwitz* collection, Rubenstein writes:[29]

> Zionism [is] the Jewish people's yearning to return to its ancient homeland, and to find a creative reunion with earth and earth's powers . . . The reestablishment of Israel marks the rebirth of the long forgotten gods of the earth within Jewish experience.[30] Increasingly it means that the earth's fruitfulness, its engendering power, will once again become the central spiritual realities of Jewish life . . .[31] No more will God be seen as the transcendent Lord of nature controlling it as if it were a marionette at the end of a string. God will be seen as the source and life of nature.[32]

The sad fact is that Rubenstein's portrait is accurately drawn. However, we can now include in his depiction not only labour Zionists like A. D. Gordon (ideologue of the movement) who, utilising the *axis mundi* imagery, wrote:

It is life we want, no more and no less than that, our own life feeding on our own vital sources, in the fields and under the skies of our Homeland . . . We want vital energy and spiritual richness from this living source. We come to our Homeland in order to be planted in our natural soil from which we have been uprooted, to strike our roots deep into its life-giving substances and to stretch out our branches in the sustaining and creating air and sunlight of the Homeland . . . It is our duty to concentrate all our strength on this central spot . . . What we seek to establish in Palestine is a new re-created Jewish People.[33]

and not only Rabbi Abraham Isaac HaCohen Kook (mystic, poet, Talmudic scholar and first Chief Rabbi of Palestine) who wrote:

Eretz Yisrael is not something apart from the soul of the Jewish people: it is no mere national possession, serving as means of unifying our people . . . *Eretz Yisrael* is part of the very essence of our nationhood; it is bound organically to its very life and inner being.[34] Jewish original creativity, whether in the realm of ideas or in the arena of daily life and action, is impossible except in *Eretz Yisrael*).[35] In the Holy Land man's imagination is lucid and clear, clean and pure capable of receiving the revelation of divine truth . . . there the mind is prepared to . . . be illumined by the radiance of the Holy Spirit.[36]

but also the *Gush Emunim* (the Block of the Faithful who have settled the West Bank), a contemporary political force that has merged the mythic perspective, shared, ironically, by both Gordon and Rav Kook[37] with a potent political messianism. The rabbis of the movement repeatedly emphasise that a total sanctity rests on the earthy soil and statehood of *Medinat Yisrael* (the State of Israel) and on the political boundaries fixed in the Six Day War (1967). Rabbi Zvi Yehuda Kook (the son of the former Chief Rabbi) who was, until his death, the spiritual leader of the movement has written:

[People] speak of the beginning of Redemption . . . We are in the parlor, not in the vestibule . . . the return to Zion, the Kingdom of Israel being rebuilt anew . . . This is the revelation of the Kingdom of Heaven . . . The Israel Defense Force is total sanctity; it represents the rule of the people of the Land in His Land . . .

We must know that the Kingdom of Heaven is being revealed in this kingdom, even in the kingdom of Ben Gurion.[38]

And so the circle is joined. Ben Gurion, who expressed contempt for traditional religion is transformed into an ally of the mystical messianist, Rabbi Kook. What binds them is the fact that the Land occupies a centrally determinative place in their thinking. Along with Gordon they believe that the Land is life-giving and that by planting themselves in the homeland they will soon usher in a redemptive age. They have, each in his own way, revived the mystifying imagery of a sacred centre and provided a channel for Nachmanides to speak to our generation.

III

Over and against Nachmanides stands Maimonides (RaMBaM 1135–1204), the philosopher–physician–Talmudist from Cordoba who, as we indicated above, omits *kibbush* (conquest) and *yishuv* (settlement) from his list of 613 commandments. This refusal to admit conquest into the body of divine precepts is no accident. It is consistent with an outlook that Maimonides maintains throughout his legal *magnum opus*, the *Mishneh Torah*. In *Hilchot Terumuh* 1:5 he writes:

> All the property occupied by those who 'ascended' from Egypt that was, as a result, sanctified with an initial sanctification [*kedushah rishonah*], lost its sacred status when the Israelites were exiled. Since the initial sanctification was potentiated by conquest alone, the Land was sanctified for the moment [the duration of the conquest] and not for the future. However, when the exiles 'ascended' and occupied part of the Land, they sanctified it with a second sanctification [*kedushah shniyah*] that remains in force forever: for the moment and for the future.[39]

He further asserts:

> Why do I maintain that regarding the Temple and Jerusalem the initial sanctification is sanctified forever while with regard to the remainder of *Eretz Yisrael* for the purpose of the Sabbatical and tithes, etc. it does not? For the sanctity of the Temple and Jeru

salem was generated by the *shechinah* (Divine Presence), and the *shechinah* cannot be nullified. Behold scripture says, 'I will make your sanctuaries desolate' (Leviticus 26:31), and the sages taught 'Even though they are desolate they maintain their sanctity'. However, the Land's Sabbatical and tithing obligation derives only from the conquest by the multitudes. Since it was recaptured, the initial conquest is nullified and the Land is Torahitically exempt from tithes and Sabbatical since it is not part of *Eretz Yisrael*. When Ezra ascended and sanctified the Land he did not sanctify it through conquest but through *chazakah* (occupation), the settlement of the Land. Therefore, every place that the Babylonian returnees occupied, that was sanctified with the sanctification of Ezra – the second sanctification – is still sanctified today even though the Land has been retaken from us. As a result, one is obligated to observe the Sabbatical and give the tithes as has been elucidated in the Law of *Terumah*.[40]

Upon analysis of the many Talmudic discussions[41] Maimonides has decided that Joshua's conquest was time-limited and was terminated by Nebuchadnezzar's destruction. On the other hand, the sanctity of the Land effected by Ezra's peaceful *aliya*, under the protection of Persian King Cyrus, is enduring. Joseph Karo in his comprehensive commentary to the *Mishnah Torah* is bewildered by the master's decision. 'I don't understand', he writes, 'the way in which the power of occupation is superior to the power of conquest. Why should we not argue regarding occupation as well that when the Land was retaken from us the *chazakah* was nullified? Moreover, initially when the Land was sanctified through conquest did that not include occupation? Is then occupation without conquest really preferable to occupation with conquest?'[42] Karo it seems is reasoning out of a Nachmanidean frame. More precisely, the mystically messianic atmosphere that surrounded him in the Safed community of Spanish exiles, where the practice of rabbinic ordination was revived and where Karo himself was one of the ordainees, appears to have affected his ability to distinguish clearly between the efficacy of occupation as compared to the power of conquest. Maimonides, sophisticated political philosopher that he was, understood fully the limits of power. It was clear to him that the authority gained by conquest was only as potent as its source while the authority of 'peaceful conquest' (settlement) is everlasting. Perhaps he sensed the inherent contradiction involved in Karo's assertion that *kedushah* (sanctity) derived from conquest is the equivalent of *kedushah* derived from gradual, peaceful and moral process of settlement.

The Maimonidean formula for the messianic age follows a similar pattern.

> Let no one think that in the days of the Messiah any of the laws of nature will be set aside or any innovation be introduced into creation. The world will follow its normal course . . . They will all [all nations] accept the true religion, and will neither *plunder nor destroy* and together with Israel earn a comfortable living in a legitimate way . . . Said the rabbis: The sole difference between the present and the Messianic days is delivery from servitude to foreign powers (B. T. Sanhedrin 9lb).[43]

There will be no cataclysm, no miraculous intervention, no 'transcendence breaking in upon history',[44] no apocalypse. Salvation results not from a rupturing of the natural order but is an historical process mediated by a human community that evolves better social and economic conditions accompanied by political security and peaceful coexistence.[45]

Given Maimonides's predisposition to a peaceful rather than to an eruptive messianism it follows logically that he would prefer *chazakah* to conquest as a means of establishing abiding sanctity in the Land. Furthermore, the *telos* of the messianic age is absolutely inconsistent with a sanctity achieved by means of conquest, as we read:

> The Sages and prophets did not long for the days of the Messiah that Israel might *exercise dominion* over the world, or rule over the heathens, or be exalted by the nations, or that it might eat, drink and rejoice. Their aspiration was that Israel be free to devote itself *to the Torah* and its wisdom, with no one to oppress or disturb it.[46]

The messianic age will be distinguished by an intensification of spiritual pursuits and by dedication to Torah study and to its realisation. Such a climate of piety and spiritual seeking could never be induced by conquest. Maimonides thus rejects what has been demonstrated to be a cornerstone of the mythic doctrine of the Land.

Not only is conquest inconsistent with the ultimate end, it is also irrelevant to — and, possibly, undermining of – the immediate purpose of dwelling in the Land which is to make it holy by observing the specific commandments that apply to the Land (*mitzvot hatluyot ba'aretz*). Accordingly, the sanctity of which the Talmud speaks is not an inherent sanctity but one that is conditioned on human dedication to the principles of Torah. The Land is not so much a sacred centre as it is a *centre of sacred behaviour*. It is not the Land that holds the key to holiness but the human community inhabiting the Land — most specifically the Jewish people — that is charged with maintaining the Land's holiness. Although it is settlement that generates holiness, the purpose of this *kedushah* is to create a state of obligation requiring the observance of a series of agricultural commandments including the laws of the Sabbatical Year (*sheviit*),[47] the heave-offering (*terumah*),[48] the tithes (*maserot*),[49] the corner of the field (*peah*),[50] the gleanings (*leket*),[51] the forgotten sheaves (*shikchah*),[52] the dough-offering (*challah*),[53] the fruit of the young trees (*orlah*),[54] the first-fruits (*bikkurim*),[55] the diverse kinds (*kilayim*)[56] and the new grain (*chadash*),[57] as we read:

> There are ten degrees of holiness. The Land of Israel is holier than any other land. Wherein lies its holiness? In that from it they bring the offerings of the *omer* [sheaf], the first fruits, and the two loaves, which they may not bring from any other land.[58]

This famous *mishnah* passage continues to list, in ascending order, the various holy locales with each degree of holiness determined by a particular legal restriction. In other words, it is the applicability of Torah law to the Land that assures its special holiness.[59]

In still another striking text the Talmud, adapting sacred centre imagery, fixes the location of the *Sanhedrin* within the Temple precincts and asserts:

> Your navel is like a round goblet (Canticles 7:3). Your navel: that is the *Sanhedrin*. Why is it called 'navel'? Because it is at the navel point of the world.[60]

Centrality and holiness is thus explicitly linked to justice and morality. Sacred centres must be centres of justice. Scripture warns again and again that failure to uphold the law and neglect of God's commandments will result in pollution, defilement and banishment from the Land:

So let not the land spew you out for defiling it, as it spewed out the nation that came before you (Leviticus 18:28).

If, then, you agree and give heed, you will eat the good things of the earth; But if you refuse and disobey you will be devoured by the sword (Isaiah 1:19).

And when you announce all these things to that people, and they ask you, 'Why has the Lord decreed upon us all this fearful evil? What is the iniquity and what is the sin that we have committed against the Lord our God?' say to them, 'Because your ancestors deserted Me — declares the Lord — and followed other gods and served them and worshipped them; they deserted Me and did not keep My Torah' (Jeremiah 16:10–11).

And the rabbis add:

'So let not the land spew you out' (Leviticus 18:28): The Land of Israel is not like any other land; it neither sustains nor tolerates violators of God's law.[61]

Not only does the Land seem convulsively to expel those who do not keep the particular agricultural laws but – more importantly – the rape of the Land and the ensuing exile result from moral depravity, most especially from an indifference to the kinship laws that are intended to structure and preserve the social order. In fact, the dynamic principle behind most of the agricultural laws, from the rabbinic perspective, is to develop a moral society as evidenced by the Sabbatical year with its concommitant cancellation of debts (Deuteronomy 15:16), the requirement to leave a corner of the field to be harvested by the poor (Leviticus 19:9), and the poor-person's tithe (Deuteronomy 14:28–9).[62] Agricultural law and moral law are one in the same. The recognition of God's sovereignty over the Land that is the basis of the Sabbatical legislation, 'for the Land is Mine' (Leviticus 25:23), is part of an elaborate design whose aim is to create a moral eco-system that links stewardship of the earth's resources (the commandment to let the earth lie fallow every seventh year) with moral uprightness. To observe the Sabbatical properly brings sanctification to both the Land and to the people; to disregard the Sabbatical profanes the Land and corrupts society, engendering an environment of chaotic disruption that will ultimately devour the earth and its inhabitants. This is the main thrust of the apocalyptic rebuke (*tochachah* as it is called in the synagogue) that follows immediately upon the Sabbatical and land redemption legislation (Leviticus 26:3–46). If Israel is faithful to God then, 'I will grant your rains in their season' (Leviticus 26: 3), But if Israel spurns God's rules then, 'I will make your skies like iron and your earth like copper . . . You shall eat the flesh of your sons I will lay your cities in ruins . . .' (Leviticus 26: 19, 29, 31). The law is the means by which Israel enters into a harmonious relationship with nature. Ecological wellbeing is dependent upon Israelite justice. The Psalmist's poetic juxtaposition of the glory of the created universe, 'The heavens declare the glory of God' (19:2), with the perfection of the Law, 'The teaching of the Lord is perfect, renewing life' (19:8), articulates this doctrine: Israel has an opportunity to integrate itself into the natural order by upholding God's law. The specific space where the Jewish people is to enact this harmonious symmetry is the Land of Israel. And the only place where Jews can fulfil all their laws is in the Land.

The Land of Israel is then the place of completeness and harmony: harmony with nature, harmony with one's community and harmony with God. That which effects the harmony is the Law. A complete Jewish life under God's law is possible only in the Land. One's Jewishness is emaciated, incomplete, outside the Land. *Aliya* might then mean going up to the Land in order to attain an elevated state of completeness within the Law, a state of wholeness — i.e., holiness, sanctification. The Land is the staging ground for the unification of human will with Divine will through the agency of the Law.

In sum, the role of the Land is 'to concretize and implement the values and the way of life given to Israel at Sinai'.[63] The irony of this comment by David Hartman is that he suggests that the return to the Land is actually the road back to Sinai.[64] Enlandisement is but the means for the establishment of the heavenly-other-worldly Sinai, on earth.[65] We departed from Sinai in order to bring Sinai's Torah into the Land. Conquest by arms is not the key to holiness, but subduing the earth by means of the Law is the goal. The sanctification of the *Land* of Israel is but a tool for the sanctification of the *people* of Israel. In contrast with the mythic outlook, the *halachic-*legal view understands the Land not as an end, not as deified nature *à la* Rubenstein, but as a means of approaching God through God's law. Whereas Rubenstein's theology reverts to Biblical Israel, and to its syncretistic nature worship, consequently conceiving of exile as a disjuncture in the normal course of Jewish history, Hartman's Judaism is formulated in terms that are continuous with the rabbinic past and that define a modern Israel that represents the culmination of a spiritual process. For Rubenstein, sovereignty is a function of monarchic rule, while for Hartman it is to be determined by our reapplication of God's law to the Land. For Rubenstein, the establishment of the State of Israel implies the return of the Jewish people to nature while for Hartman it implies the return to a reinvigorated political life under the Law. For Rubenstein the existence of the State means the *recovery of power* — the loss of which had occasioned two millennia of Jewish suffering in exile, while for Hartman it means the quest for the *morality of power* — the absence of which jeopardises the entire enterprise. From Hartman's perspective, therefore, the State of Israel provides the Jewish people with the opportunity to generate a Jewish politics that is nurtured by Talmudic law. Such a politics will complete the fabric of Jewish law that has been rent by centuries of exile. Such a politics will help mark a further stage in the development of the sanctified body of Israel. As a result, the critical issues facing Jews in the contemporary world are: How does our consciousness of the Torah's call for justice and righteousness influence our drive to correct the evils that derive from a modern state's needs for security and power? How can we protect the rights and honour of the stranger in our midst while we are threatened by the constant dangers of war? Can we learn from the tradition possible ways of interlacing the costs of security with a sensitivity to the requirements of the needy, in spite of the economic crises?

It is Israel's historical task to confront these challenges by drawing from and applying the teachings of the entire intellectual and spiritual heritage of Judaism. Only then will her future as a dynamically moral society covenanted with God be vouchsafed.

Abbreviations, Notes and References

B.T. – Babylonian Talmud.
M.T. – Mishneh Torah.
1. A. J. Heschel, *The Sabbath*, pp. 8–10.
2. G. Von Rad, *The Problems of the Hexateuch and Other Essays*, pp. 85 ff.
3. Jonathan Z. Smith, 'Earth and Gods', in *Map Is Not Territory*, (Leiden: Brill, 1978) p. 110.
4. B.T. *Ketuboth* 110b.

5. B.T. *Kiddushin* 49b.
6. *The Holy Letter*, Seymour Cohen (trans.), ch. 2, pp. 41–2.
7. See Richard Rubenstein, 'The Cave, the Rock and the Tent: The Meaning of Place' in *Continuum*, 6 (1968) pp. 143–55, and 'The Rebirth of Israel in Contemporary Jewish Theology' in *After Auschwitz*, pp. 131–144.
8. Smith, 'Earth and Gods', pp. 109–10.
9. *Bereshit Rabbah* 6:5.
10. B.T. *Chagiga* 3b.
11. Tosephta, Avodah Zarah, 5:5.
12. Torat Hamelukhah, p. 108 quoted in Uriel Tal, 'The Land and the State of Israel in Israeli Religious Life,' Proceedings of the Rabbinical Assembly, 38 (1976) pp. 1–40.
13. Commentary to Numbers 33:53, Charles Chavel (trans.), pp. 385–6.
14. *Sefer Hamitzvot* (ed.), *Charles Chavel, Positive Commandments omitted by Maimonides* #4, pp. 244–6.
15. 'And who was it who told David to worship other gods. Scripture has therefore come to teach that whoever dwells outside the land, it is as if that person is an idolator' (B.T. *Ketuboth* 110b).
16. Numbers 33:53.
17. *Sefer Hamitzvot*, pp. 244–6.
18. See, Uriel Tal, 'Historical and Metahistorical Self-Views in Religious Zionism', in *Religious Zionism*.
19. Chavel (trans.) pp. 271–2.
20. Commentary to Deuteronomy 11:18, Charles Chavel (trans.), pp. 134–5.
21. W. D. Davies, *The Territorial Dimension of Judaism*, (Berkeley: University of California Press, 1982 p. 3).
22. Quoted in M. Eliade, 'The World, The City, The House', in *Occultism, Witchcraft and Cultural Fashions* (Chicago: University of Chicago Press, 1976) pp. 23–4.
23. *Tanhuma*, Buber edition, V. II, p. 78.
24. *Pirke d'Rabbi Eliezer* ch. 35, Friedlander (trans.), p. 266. See R. Patai, *Man and Temple*, pp. 85–6, 101–2, n. 100–2, for complete citations and further discussion. (New York: T. Nelson, 1947) 2 Enl. Ed. New York: KTAV, 1967.
25. Smith, 'Earth and Gods', p. 113.
26. B.T. *Baba Bathra* 158b.
27. See above, n. 7.
28. *Ibid.*, p. 153.
29. 'The Rebirth of Israel in Contemporary Jewish Theology', p. 134.
30. *After Auschwitz*, p. 30.
31. *After Auschwitz*, p. 106.
32. *After Auschwitz*, p. 139.
33. Translated in A. Hertzberg, *The Zionist Idea* (New York: Atheneum, 1976) pp. 382–3.
34. *The Zionist Idea*, p. 419.
35. *The Zionist Idea*, p. 420.
36. *The Zionist Idea*, p. 421.

37. Perhaps that is why Rav Kook exhibited such tolerance towards secular Zionism.
38. Quoted in Uriel Tal, 'The Land and the State', p. 9.
39. M.T. *Zeraim* (Book of Agriculture), Laws of the Priestly Offering, 1:5.
40. M.T. *Avodah* (Book of the Temple Service), Laws of the Temple 1:16.
41. B.T. *Chagiga* 36, *Megillah* 10b, *Shevout* 16a, *Chullin* 10a, etc.
42. *Kesef Mishneh* to M.T. Laws of the Temple 1:16.
43. M.T. *Shofetim* (Book of Judges), Laws of Kings and Wars 12:1–2.
44. Gershom Scholem, *The Messianic Idea in Judaism, and other essays on Jewish Spirituality* (New York: Schocken, 1971) p. 10.
45. For a far more elaborate and articulate presentation of this analysis see David Hartman, 'Maimonides' Approach to Messianism and its Contemporary Implications', in *Daat* 2–3 (1978–9). Hartman's approach has greatly influenced the direction of this chapter.
46. M.T. Law of Kings 12:4.
47. Leviticus 25:1–7.
48. Numbers 18:8, 11–12.
49. Numbers 18:21–4.
50. Leviticus 19:9–10.
51. Leviticus 19:9–100.
52. Deuteronomy 24:19–22.
53. Numbers 15:17–21.
54. Leviticus 19:23.
55. Deuteronomy 26:1–11.
56. Deuteronomy 22:9–11.
57. Leviticus 23:14.
58. *Mishnah, Kelim* 1:6.
59. See Davies, *The Territorial Dimension*, pp. 34–9 for a full discussion.
60. B.T. *Sanhedrin* 37a.
61. *Sifra, Kedoshim* (11:14).
62. See *Sifre* Deuteronomy, 109.
63. David Hartman, 'Israel and the Rebirth of Judaism', in *Joy and Responsibility: Israel, Modernity and the Renewal of Judaism*, pp. 279–80.
64. David Hartman, 'The Sanctity of the Land', *Yediot Achronot*, (Heb.) 5 March 1982.
65. In this connection, it is imperative to note that Jewish tradition never claimed to know exactly where Sinai is located. Nor for that matter was it really important to any of the rabbis but the mystically messianic former Chief Rabbi, Shlomo Goren.

Addenda

I

Upon further reflection, it would seem that what I have termed the *halachic*-legal approach is a direct consequence of the exilic experience. The *halachists* are those – like Maimonides and his contemporary champion, David Hartman – who see themselves as part of a chain of tradition that has survived by consistently adapting to new realities. The mythic-messianists, on the other hand, have a rapturous view of history that involves them in sustaining the fantasy that they are reliving a period that once was. For them, reality is a foil that must be overcome and transcended. Their universe is the world of the supernatural and the miraculous. Whereas the *halachic*-realists have accepted exile and have been willing to consider its positive lessons, the mythic-messianists have rejected exile as a source of Jewish teaching. They recount a pulsating Jewish history that is comprised of ancient Israel's *heilsgeschichte* and of the modern effort to reexperience the sacred past. All other moments harbour negative meaning (anti-history)[1] or are simply meaningless. The *halachic*-realists, on the other hand, view Jewish history as a stream flowing rhythmically through an historical time that is suffused with meaning.

One of the most significant byproducts of Israel's doctrine of the Land is the Exile. It is with a tinge of the tragic that one might say that Israel's genuinely unique contribution to the history of ideas and to the sociology of culture is its rich tradition of Exile rather than its ideas regarding the Holy Land. As David Vital has noted, 'Exile has been the distinctive characteristic of Jewish life'.[2] If only for the simple reason that most of our history has been perceived to be in exile, we have been compelled to develop a theology that invested the Exile with various levels of meaning. Aware of this Jewish tradition, many contemporary national groups have adopted this Judaic concept in order to describe their own experience. Ironically, the Palestinians now use the Jewish categories of exile and return to define their own circumstances.

A particular Jewish twist to the doctrine of the Exile has, however, evolved. Rather than view the loss of sovereignty and banishment from one's land as an unmitigated tragedy, there developed a tendency to uncover some of its positive dimensions. James Sanders, in a penetrating insight rooted in his penchant for redaction criticism, has observed that there is a hint of accommodation to exile already evident in the editing of the *T'nak*. While attempting to elucidate the reason that the Biblical authors chose to close the Torah with Deuteronomy rather than with Joshua (which forms a natural ending to the Hexateuch), he avers that the crisis of the sixth century B.C.E. in which Land, Temple and Jerusalem were lost forced the editor to conclude the narrative prior to the conquest, as Moses looks to the Promised Land. The editor thereby asserts that because the old symbols had ceased to sustain Israel, the Sinaitic covenant of the Law, which is the substance of the Torah's Mosaic age, was the appropriate source to look to for the authoritative norms that give life to the people.[3]

During the monarchic period, when Israel's commitment to YHWH had waned, it was quite common for the prophets to voice romantic sentiments that idealised the state of intimacy that Israel was able to attain with its God during the yeas of wandering in the desert. Jeremiah's nostalgic admiration for the innocence of the wilderness:

> Thus said the Ruler: I accounted to your favour. The devotion of your youth, Your love as a bride – How you followed Me in the wilderness, In a land not sown (Jeremiah 2:2).

is but one example of a familiar theme. In retrospect, it seems as if God and Israel had enjoyed an uncomplicated relationship of mutual love before Israel entered the Land. Upon conquest, the Land competed with God for Israel's loyalties. The unsettled desert was also the place of revelation and the place that Israel was elected. It was, in reality, no place and every place. It was exile.

Jacob Neusner, applying a type of structural analysis to the Talmud that is similar to Sanders's redactional criticism, observes that although the *Mishnah* deals at length with the agricultural laws of the Land and with purities (one cannot sustain purity outside the Land of Israel), both areas are omitted from the *Babylonian Talmud*. This leads him to conclude that the theology of the *Mishnah* as that of the *T'nak* before it, is that 'Israel can be Israel only in the Land of Israel':[4]

> for the *Mishnah*, to be Israel and clean, so holy, is to live in the Land and to eat, so share its bounty with God, the owner, in a relationship of mutuality and reciprocity.[5]

The Babylonian experience of exile, however, inspired a Talmudic tradition that knows without a doubt that we can be a holy people anywhere. By ignoring the repertoire of laws dealing with cultic cleanness and those pertaining to the Land, the Talmud, in Neusner's words, transforms the *Mishnah* 'into a system serviceable everywhere and restricted to nowhere'.[6]

In spite of the Exile and the destruction of the Temple the people can still function as Jews. The *Shechinah* (Divine presence) resides with every exiled fragment of the Jewish people. One need not worry about the absence of sacrifices for atonement:

'My son', said Rabbi Yochanan to Rabbi Joshua, 'be not grieved. We have another atonement as effective as sacrifice. And what is it? It is acts of loving-kindness, as it is said, 'For I desire mercy and not sacrifice' (Hosea 6:6).[7]

In fact, prayer is superior to sacrifice as we read:

God said to Israel: 'Be steadfast in prayer, it is greater than all sacrifices'.[8]

Here is the turning point; a gradual movement away from a theology of tragedy to a reconciliation with exile and a recognition that it provides new opportunities for religious expression. Rather than reliance on the priest and his mediating sacrificial service, the Jew could focus his or her attention directly and exclusively on the Divine through a developing liturgy. No longer were the people dependent upon a central sanctuary and its cult. Now prayer and Torah study dominated Jewish life and allowed for the evolution of religious self-sufficiency and independence. The destruction and exile, from this perspective, emancipated the Jew from his or her childhood dependencies and stimulated a process of spiritual maturation that led to the flowering of Torah study and the life of the intellect:

Rav, and some say Rav Shmuel bar Marta, taught: The study of Torah takes precedence over rebuilding the Temple. For, as long as Baruch ben Neriya [Jeremiah's scribe here viewed through rabbinic eyes as a Talmudic scholar] was alive Ezra did not leave him to ascend to the Land [and participate in rebuilding the Temple].[9]

The loss of the Land was transcended and, herein, a suggestion made that despite the experience of tragedy, the Jewish people was better off with its Torah (shades of Jeremiah). All of the spiritual qualities heretofore reserved for the Land were ascribed by the rabbis to Torah (in its expansive sense). It became the fertile soil tilled by Jewish minds with passionate devotion for centuries. It was, in Neusner's words, 'a mobile land' and 'a map without territory'.[10]

The apex of this spiritualising trend was reached in the Chasidic thought of the late eighteenth century when the Maggid of Mezritch (successor to the Baal Shem Tov, the founder of the movement) proclaimed that 'in exile it is easier to attain the holy spirit and the union with God than in the Land of Israel'.[11] Such an extraordinary statement metamorphosed all the spheres of Judaism into spheres of the soul. The concept of exile was turned completely on its head. No longer a description of place, it was transformed into an existential state that could be overcome through inner-directedness. The primary emphasis was on individual communion with God which, when effected, constituted a redemptive experience. Chassidim were charged with the task of uncovering the godliness that inhered in *all places* and *all things*. It was thus absolutely necessary to live outside the Land. Salvation (*geulah*) was, therefore, a function and a consequence of exile (*galut*).

This transvaluation of and accommodation to exile necessarily resulted in the Chassidic rejection of the Zionist alternative. Land-centredness – and, to a lesser degree, even Torah-centredness – gave way to God-centredness, and God's immanence made God accessible everywhere. A striking example of the notion of Divine mobility is to be found in a teaching of R. Moshe Chaim Ephraim of Sudlikov (grandson of the Baal Shem Tov) who writes:

> It was for this reason that the Torah hinted at the word 'tent' in the phrasing of this verse, showing that the Sabbath too is a form of tent or tabernacle. The word *le-dorotam* also hints at the notion of 'dwelling' [DoRoTaM = DiRaTaM], as in the dwelling of a Temple. In this way, God dwells in our midst, and that is why Scripture continues, 'as an everlasting covenant' by means of the Sabbath, the Lord, blessed be God, dwells in our midst . . . and the words *Ot Hi L*'olam again form the word *OHeL* [tent], showing that this sign goes on without interruption. Even in times when there is no Temple, the Sabbath has not been negated, and it is the Temple.[12]

God's presence remains in our midst in spite of the destruction of the Temple and the Exile. Where previously God's dwelling was localised, now God could be carried with the people of Israel wherever they dwelt: the Temple was no longer a spatial palace, it became an inner sanctuary shaped by each individual Jew. Exile was declared the fertile ground for redemptive works.

II

No discussion of the doctrine of the Land can be complete without reference to Nachmanides's opening comment to Genesis 1:1:

> In the beginning God created. Rabbi Yitzchak said: The Torah, which is the book of laws, should have begun with the verse, 'This month shall be unto you the first of the months', which is the first commandment given to Israel. What then is the reason that it begins with the creation? 'God has showed God's people the power of God's works, that God may give them the inheritance of the nations' [Psalms 111:6]. Should the nations of the world say to Israel, 'You are robbers because you took unto yourselves the lands of the seven nations of Canaan', they [Israel] may reply to them, 'The whole world belongs to the Holy One, blessed be He. He gave it to whom He pleased, and according to His will. He took it [the land] from them and gave it to us'.

> This is a homiletic exposition as quoted by Rabbi Shlomo (RaShI) in his commentaries.[13]

RaMBaN proceeds to explain that the force of Rabbi Yitzchak's question is that given the mysterious and deeply mystical significance of the opening chapters, their true meaning can only be known: 'Through the tradition going back to Moses . . . and those who know it are obligated to conceal it'. For this reason, there is no great need for the introductory narratives. People who uphold the Torah would believe in the general statement mentioned to them in the Ten Commandments (Exodus 20:11) while only those with access to esoteric traditions would have knowledge of the process of creation:

> Rabbi Yitzchak then gave a reason for it. The Torah began with the chapter of 'In the beginning God created' and recounted the

whole subject of creation until the making of man, how He [God]
granted him dominion over the works of His hands, and that He
put all things under his feet; and how the Garden of Eden, which
is the choicest of places created in this world, was made the place
of his abode until his sin caused his expulsion therefrom; and how
the people of the generation of the flood were completely expelled
from the world on account of their sin, and the only righteous one
among them, he [Noah] and his children were saved; and how the
sin of their descendants caused them to be scattered to various
places and dispersed to different countries and how subsequently
they seized unto themselves places 'after their families, in their
nations', as chance permitted. If so, it is proper that when a people
continues to sin it should lose its place and another people should
come to inherit its land, for such has been the rule of God in the
world from the beginning. This is true all the more regarding that
which is related in Scripture, namely that Canaan was cursed and
sold as a servant forever. It would therefore not be proper that
he inherit the choicest of places of the civilised world. Rather, the
servants of God – the seed of His beloved one, Abraham – should
inherit it, even as it is written. 'And He gave them the lands of
the nations, and they took the labor of the peoples in possession;
that they might keep His statutes, and observe His laws'. That is
to say, He expelled those who rebelled against Him, and settled
therein those who served Him so that they know by serving Him
they will inherit it, whereas if they sin against Him, the land will
vomit them out, just as it vomited out the nation before them.[14]

According to RaShI (1040–1105, France) the Torah began with the
creation narrative because it is a record of the fulfilment of God's
promise of the Land and not a book of laws. Since God was the
Creator, God is then responsible for assigning lands to all peoples
and has the full authority to give Israel the inheritance of the nations
– i.e., *Eretz Yisrael*. This interpretation suggests that God's pledge
was absolute and that no moral consideration has any weight against
it. God has the power to do with the Land as God desires. Long ago
God indicated that God wants Israel to have the Land. Nachmanides,
however, is not pleased with RaShI's understanding. If the sole
purpose of Genesis were to establish God's credentials as Creator,
he argues, the mere statement to that effect in the Ten Commandments would have sufficed. The Book of Genesis, according to Nachmanides, is in its entirety intended to teach us that our tenure in the

Land is *conditioned* on our obedience to the word of God. Genesis describes for us again and again circumstances of expulsion that were the result of the sinful disregard of God's moral law. Israel, too, is not exempt from this fate if it should reject God's ways.

In light of Nachmanides's analysis it is important to note Abraham Ibn Ezra's (1092–1167, Spain) comment on the significance of 'the *power* of God's works' (Ps. 111:6): 'The meaning is that God acts with benevolence, justice and righteousness. This is what God showed to God's people so that they would follow God's example and gain the inheritance'.[15] That is, Ibn Ezra would couple Psalms 111:6 ('God has showed . . .') with the following verse, 7, 'the works of God's hands are truth and justice; all God's commandments are trustworthy'. God's power is thus defined as moral power. God grants Israel the right to the Land only if Israel will act in accordance with the principles of truth and justice.[16]

In a similar vein does the Chasidic Master Rabbi Levi Yitzchak of Berditchev comment:

> God gave to God's people the power, the essence of everything, which is the *mitzvot*. That is the meaning of 'The power of God's works . . .' Would that God would give us a pure heart to know the *mitzvah* of each and every thing, Amen.[17]

Once again, power is identified with *mitzvah*. In the Chassidic sense it is the particular *mitzvah* that is attached to every created thing. The conclusion, however, is the same: Israel received the Land in order to sustain it through adherence to God's *mitzvot*. If Israel fails to sustain the law, Israel loses her right.

What emerges from Nachmanides's presentation is that the contemporary debate is prefigured in the medieval exegesis. RaShI can be utilised to justify the uncompromising position of *Gush Emunim* that holds the Land to be an absolute value, while Nachmanides's interpretation of the text is more consistent with the humanistic tradition that considers the Land to be within the system of God's moral law.[18]

Notes and References

1. Consider, for example, the doctrine of *shelilat hagolah* (negation of the exile) that has been a consistent theme in Zionist thought.

2. D. Vital, *The Origins of Zionism* (Oxford: Clarendon Press, 1975) p.1.

3. James Sanders, *Torah and Canon* (Philadelphia: Fortress, 1972) pp. 25–48. Sanders's observation is most interesting in light of the land–law dichotomy posited in the main body of the chapter. Perhaps the Torah is itself the best evidence of the inherent correctness of the RaMBaM–Hartman approach; the narrative description of the *Kibbush* is separated from the Torah and its laws.

4. Jacob Neusner, 'Sympesium and the Territorial Dimension of Judaism', *Midstream* (March 1983), pp. 38–9, and 'Map Without Territory: Mishna's System of Sacrifice and Sanctuary', *History of Religions* 19 (1979) pp. 103–27.

5. 'Map Without Territory'.

6. 'Map Without Territory'.

7. *Avot d'Rabbi Natan*, ch. 6.

8. *Tanhuma, Vayera* 1, Buber edn, p. 420.

9. B. T. *Megillah* 16b.

10. Neusner, 'Map Without Territory', p. 125.

11. *Maggid Devarar l'Yaakov* (Koretz) p. 9b quoted in G. Scholem 'Neutralization of Messianism in Early Hasidism', *The Messianic Idea in Judaism, and other essays on Jewish Spirituality* (New York Schocken, 1971), p. 201.

12. *Degel Machaneh Ephraim* (Jerusalem), pp. 135–6. A full discussion of this beautiful passage is to be found in Art Green, 'Sabbath as Temple Some Thoughts on Space and Time in Judaism', in *Go and Study: Essays Presented to Alfred Jospe*, (edited by Raphael Jospe and Samuel C Fishman (Washington, DC: B'nai B'rith Hillel Foundations, *c.* 1980) pp. 301–2.

13. Nachmanides, Commentary to Genesis 1:1, Charles Chavel, (trans.) pp. 17–20.

14. Nachmanides, Commentary to Genesis 1:1, pp. 17–20.

15. Commentary to Psalms, *Mikraot Gedulot*.

16. For a full discussion of all the issues pertaining to Nachmanides see Uriel Simon, 'Religion, Morality and Politics', in *Forum*.

17. *Kedushat Levi* (Warsaw) p. 5.

18. Although I argued above that Nachmanides's relationship to the Land is that of the mythic-messianist, his mythically mystical inclinations cannot override the moral–ethical considerations of the law. He is, after all thoroughly committed to Talmudic law and ethics.

A Christian Response to Chaim Seidler-Feller: The Land of Israel: Sanctified Matter or Mythic Space

Heidi Singh

Before I begin, I would like to state what a tremendous honour it is to respond to Rabbi Seidler-Feller's extraordinary chapter. It is an honour and a great responsibility: there is so much material and food for thought here that a ten-minute response does not do the chapter justice. I also feel an awesome sense of responsibility presenting 'a Christian view', as John Cobb has already stated. I, too, have to emphasise I am speaking for myself, and not in the totality of Christianity or even of Catholicism.

Besides responding to certain points in Chaim's chapter, I will be going on a short excursion, using this material as a point of departure. Permit me to travel from Point A to Point C, via Point B and various stops in between. I will be arriving eventually at a relevant conclusion, based on some things I have been pondering these last two days, and one or two items related to the process of dialogue in general.

Reading Chaim's chapter, I was struck by the rich imagery he has used, in conveying the longing for the Land of Israel that has been with the Jewish People over the centuries. On pp. 138–9, for example, we read, 'Our longing for the Land and its comforting beauty continues to be expressed in the liturgical corpus fashioned by the [rabbis]'.

Then on p. 140 there is a statement that is particularly moving:

What could have very easily deteriorated into a dysfunctional state of mind had a positive effect on Jewish life. By focusing our attention on a distant geographic locale we were able to transcend the temporal misery that surrounded us and forge a national community that generated a unique identity.

Thus, by this remembrance of the Land, the misery of life in the diaspora, in an often hostile environment, was somewhat alleviated. I will return to this point in a moment, because it is extremely significant.

Chaim tells us about the mythic dimension of the Land, and relates Israel to the '*axis mundi*' concept from history of religions terminology. One is moved by the 'visceral connection with the land' mentioned on p. 142. The idea of settling the land as a *mitzvah*, furthermore, is most enlightening.

This chapter is a profound examination of the development of the notion of Israel in rabbinic thought and other aspects of Jewish tradition, in both the mythic and legal dimensions of that notion. As such, the chapter is a rich treasure and a valuable resource work, particularly for a Christian who wishes to understand the importance of the Land in Judaism. For this, we can all be most grateful to Chaim.

There is a final point in the chapter which deserves our attention. On p. 154, we read:

> For Rubenstein the existence of the State [of Israel] means the *recovery of power* – the loss of which had occasioned two millenia of Jewish suffering in exile, while for Hartman it means the quest for the *morality of power* – the absence of which jeopardises the entire enterprise. From Hartman's perspective, therefore, the State of Israel provides the Jewish people with the opportunity to generate a Jewish politics that is nurtured by Talmudic law.

On p. 154 Chaim concludes:

> It is Israel's historical task to confront these challenges by drawing from and applying the teachings of the entire intellectual and spiritual heritage of Judaism. Only then will her future as a dynamically moral society convenanted with God be vouchsafed.

In reading this section of the chapter in particular, and having the good fortune to know Chaim as a colleague, I felt how truly unfortunate it is that all those reading his words do not know him personally. I would therefore like to call upon Chaim to expand upon the ideas in this chapter, especially how he views the application of the morality mentioned here, and what he feels is its foundation. I am aware that this notion has been a point of great interest, indeed, a 'wrestling for Chaim, and if he would like to expand on the ideas already presented it would be most enlightening for all of us.

My basic point of departure is the statement I mentioned earlier found on p. 140:

> What could have very easily deteriorated into a dysfunctional state of mind had a positive effect on Jewish life. By focusing our attention on a distant geographic locale we were able to transcend the temporal misery that surrounded us and forge a national community that generated a unique identity.

I found this portion of the text incredibly striking, and immediately I asked myself – what equivalent would there be in Christian terms? How could I as a Christian resonate with this statement?

And I realised that indeed there is a parallel notion in Christian thinking, wherein the world to come is viewed as the New Jerusalem. In this context there is a longing expressed for that next world beyond this, beyond 'the temporal misery that surrounds us'.

(Let me interject here my own perspective as a Catholic, and one whose spiritual orientation is mystical and experiential, indeed informed by Carmelite spirituality in particular. In Catholicism, it must be noted, we have an entire faith development that is non-Scriptural and is called Tradition, embodying doctrine, dogma, etc. We also have a fully accepted notion of the '*scientia cordis*', the science of the heart, wherein it is acknowledged that God 'speaks' to the heart of an individual through the practice of prayer, of meditation.)

For Catholics, this idea of the 'New Jerusalem', the next existence, has always had a strong appeal. And it can also be said that it spawned the oft-criticised 'otherworldliness' of Christianity. But it struck me, upon reading Chaim's description of the function of the focus on 'a distant geographic locale' for generations of Jews in the misery of the diaspora, that one could view this similar 'New Jerusalem' focus in Christianity in two ways: one, as a negative concept which entails abdication of responsibility for what happens on this earth (upon which I do not want to focus here) and two, as a valuable, functional concept which serves not only as a source of comfort but also as a means by which the transitory nature of earthly existence is kept in perspective.

What, then, is the significance of this 'other worldliness' for me, in my personal life, and in my life's work, my personal and professional commitment to interfaith dialogue? It struck me these last two days, as perhaps never before, that this 'otherworldly' focus has served as a bridge for dialogue with the great Eastern traditions, specifically Hinduism and Buddhism. And this addresses Rabbi Fred Krinsky's earlier point, namely, how do the various Christian traditions relate to other world religions not included in this trialogue and their continuing validity? I can assert that the Catholic Church answers this question very positively.

It has to be noted that our unique, mystical, 'otherworldly' Catholic peculiarities – such as our monastic tradition, our celibate priesthood, our emphasis on contemplation, etc. whatever their value – have served as foundations for dialogue with the Eastern religions. The three religions represented here (the so-called monotheistic faiths) 'find the end or goal of human life not in contemplation but in ethical social action in the service of God', as it was stated elsewhere. But, indeed, in Catholicism there is a monastic tradition over 1000 years old that does find contemplation the pre-eminent way in which to worship God in this very existence. And in this context, the practice of meditation is of immense importance.

Thus, while dialogue is going on all over the world between Catholics and other 'western' religions, there are innovative experiments occurring also with the Eastern religions, such as Zen Buddhist meditation masters training Catholic monks in *zazen* here in the United States, in Europe and most notably in Japan. There are experiments with Christians living in Hindu ashrams in India, as another example. In addition, Catholics concerned with peace and justice issues are finding increasing inspiration in the practice of non-violence as taught by Gandhi and by the Eastern traditions themselves.

How does all this relate to the topic of 'earth' before us today? Precisely in that I contend aspects of the Catholic view of the 'world' are in some important respects similar to those found in the Eastern traditions. Moreover, not only does this similarity function as a basis for a dialogue 'condoned' by the Church, indeed, we are given a *mandate* to dialogue with these traditions. I quote from the Vatican II 'Declaration on the Relation of the Church to Non-Christian Religions' (*Nostra Aetate*) dated 28 October 1965:

Thus, in Hinduism men explore the divine mystery and express it both in the limitless riches of myth and the accurately defined insights of philosophy. They seek release from the trials of the present life by ascetical practices, profound meditation and recourse to God in confidence and love. Buddhism in its various forms testifies to the *essential inadequacy of this changing world*. It proposes a way of life by which men can, with confidence and trust, attain a state of perfect liberation and reach supreme illumination either through their own efforts or by the aid of divine help. So, too, other religions which are found throughout the world attempt in their own ways to calm the hearts of men by outlining a programme of life covering doctrine, moral precepts and sacred rites.

The Catholic Church rejects nothing of what is true and holy in these religions. She has a high regard for the manner of life and conduct, the precepts and doctrines which, although differing in many ways from her own teaching, nevertheless often reflect a ray of that truth which enlightens all men . . . The Church, therefore, urges her sons to enter with prudence and charity into discussion and collaboration with members of other religions. Let Christians, while witnessing to their own faith and way of life, acknowledge, preserve and encourage the spiritual and moral truths found among non-Christians, also their social life and culture.[1]

It is significant that in *Nostra Aetate*, Hinduism and Buddhism are mentioned first, then there is a section on Islam and a long section on Judaism, and following that, a separate section entitled, 'Guidelines on Religious Relations with the Jews'.

This brings me to my final point. There is a repeated reference in all the conference papers to '*the* three monotheistic traditions'. But I have to register with some distress that there is a fourth not even mentioned here (and sadly, not mentioned in *Nostra Aetate*, although certainly implied) – a religion whose adherents assert that there is one God (*Ek Onkar, Sat Nam*: 'There is one God, His Name is Truth'). That religion is Sikhism. While Sikhs are a minority everywhere, even in India, there are about 15 million around the world. Why is Sikhism important to me? Because I am married to a Sikh. I mention this because, while some or all of my colleagues here may be comfortable with the notion of '*the* three monotheistic faiths', I want it to be on the record that this limitation is not endorsed by me.

Over and above Sikhism, moreover, the other traditions have to be acknowledged – Hinduism and Buddhism among them, and there are others as well. While some of my colleagues may see this as problematic, it must be noted that even in official documents, the Catholic Church regards these religions with great respect and, further, finds valuable and relevant certain aspects of these religions which she urges her children to discover and encourage.

I have to insist that we do not operate in a vacuum in this world. While a trialogue such as this one has its own tremendous value, and indeed the three traditions represented here *must* dialogue with one another, nevertheless there is a real danger in defining ourselves 'against' other groups. I continue to see this negative defining process all the time in numerous interfaith activities.

For years we Catholics and Protestants have defined ourselves as 'against' one another. Now we are talking, struggling with the ecumenical question of unity. We are still struggling with our very real differences, but we now confront them and get on with the work before us. And now we realize that we are not alone.

As for Jews and Christians: Jewish–Christian dialogue has enriched my life more than I can say, and it is an incredibly valuable phenomenon. However, sometimes Jews and Christians get to the point where the dialogue becomes, 'I'm okay, you're okay – and the heck with everybody else'.

And now we are three – Jews, Christians and Muslims. To be sure, we must have these trialogues, and we must speak, the three of us, to one another. But to box ourselves in philosophically – for whatever reasons, even our historical connections – and to exclude all others, to define ourselves as '*the* three monotheistic faiths' – misses the point entirely in the face of reality as it is, whether one wants to confront the impending (God forbid) nuclear holocaust, or even just the living of our lives in a truly pluralistic society as is the situation in the United States.

This defining 'against' others is a reprehensible aspect of interfaith dialogue that should be avoided at all costs. And I caution Jews and Christians in particular: much has been said in the papers of this conference about Hinduism and Buddhism specifically which is totally irresponsible and indeed inaccurate. This has been done simply as a means to *define* ourselves *against* 'them'.

And so once more I must register my feelings that as a Catholic – both with a capital 'C' and, more important with a small 'c' – I have to protest and express the fact that to maintain exclusivity and religious arrogance in the context of trialogue, in this day and age, is *to me* completely unacceptable.

Reference

1. *Vatican Council II: The Conciliar and Post Conciliar Documents*, Austin Flannery, O.P. (ed.) (New York: Costello Publishing, 1979) p. 739, emphasis mine. (The sexist language of these translations is another issue.)

A Muslim Response to Chaim Seidler-Feller: The Land of Israel: Sanctified Matter or Mystic Space

Ismail K. Poonawala

Like all political movements, Zionism not only perpetuates its myth but also uses basic myths to justify its goals and to legitimise its action. This chapter, written with an explicit purpose to justify the creation of the Zionist State and to confer legitimacy upon it, is a case in point. Rabbi Chaim Seidler-Feller uses the myth of the land of Israel to equate obligations to Zionism with Judaism. His presentation gives the impression that Zionism is the natural outcome of the whole of Jewish history and that it is also the intrinsic core of Judaism to which all Jews owe their allegiance. The author views the doctrine of the Land from two perspectives – mythic and legal – and employs preconceived ideas without discussing all their implications. The so-called 'legal perspective' is nothing but Zionist sophistry.

What is most disturbing about this chapter, written by a Rabbi and presented at an interfaith dialogue (to promote better understanding of the other man's faith), is that the moral issues involved in the creation of Israel have been totally brushed aside. How can one deny the fact that the very creation of Israel has caused one of the grimmest human tragedies of our times? Has the author ever thought about Zionism from the standpoint of its victims, the Palestinian refugees? The chapter indicates neither moral sensitivity nor awareness of a vast body of scholarly literature on this thorny question. In his endeavour to promote Zionism, Rabbi Seidler-Feller has clouded the basic issues and has selected a certain interpretation projecting his own ideas into the past.

The basic notion underlying my comments is that no living religion remains static, but it is constantly changing in the sense that its followers interpret its principles, practices and rituals according to the need of their own time. All the modern movements in Judaism, including Zionism, are therefore responses to the modern world.[1] Judaism can be viewed from different perspectives, and to define it by one form to the exclusion of others is to impose only one view and to ignore the complexity of the subject.

I will start with the millennial Jewish vision of the return to Zion (the poetic term for the Holy Land), the nostalgia for the lost home-land portrayed in Jewish literature and folklore. The role of the land of Israel is, of course, closely related to the concept of Israel as the chosen, or Covenant people. Following the destruction of Jerusalem by the Romans in 70 A.D. the dispersed Jews not only continued to cherish the land, but made it a symbol of fulfilment. Their return to Palestine was thus looked upon as an integral part of messianic restoration. Although the return to the Holy Land was idealised in literature, it was viewed primarily in eschatological terms – at the end of time. In a Biblical perspective, the Jews have been going in and out of Palestine for almost 3000 years. They first migrated from the Euphrates under Abraham; returned from Egypt under Moses; came back again from Babylonian captivity, and were dispersed again when Jerusalem fell to the Romans. The Promised Land referred to in *Genesis*, states I. F. Stone, thus seems anachronistic. He adds:

The Bible is still the best guide to it. Nowhere else can one find a parallel for its ethnocentric fury. Nowhere that I know of is there a word of pity in the Bible for the Canaanites whom the Hebrews slaughtered in taking possession.[2]

It was not until the nineteenth century that the land began to play a role other than the goal of pilgrimage or of occasional settlement by pietists and mystics. During this period several factors contributed to the rise of Zionism. Drawing on the general currents of European nationalism, Zionism reinterpreted religious aspirations which hinged upon a messianic vision of the end of time (when the final golden age would unfold in Palestine) in terms of modern nationalism. The Zionist political movement reflected a dissatis-faction with the view that the Jews were merely a community of religious believers, an interpretation that had become dominant following the political emancipation of the Jews after Napoleon.

Theodore Herzl, the founder of this movement, who is stated to have confessed in 1899 that the Dreyfus affair had made him a

Zionist,[3] posed the Jewish question as a national problem to be solved through international political action.[4] He identified the Jewish question in all its aspects with the fact of antisemitism, which he conceived of as the natural rejection by all peoples, always and everywhere, of the very existence of Jews. Inspired by European nationalism, he believed that the Jewish question could be solved by finding a homeland whereby the exclusive element could be reintegrated into the family of nations. Moreover, he saw nation states as immutable structures of reality. Differences in class structure, differences between political parties, and differences between various countries at various times in history did not exist for Herzl. Although both Argentina and Palestine were mentioned in his *Der Judenstaat* (*The Jewish State*, 1896) as possible sites for the Jewish homeland, he entertained no doubts that the idea of a return to Palestine would have the symbolic significance and psychological power for the eventual ingathering of the Jewish masses. Earlier efforts at colonisation were not successful in attracting large numbers of Jews. Hence, he thought, what was needed was a grant of 'exclusive sovereignty' by a powerful nation over a 'neutral piece of land'. He stressed that mere immigration to the land was insufficient without the political relationship necessary to secure the legal right to it. This sovereign right over Palestine has never been unconditionally granted, nor has it ever been accepted by the Palestinians, the victims of the creation of Israel.[5]

The founding fathers of Zionism did not share the religious fervour of devout Jews as theirs was primarily a secular quest. As they stressed the national concentration of Jews in a secular state, it was an example of secularisation of Jewish life and of Jewish messianism. It is, therefore, not surprising that it aroused considerable opposition and that for many years the Zionists had no more implacable enemies than the rabbis. In fact the location of the First Zionist Congress (1897) was moved from Munich to Basle, mainly because of a strong anti-Zionist reaction from the German Rabbinic Council and local Jewish community. It would be wrong to state that political Zionism captured the imagination of the whole of Jewry from its inception. From the very beginning, Zionism met with opposition within Jewry for a variety of reasons. Opposition from Orthodox Judaism stressed the distinction between religion and politics, between the words of the Torah and the mundane ramblings of politicians. The formation of the Agudath Israel movement (1912) articulated the Orthodox position. In its essay entitled 'The Challenge to Israel', the Agudath movement states:

> Political Zionism comes with empty hands to the land of our fathers . . . [it] is unable to bring to unfoldment the national culture of God's kingly law, for which the nation and the land have sighed for 2000 years.[6]

Another voice of opposition came from Reform Judaism (in America, Germany and eastern Europe). Although their opposition stemmed from socioeconomic reasons, they based their antagonism upon theological grounds. They argued on the same lines as the Cromwellian supporters of a Jewish resettlement had done before in England by stressing the universalism of Israel and by maintaining that the propagation of prophetic Judaism was the mission of all Jewry. Such a mission, they further argued, demanded the dispersal of Jewry rather than centralisation in Palestine. They also stressed that Zionism was a secular, nationalistic ideal opposed to their concept of Judaism. It is worth noting that in Reform Judaism all references to the doctrine of the 'Chosen People' and all references in the traditional prayers to a return to Zion were excised from its liturgy. The traditional messianic doctrine, a central theme in earlier Judaism, was transformed into a universal hope of a messianic age for all mankind with the establishment of the Kingdom of truth, justice, and peace. This change was combined with the rejection of the notion of Jewish nationhood (i.e., return to the land of the forefathers and the restoration of a Jewish state), and the Jews were designated as a religious community.[7] Such a view was not new. Isaiah (the prophet in the second half of the eighth century B.C.) too had maintained that the political status of Palestine was of little concern to the Jewish religion as its mission was bound by spiritual ties and not dependent on physical conditions.[8] The Central Conference of American Rabbis, in their 1897 resolution, expressed their disapproval for the Zionists' attempt to establish a Jewish state.[9] For a good number of Jews, Zionism could not be a lasting solution for the Jewish question. There were others who saw a total assimilation of the Jews into society as the only solution. Hence, they opposed Zionism as yet another factor separating the Jews from their neighbours.

Some Jews accused Herzl of being an inexperienced novice in the field of Zionism, with no real understanding of the problems involved. Orthodox rabbis decried his attempt as doing the work of the Messiah, while Reform rabbis proclaimed their opposition to his negation of the Jewish mission. The bitter debate that ensued at the birth of political Zionism and which continued after the Balfour Declaration (1917)[10] was brought to an abrupt end by the events in Nazi Germany. It is a tragic dialectic of history that Israel would not have been born without Hitler. It is also an irony that it took the murder of six million to awaken sufficient nationalist zeal in Jewry to bring a Jewish state into existence.[11]

As stated above, Zionism has reinterpreted religious aspirations in terms of modern nationalism; hence it is viewed as the secularisation of a religious tendency. Irrespective of how one views Zionism, it is irrelevant in defining the basis of the Arab–Israeli conflict. Historically, the origin of the conflict lies in the settlement of a radically new population on a land already occupied by a people. This is an undeniable fact. Maxime Rodinson has eloquently argued and given strong support to this basic Arab historical contention.[12] He sums up his arguments by stating:

> When a people is subjected to foreign conquest, the moral wound it receives is in no way alleviated by the spiritual tendencies observable within the conquering group, nor by the motives for the conquest, or the aspirations which they express.[13]

Israel is a colonialist implantation in the Arab world, supported from the beginning by imperialist power. Zionism, from its inception, tried to gain its aims by offering to serve as an outpost in the Middle East for one of the great empires. Herzl tried to convince first the Ottoman Sultan, then the Kaiser by such arguments.[14] Considerations of imperial strategy finally won the Balfour Declaration from Britain. The Ottoman defeat brought Palestine under the British Mandate (in 1919), which facilitated Jewish immigration in spite of growing Arab resentment. Hitler's rise to power in 1933 accelerated the rate of Jewish immigration to Palestine. Referring to this immigration, I. F. Stone states that compassion was not strong enough to open the gates of the West to Jewish immigration, the Capitalist West and the Communist East preferring to displace (the Palestinian) Arabs rather than welcome the Jewish persons from Europe's postwar refugee camps. Morally one uprooting cannot be equated with the other.[15]

In 1947, the United Nations – led by the Western powers and the

Soviet Union, in spite of the opposition of third world countries – decided to partition Palestine between its Arab and Jewish inhabitants. The Arab inhabitants owned more than 90 per cent of the land, while the Jewish inhabitants, most of whom were newly-arrived immigrants, owned less than 7 per cent. The United Nations partition plan, nevertheless, gave more than 56 per cent of the territory to the Jewish inhabitants.[16] When they unilaterally proclaimed the State of Israel on 14 May 1948, without defining its boundaries, fighting ensued. Most of the Palestinian inhabitants abandoned their homes and lands. They cite the massacre of Deir Yassin, where the forces of Menachem Begin killed 254 Arab men, women and children and then paraded wounded survivors through other Arab villages as a warning of what could happen to them if they chose to remain inside Israeli lines. Memoirs of Yigael Allon and other Israeli generals also describe the forcible evacuation of Arab villages. The Israelis were glad to see the departure of a population which presented an obstacle to the realisation of the Jewish State projected by the Zionists. When the fighting ceased, the Israelis had increased the land they held to 77 per cent, and about one million Arab Palestinian occupants of those territories were barred by the Israelis from returning to their homes and lands.[17]

Zionism has degenerated into what Martin Buber called a '*sacro egoismo*', deviating from the Jewish ethic by making an idol of the people.[18] It is this moral myopia that makes it possible for Zionists to dwell on the 2000 years of Exile in which the Jews have longed for the return to Zion, at the same time dismissing the Palestinian refugees' longing for their homeland, so fresh in their memories, as totally worthless. 'Homelessness' is the major theme of Zionism, but this pathetic passion is denied to Palestinian Arab refugees. In the outside world, the welfare of Jewry depends on the preservation of secular, non-racial, pluralistic societies, but in the Zionist State they have to defend a society in which mixed marriages cannot be legalised, and in which the Arabs are barely tolerated even as second-class citizens. In Israel, the ideal is racial and religious.[19]

The aforementioned viewpoints, from such opposite groups of Judaism as Orthodox and Reformists, might be criticised today as being irrelevant or no longer popular, since the symbols of Judaism and religious ideology have become intertwined with symbols and aspirations of the Zionist State. As the Zionist outlook became predominant among Jewry, various shades of opinion about Judaism and Zionism were considered non-kosher. Both the Agudath Israel

and the American Reform movement have forsaken their opposition
to the fundamental tenets of political Zionism and have gradually
entered into a working compromise with it.[20] Consequently, they
partake of political influence and power, either in Israel or in
America. Many Orthodox Jews and a few Hassidic sects still maintain
their hostility to the secular nationalism of the Jewish State.
Although overt opposition to government policies did not engender
mass support in the past, the Israeli invasion of Lebanon (in June
1982) has changed the situation so drastically that a vocal minority
has vehemently protested against the invasion. Israel stands practically alone as far as the United Nations and world opinion are
concerned. Only the United States still supports Israel. Paradoxically
it is Israel's special relation with America, and its links with South
Africa and other repressive regimes of Latin America, which reveal
the true nature of the Zionist State. These relations are well docu-
mented and brilliantly analysed by Noam Chomsky.[21] Many Israeli
writers are far ahead of American Jewish and non-Jewish writers in
exposing Israeli society as racist, and oppressive to the Arabs.[22]

In his self-searching article written after the Israeli invasion of
Lebanon and just before he died, Nahum Goldmann, President of
the World Jewish Congress for many years, states:

> Both the holocaust and the creation of the Jewish State justified
> the assumption that the Jewish question had finally been resolved
> . . . The establishment of Israel, on the other hand, led radical
> Zionists to believe in Theodore Herzl's naive and ingenious simpli-
> fication of the Jewish question . . . Both expectations were false.

Finally, he concludes:

> Contemporary Israel runs the risk of making the Jewish question
> banal. With its politics of aggression it robs the Jewish question
> of its unique quality . . . More and more Jews put distance between
> themselves and Israel's conduct. Some even go so far as to declare
> that they are ashamed as Jews.[23]

Notes and References

1. Joseph Blau, *Modern Varieties of Judaism* (New York: Columbia
   University Press, pp. 119–51.

2. I. F. Stone, 'For a New Approach to the Israeli–Arab Conflict', in *New York Review of Books*, 3 August 1967; reprinted in Gary Smith (ed.), *Zionism: The Dream and the Reality, A Jewish Critique* (New York, 1974) p. 199.

3. W. Polk, D. Stamler, and E. Asfour, *Backdrop to Tragedy: The Struggle for Palestine* (Boston: Beacon Press, 1957) p. 148. The Dreyfus affair created a political crisis for the French Third Republic between 1894 and 1906, about the guilt or innocence of army captain Alfred Dreyfus, who was Jewish and was convicted of treason for selling military secrets to the Germans.

4. Hannah Arendt, 'The Jewish State: Fifty Years After – Where Have Herzl's Politics Led?', in Smith (ed.), *Zionism*, pp. 72–3.

5. Gary Smith, 'Introductory Note', in Smith (ed.), *Zionism*, p. 17.

6. Smith (ed.), *Zionism*, p. 14. Herzl's program was entirely secular, see also Blau, *Modern varieties*, p. 141.

7. Blau, *Modern Varieties*, pp. 38–9.

8. See the prophetic book Isaiah in the Bible; *Encyclopaedia Britannica*, IX, p. 908.

9. Polk *et al.*, *Backdrop to Tragedy*, p. 147.

10. Polk *et al.*, pp. 160–70; Ronald Sanders, *The High Walls of Jerusalem: A History of the Balfour Declaration and the Birth of the British Mandate for Palestine*, New York: Holt, Rinehart and Winston, c. 1983 (London, 1983); and its review in *New York Review of Books*, 15 March 1984.

11. Stone, 'For a New Approach', pp. 210–11.

12. Maxime Rodinson, *Israel and the Arabs*, M. Perl (trans.), (1st American edition New York: Pantheon, 1968), especially ch. 9. See also *Les Temps Modernes* special issue on *Le conflit israélo–arabe* (Paris, 1967).

13. Rodinson, *Israel and the Arabs*, p. 219.

14. Rodinson, *Israel and the Arabs*, pp. 13–14; Polk *et al.*, *Backdrop to Tragedy*, pp. 150–4.

15. Stone, 'For a New Approach', pp. 208, 210–11.

16. John Kimball, *The Arabs 1983* (Washington, 1983) p. 32.

17. Kimball, *The Arabs*, p. 32.

18. Smith (ed.), *Zionism*, p. 17.

19. Stone, 'For a New Approach', p. 209.

20. Smith (ed.), *Zionism*, p. 15; Moshe Menuhin, *The Decadence of Judaism in Our Time* (New York: Exposition Press, 1965) pp. 325–61, 542–54.

21. Noam Chomsky, *United States, Israel and Palestine: A Fateful Triangle* (New York, 1983); Noam Chomsky, Peace in the Middle East? Reflections on Justice and Nationhood (New York, 1974); Lenni Brenner, *Zionism in the Age of the Dictators* (London, 1983; this sets the stage for a better understanding of the direction of Israeli politics).

22. Arie Bober (ed.), *The Other Israel: The Radical Case Against Zionism* (New York, 1972); Uri Davis and N. Mezvinsky, *Documents from Israel, 1967–1973* (London, 1973); Uri Davis, A. Mack and N. Yuval-Davis, *Israel and the Palestinians* (London, 1975); Felicia Langer, *With My Own Eyes* (London, 1975); Roberta Feuerlicht, *The Fate of the Jews: A People Torn Between Israeli Power and Jewish Ethics* (New York,

1983; this is a biting corrective to the various forms of Israeli and Zionist brainwashing and confronts the Jews with painful truths). See also Edward Said, *The Question of Palestine* (New York, 1979, by a Palestinian Arab); *Arabs Under Israeli Occupation*, series published by Institute for Palestine Studies; see also news reports by M. Kubic in *Newsweek*, 13, 20, 27 February, 1984.

23. N. Goldmann, 'Where is Israel Going?', in *New York Review of Books*, 1 October 1982. See also Bernard Avishai, 'Can Begin Be Stopped?' in *New York Review of Books*, 2 June 1983; Meron Benvenisti, 'The Turning Point in Israel', *New York Review of Books*, 13 October 1983.

Editors' Note

Because this statement presents one side of a highly controversial political issue, it is appropriate to append a brief bibliography of works which can be consulted for alternative perspectives:

Encyclopedia Judaica, vol. 9 'Israel, Land of (History)', cols. 237–301; 'Israel, State of (Historical Survey)', cols 302–472.

Joan Peters, *From Time Immemorial* (New York: Harper & Row, 1984).

James Parkes, *Whose Land? A History of the Peoples of Palestine*, 2nd edn. (Harmondsworth, 1970).

7 The Essence of Judaism
David Ellenson

There is a famous talmudic story, involving a prominent first-century rabbi named Hillel the Elder. In this tale a pagan, interested in converting to Judaism, approached Hillel and challenged the rabbi to define the essence of the Jewish religion while standing on one foot. I, of course, am not standing on one foot. Indeed, I am sitting on a chair. Nevertheless, in this brief opportunity to explain the core of my faith as a Jew to all of you, I feel I am placed under the same kind of constraint Hillel was at that moment. Moreover, I suspect that I cannot markedly improve upon the answer Hillel is reported to have given to his interlocutor. For, in replying to this potential convert to the Jewish fold, Hillel stated the Jewish version of the Golden Rule, 'That which is hateful to you, do not do unto others'. This, Hillel felt, was the 'essence' of Judaism. However, he quickly added, 'The rest is commentary. Now, go and study the commentary'. As you can imagine, the commentary in Judaism, as in other scriptural religions, is seemingly endless. Therefore, what I propose to do is to expand upon Hillel's statement, and provide a bit of that commentary.

Hillel, I believe, was able to offer his version of the Golden Rule to the would-be proselyte precisely because Judaism holds that humanity – men and women – was created in the image of God. This belief, stated in the first book of Genesis, is perhaps the cardinal precept upon which Judaism is established. It signifies that we as individuals have been granted the gift of ratiocination and free-will by God. In addition, we possess the ability to empathise, 'to place ourselves in the place of another' and, consequently, to feel his or her pain or joy. In short, we as human beings are blessed with the ability to 'repair the world' – the ability to see to it that moral and ethical precepts become enacted in the world – or, conversely, the opportunity, if our inclinations so direct us, to reject God's word and not strive to make the world a good and better place. The mission of Judaism, then, is best summed up in Leviticus 19:2, where the Jewish people are instructed by God to be *kedoshim*, holy

persons. The major aim of Judaism is the attempt to transform the
world into a holy place, and a principal belief is that humanity has
the capabilities to perform this act. This sense of messianic mission
– that the world of 'is' can be transformed into the realm of 'ought'
– lies at the heart of Judaism. The Jew, spurred on by the Jewish
religion, strives to make the world a place where, metaphorically,
God would feel at home. How, though, does the Jew accomplish
this task? How does the Jew receive guidance in this quest to make
the world a holy place?

The answer, from the Jewish perspective, is that the Jew and all
humanity realise this goal of promoting holiness in the world through
a partnership with God. This notion of partnership – that God and
humanity together labour in the creation of a better world – is
expressed in Judaism through the biblical concept of *b'rith*, or
covenant. In Genesis, immediately after the story of the Flood, it is
stated that God establishes a covenant with all humanity through
Noah. This covenant, known in rabbinic tradition as the Noahide
Covenant, holds that God issues seven commandments, *mitzvot*, to
all humankind. These include prohibitions against idolatory, incest,
murder, robbery, tearing a limb from a living animal and taking the
Lord's Name in vain. In addition, all humanity is instructed to establish courts of justice in society. In this way, justice will be reached
and, in the words of Rabbi Marcus Horovitz (1844–1910), a German
Orthodox rabbi, gentiles, as well as Jews, will participate in the acts
of *tikkun olam*, repair of the world.

There is, moreover, a second covenant which God establishes, a
covenant between God and the Jewish people alone. This covenant
is expressed through the revelation which God bestows upon Israel
at Sinai, the gift of Torah. This Torah – which means 'instruction'
– consists, in rabbinic tradition, not only of a Written Law, but,
remarkably, an Oral one as well. The Oral Torah, which provides
commentary upon the Written Torah, allows for continuous
interpretation of the Law. It permits Judaism to adapt, to grow, to
live: and it allows the Law, and the traditions of the people, to give
guidance to the Jew in all his or her habitations. While Orthodox
and non-Orthodox Jews differ over the meaning and significance of
this Oral Law, the key concept which needs to be stressed is that
Law comes to be the way in which Covenant – the partnership
between God, Israel and humanity – is expressed in Judaism. For
Law, in Judaism, is not the antithesis of love and caring. Rather,
Law becomes the manner, the path (*Halakhah*), in which the values

of Judaism – those values of human dignity which call upon the Jew to make the world a holy place – come to be concretised in the world.

Therefore, in concluding, I would like to assert that what Judaism attempts to do is make holy the profane. For Judaism teaches that every moment is potentially holy. That is why Jewish law attempts to address every facet of a person's life. No detail in a human being's life is too insignificant for God's concern. The classical codes of Jewish law thus instruct individuals on everything they should do from the time the individual arises in the morning, to the manner in which they should pray, to the way in which they should conduct themselves in business. The idea which undergirds all this – the notion which permits the Jew to act in a manner which attempts to maximise the dignity and integrity of every human being, and which instructs the Jew on how to behave so as not to act hatefully towards another – is the concept of Covenant, which finds its expression in Law. For it is through these laws, these *mitzvot* (commandments), that Jewish values become actualised in the world.

8 The Heart of the Christian Faith for Me

James A. Sanders

My understanding of the Christian faith is founded on a theocentric reading of Scripture, with *equal* emphasis on God as creator and redeemer.

God is One. God is the Integrity of Reality. God is the continuing creator of all that is; and God is the continuing redeemer of creation. God is the creative redeemer and the redemptive creator. God is also sustainer, judge and re-creator. He is the God of life and of death. There is no other. *Hu' memit vehu' meḥayeh.*

It is the same God who threw up the valadium vaults and cast the planets in their orbits who paid a pastoral call on Abraham and Sarah, sojourned in the huts and hovels of the slaves in Egypt and crouched into the cradle of Jesus, a Jew, in the first century. God judged the ancient states of Israel and Judah and out of their deaths in the eighth and sixth centuries resurrected a new Israel, Judaism. Just before the demise of the early Jewish state in Palestine in the first century God appointed a few scholars, two priests, a young political activist and an inept Roman provincial governor to bring about the fall of his Son, Jesus Christ, for the sake of them all, indeed, for the sake of all creation.

Just as the concept of the *sōd'elohîm* or *sōd 'adonai* in the Old Testament was a means of monotheising in the Iron Age and Persian period, so the Trinity became for early Christianity a means of monotheising in the hellenistic–Roman period. God is one. The trinitarian formula is a feeble human attempt to understand God as creator and redeemer – as well as judge and sustainer.

God is not an abstract principle but the divine person who in ancient Israel, Judaism and climactically in Christ, rendered himself vulnerable to human sinfulness. In Christ, God permitted himself to get crushed between the zealots and the establishment for the sake of them both and for the sake of us all. It was the God who earlier had rendered himself vulnerable in his identification with the people of ancient Israel who in Christ rendered himself vulnerable by full

185

identity with Christ – yet remaining fully God. Human language is so limited that it takes a paradox to express the mystery.

God is the God of death and of life. Death is not a god like *mot* or *abaddon*. There is only one God. God in Christ, the Holy Warrior, utterly defeated death and is the victor finally over all the forces of chaos and evil.

God, in Christ and through his Holy Spirit, is the sole sovereign of all that is. He is the Integrity of Reality. All who believe in him are commanded to pursue that integrity in their lives and in their living. They are called upon to be good stewards of the precious life they are given. They fully realise that all they have is a gift of God – body, mind, spirit, family and whatever of this world's goods. They are stewards and others of land and earth. They anticipate an ultimate accounting of that stewardship.

The Church of Jesus Christ is called with others, Judaism and Islam, to be witness to the Integrity of Reality, to proclaim God's unlimited grace to all who would listen. The true Christian does not worry about whether others are lost but stays her or his mind on the joy of the faith and the pursuit of the Integrity of Reality in her or his life with hope in the promise that that very integrity will be God's ultimate and final gift to the believer and to all humankind.

9 Islam: A Brief Look[1]
Jamāl Badawi

All grace is due to Allah, Creator and Sustainer of the universe, and I bear witness that there is no god but Allah and that Muhammad is His Servant, messenger and the seal of all the prophets and messengers in history. May Allah's peace and blessing be upon them all.

I'd like first to express my thanks and appreciation to those who arranged this seminar, and I do hope that we leave it with a better understanding of each other and with more positive attitudes.

Now I'd like to share with you eight basic points, consideration of which is imperative in understanding Islam: the meaning of the term 'Islam'; the Islamic monotheism; nature of the human; the relationship between the human and Allah; the special role of Muhammad; accountability and salvation; the applied aspect; and finally some conclusions.

I MEANING OF 'ISLAM'

'Islam' is not derived from the name of any particular person, race or locality. A Muslim considers the term used by some writers, 'Mohammedanism', to be an offensive violation of the very spirit of Islamic teaching.

Prophet Muhammad, peace be upon Him, is not worshipped, nor is he regarded as either the founder of Islam or the author of its Holy Book, the Qur'an. The term 'Islam' is given in more than one place in the Qur'an itself. It is derived from the word that means 'peace' or 'submission'. Indeed, the proper meaning of 'Islam' is the attainment of peace, both inner and outer peace, by submission of oneself to the will of Allah. And when we say 'submit', we are talking about conscious, loving and trusting submission to the will of Allah, the acceptance of His Grace and the following of His path. In that sense, the Muslim regards the term 'Islam', not as an innovation that came in the seventh century (Christian era) with the advent of the Prophet Muhammad, but as the basic mission of all

187

the prophets throughout history. That universal mission was finally culminated and perfected in the last of these prophets, Prophet Muhammad, peace be upon Him.

II   ISLAMIC MONOTHEISM

The next essential concept that needs to be clarified is the term 'Allah'. What does it mean? It should be emphasised first that the term 'Allah' has no connotation at all of a tribal god, an Arabian or even a Muslim god. The term 'Allah' in Arabic simply means the One and Only True, Universal God of all. To think that Allah is different from God, with a capital 'G', is no more valid than saying the French Christians worship a different god because they call him 'Dieu'.

What are the basic attributes of Allah? The Qur'an mentions the 'most beautiful names' (or attributes) of Allah. Instead of enumerating them all, let's examine a few. Some attributes emphasise the transcendence of Allah. The Qur'an repeatedly makes it clear that Allah is beyond our limited perception. 'There is nothing whatever comparable unto Him' (al-Shura 42:11). 'No vision can grasp Him but His grasp is over all vision' (al-An'ām 6:103). A Muslim never thinks of God as having any particular image, whether physical human, material or otherwise. Such attributes as 'The Perfectly Knowing', 'The Eternal', 'The Omnipotent', 'The Omnipresent' 'The Just' and 'The Sovereign' also emphasise transcendence. But this does not mean in any way that for the Muslim Allah is a mere philosophical concept or a deity far removed. Indeed, alongside this emphasis on the transcendence of Allah, the Qur'an also talks about Allah as a 'personal' God who is close, easily approachable, Loving Forgiving and Merciful. The very first passage in the Qur'an which is repeated dozens of times, is 'In the name of Allah, Most Gracious Most Merciful . . .'. The Qur'an tells us that when Allah created the first human 'He breathed into him something of His spirit', (al Sajdah 32:9) and that 'Allah is closer to the human than his jugular vein'. In another beautiful and moving passage we are told, 'When my servants ask you [O Muhammad] concerning me, then surely am near to them. I listen to every suppliant who calls on Me. L them respond to My call and obey My command that they may b led aright'.

To the Muslim, monotheism does not mean simply the unity of

God, because there can be different persons in unity. Monotheism in Islam is the absolute Oneness and Uniqueness of Allah, which precludes the notion of persons sharing in Godhead. The opposite of monotheism in Islam is called in Arabic *shirk*, association of others with Allah. This includes not only polytheism, but also dualism (believing in one God for good or light and another for evil or darkness). The concept of *shirk* also includes pantheism, the idea that God is in everything. All forms of God-incarnate philosophies are excluded by Islam's monotheism, as is blind obedience to dictators, to clergy or to one's own whims and desires. These all are regarded as forms of 'associating' others with Allah (*shirk*), whether by believing that such creatures of Allah possess divinity or by believing that they share the Divine Attributes of Allah.

It should be added that, to the Muslim, monotheism is not simply a dogma. Islam's pure, pristine and strict monotheism is much more than a thought or a belief; it is something that deeply influences the Muslim's whole outlook on life.

III NATURE OF THE HUMAN

We have talked about Allah. What about you and me? Who is the human being? Who are you and I? And why are we here on earth? The Qur'an teaches that we humans are created of three components. We are created from clay, representing the material or carnal element. We are endowed with intellect that is Allah-given to be used, not to be put on the shelf. Reason may be insufficient but it is not the antithesis of faith, either. And thirdly, we are endowed with the spirit of Allah, which was breathed into us (al-Sajdah 32:7, al-Baqarah 2:31, al-Hijr 15:29). The Muslim does not see human existence here on earth as punishment for eating from the forbidden tree. That event is regarded as an experiential lesson for Adam and Eve before they came to earth. The Qur'an teaches that even before the creation of the first human it was Allah's plan to establish human life and civilisation on earth (al-Baqarah 2:30). The Muslim thus does not view the human as all evil, nor as all good, but rather as responsible. It is stated in several places in the Qur'an that Allah created the human to be His 'khalifah', His trustee or viceregent on earth. Humankind's basic trust, our responsibility, is to worship Allah. Worship for the Muslim is not only engaging in formal rituals, it is any activity in accordance with the will of Allah

for the benefit of oneself and of humanity at large. The Muslim thus
views the earth, its resources and ecology as a gift from Allah to
humans to harness and use in fulfilment of the trust for which we
shall all be held responsible. That is why the Qur'an speaks highly
of learning. The first word revealed of the Qur'an was, 'Recite', or
'read'. As long as they were true to their faith and to Qur'anic
injunctions about learning, Muslims established a civilisation that
saw great advances in science and in the humanities. Not only did
they preserve earlier scientific heritage but they also added to it
and paved the way for European renaissance. When Muslims again
become true to their faith such history is bound to repeat itself.

IV ALLAH–HUMANKIND RELATIONSHIP

We talked of Allah and of humankind. Now we must ask what is
their basic relationship. The Qur'an teaches us that the human race
is given an innate pure nature called 'fitrah'. Knowledge of Allah
and innate spirituality can betray us if it is not led in the right
direction. To depend on a merely human feeling of the guiding Spirit
is dangerous. Many groups, even cults, claim to be guided by the
spirit or by God or by revelation, yet these groups hold divergent,
even contradictory, beliefs. We find people behaving in contradictory
ways who claim nonetheless that each is doing the will of God. '
feel', they say 'that the spirit guides and directs me'.

A credible source of revelation is imperative. Throughout history
Allah has selected particular individuals to convey His message, to
receive His revelation and to exemplify it for mankind. For some of
these prophets, holy books or scriptures were given revealing Allah'
commands and guidance. For most of you the names of these
prophets found in the Qur'an will sound familiar: Noah, Abraham,
Ishmael, Isaac, Jacob, Joseph, Moses, David, Solomon, John the
Baptist, Jesus and, finally, the last prophet, Muhammad, peace be
upon them all. These prophets carried the same basic message: 'No
an apostle did We send before you without this inspiration sent by
Us to him: that there is no god but I; therefore worship and serve
Me' (al Anbiyā 21:25). Further, the Qur'an insists on calling all those
prophets Muslims, because a Muslim is one who submits to the will
of Allah. Their followers are called Muslims as well. Thus it is an
article of faith for a Muslim to believe in all these prophets. Indeed
Muslims are warned that anyone who accepts some prophets and

rejects others in fact rejects them all. For a Muslim, to believe in Moses while rejecting Jesus or Muhammad is against the very teaching of Moses. And to believe in Jesus but reject Moses or Muhammad is to violate what Moses, Jesus and Muhammad stood for. For a Muslim to believe in Muhammad and reject either Moses or Jesus is to violate his own Holy Book. 'Those who deny Allah and His apostles, and [those who] wish to separate Allah from His apostles, saying: "We believe in some but reject others", and [those who] wish to take a course mid-way. They are in truth [equally] unbelievers and We have prepared for unbelievers a humiliating punishment' (al-Nisa' 4:150–1). Recognition of all prophets is an article of faith, not a mere social courtesy or diplomatic statement. I do hope that with open minds, open hearts and further careful, honest study there may be more such mutual recognition.

V THE SPECIAL ROLE OF MUHAMMAD

But why do Muslims in their testimony of faith say, 'I bear witness that there is no god but Allah and that Muhammad is His messenger'? Does that mean that they in fact reject other prophets? Indeed, the special role played by Muhammad as the seal and last of all the prophets puts the Muslim in the position whereby honouring Muhammad implies honouring those who came before him as well. Muslims are warned not to make fanatical or parochial distinctions between prophets (al-Baqarah 2:285). But the Qur'an also says that Allah has favoured some prophets with more significant gifts or roles than others (Al-Isrā' 17:55). All are brothers, although the only prophet with the universal mission to all humankind is Muhammad, peace be upon Him (al-Furqaan 25:11). The Muslim believes not only that Muhammad is a brother to Jesus, Moses, Abraham and other prophets, but the Qur'an states in clear terms that the advent of Muhammad was foretold by previous prophets, including Moses and Jesus, peace be upon them (al-Araf 7:157, al-Saff 61:6). Even the Bible in its present form clearly foretells the advent of the Prophet Muhammad (e.g., Genesis 21:13, 18, Deuteronomy 18:18 and 33:1–3, Isaiah 11:1–4, 21:13–17, 42:1–13 and others).

To the Muslim, the Qur'an contains the words of Allah directly and verbatim revealed to Prophet Muhammad, peace be upon Him. Many confuse the Qur'an with the 'Hadīth', or sayings, of the Prophet. The Hadīth is quite separate from the Qur'an. The latter

was dictated to Muhammad word for word through the Angel
Gabriel and immediately memorised and put down in writing. It is
important to emphasise that the Qur'an was neither written nor
composed by Muhammad, peace be upon Him. To hold such a view
would contradict what the Qur'an says of itself and of Muhammad
that the prophet is not speaking on his own but only transmitting
the revelation dictated to him by the Angel Gabriel. To suggest that
the Qur'an borrowed from or copied from previous revelations, be
it the Bible or otherwise, is, for a Muslim, an accusation of 'prophetic
plagiarism', a contradiction in terms. The fact that there are similarities between the Qur'an and previous scriptures is simply
explained by the fact that He Who spoke through those earlier
prophets is He Who revealed the Qur'an to Muhammad, the one
and only true God, Allah. However, the Qur'an is the last revealed
Holy Book, which supersedes previous scriptures and the only one
still available in the exact words and language uttered by Prophet
Muhammad.

VI ACCOUNTABILITY AND SALVATION

We have talked about Allah, about the human and about the
relationship between them. What about accountability? How can we
humans, from the Islamic perspective, overcome 'sin'? The Qur'an
teaches that life is a test, that earthly life is temporary (al-Mulk
67:2). The Muslim believes that there is reward and punishment,
that there is life hereafter and that reward or punishment do not
necessarily wait until the day of Judgement, but start immediately
after burial. The Muslim believes in resurrection, accountability and
the day of Judgement.

   To a Muslim, to demand perfection in order to gain salvation is
not practical. It is demanding the impossible and is unjust. Islam
teaches a person to be humble and to learn that we cannot achieve
salvation by our own righteousness. The reconciliation of the 'sinful'
human with Allah is contingent on three elements: the most
important is the Grace, Mercy and Generosity of Allah. Then there
are good deeds and correct belief. Correct belief and good deeds
are prerequisites for God's Grace and Forgiveness and for rising
above our common shortcomings. How can sin be washed away?
The Qur'an gives the prescription: 'If anyone does evil or wrongs
his own soul, but afterwards seeks Allah's forgiveness, he will find

Allah is Oft-Forgiving, Most Merciful' (al-Nisā' 4:110). Another moving passage reads, 'Those things that are good remove evil deeds' (Hūd 11:114). Islam teaches repentance, stopping evil ways, feeling sorry for what one has done and determining to follow the path of Allah as much as humanly possible. The Muslim does not believe in the necessity of the shedding of blood, much less innocent blood, to wash away sins. He believes that Allah is not interested in blood or sacrifice, but in sincere repentance. The Qur'an puts it clearly: 'But My Mercy extends to all things' (al-A'raf 7:156).

VII THE APPLIED ASPECT

How about the application? Are we just talking theology? Since the human is Allah's trustee, it would be inconsistent for a Muslim to separate the various aspects of life, the spiritual and the material, state and religion. We hear a lot about the 'five pillars of Islam', but they are often presented as the whole of Islam, many times in a shallow way. They are not the whole of Islam any more than one can claim to have a functional house composed exclusively of five concrete pillars. You also need the ceiling, walls, tables, windows and other things. As the mathematicians put it, it is a necessary but not a sufficient condition. The five pillars of Islam (the testimony of faith, the five daily prayers, fasting, charity, pilgrimage) are presented by most writers as matters of formal ritual. Even the pillar that is liable to appear ritualistic – daily prayers – is a purely spiritual act involving much more than simply getting up and down. It has social and political lessons to teach the Muslim. What may appear as separate compartments of life simply does not exist for the Muslim. A Muslim does not say, 'This is business and this is moral'. Moral, spiritual, economic, social and governmental are interrelated, because everything, including Caesar, belongs to Allah and to Allah alone.

VIII CONCLUSION

In conclusion and against this background, what is the implication for the Muslims in their attitudes toward non-Muslims? To start with, and we must be frank about it, the Qur'an makes it incumbent on the Muslim to convey Allah's message in its final form, the Qur'an, to all humanity. We are not talking here about conversion. I do not like that word. Indeed, to turn to Islam, the religion of all the prophets in its final form, is not to turn one's back on the preceding prophets. It is an augmentation, rather than a conversion, because it does not involve changing one's basic spiritual nature. In the Qur'an, pure human nature is a 'Muslim nature', which knows its Lord and wishes to submit to Him. The Qur'an states, 'Let there be no compulsion in religion' (al-Baqarah 2:256). My substitute for the term 'conversion' is 'reversion', in the sense of a return to the pure monotheism in which we were all created. The Muslim is thus taught to be tolerant towards others. Indeed, the Qur'an not only prohibits compulsion in religion, but it prohibits aggression as well, although it allows defence: 'Fight in the cause of Allah those who fight you, but commit no aggression; for Allah loves not transgressors' (al-Baqarah 2:190).

In addition, we find that within this broad rule of dealing with non-Muslims, 'the People of the Book' is a special term accorded to Jews and Christians in the Qur'an. Why 'People of the Book'? Because the Muslim makes a clear distinction between a polytheist or an atheist and those who follow the prophets who originally received revelations from Allah. Even though a Muslim might point out areas of theological difference, we still believe in the divine origin of those revelations in their 'original' forms.

How should a Muslim treat these 'People of the Book'? Says the Qur'an: 'Allah forbids you not, with regard to those who fight you not for [your] Faith nor drive you out of your homes, from dealing kindly and justly with them: for Allah loves those who are just. Allah only forbids you, with regard to those [others] who fight you for [your] Faith, and drive you out of your homes and support [others] in driving you out, from turning to them [for friendship and protection]. It is such as turn to them [in these circumstances], that do wrong' (al-Mumtahanah 60:8–9).

In the world today all believers in Allah are facing common dangers: atheism, materialism, secularism and moral decay. We must work together. Allah says in the Qur'an: 'If Allah had so willed, He would have made you a single People, but His Plan is to test you in what He has given you. So strive as in a race in all virtues. The return of you all is to Allah; it is He that will show you the truth of the matter in which you dispute' (al-Mā'idah; 5:51).

I hope, feel and trust that there is sufficient common ground for Muslims and others to meet, understand each other, join hands and move together in the Path of Truth, Peace and Justice, the Path of Allah.

Thank you very much for your patience and may peace be with you.

Note

1. This is a slightly revised version of a pamphlet published by the Islamic Information Foundation, Halifax, Nova Scotia, Canada.

10 Trinity and Incarnation in the Light of Religious Pluralism

John Hick

First let me indicate my angle of approach. This is a pluralistic view of the two related notions of revelation and salvation. Presenting this from a Christian standpoint, it seems to me that the relationship to God reflected in the scriptures, the worship, and the saints of the Jewish and Muslim traditions, and in the ordinary life of Jews and Muslims under the influence of their faith, leads one to conclude that Judaism and Islam are, like Christianity, responses to divine revelation and contexts within which the transformation of human existence from self-centredness to Reality-centredness, which we call salvation, is taking place. Further, this salvific transformation seems to occur to about the same extent within each of the three traditions. For neither contemporary observation nor historical memory supports the view that one of these streams of religious life and thought constitutes a manifestly more efficacious context of salvation than the others. I therefore conclude that our respective sets of scripture, theology and tradition form 'lenses' through which God is variously experienced; and that our religious cultures (comprising modes of worship, social organisations, life-styles, forms of art, etc.) embody our differing human responses to God as thus conceived and experienced. Accordingly, our religions have to be seen as products of both divine and human influences – God's presence to a human group, and that group's particular human characteristics, including its basic geographical situation, its language and thought-forms, its cultural inheritance and its historical memories – as all affecting its awareness of God. The three religions, as earthly realities, thus represent responses to the one transcendent God from within different though related strands of the one human story; and so far as we can tell none of them, taken as a totality, has been markedly more successful or markedly less successful than the others in bringing about the redemption of human life in self-giving to God.

This pluralistic understanding stands in contrast to the exclusivist or absolutist conception that there is only one authentic divine revelation and responding community – namely one's own – so that other religious traditions must be inferior and their adherents must have a second-class status in the eyes of God.

The pluralist vision is to be found at some point within each religion, though it has generally received much less emphasis than the contrary self-understanding of each tradition as uniquely superior to all others. An acceptance of pluralism is perhaps most evident in Islam, with its doctrine of Jews and Christians as fellow People of the Book. Behind this is the basic Qur'anic insistence that 'To God belong the East and the West: withersoever ye turn, there is the Presence [or Face] of God'[1] and that 'God doth guide whom He will to His Light'.[2] The Hebrew scriptures likewise contain an universal and implicitly pluralistic strand. Their sacred story begins with God' creation of the first forefather of the whole human race, and shows through the ages God's fashioning of Israel to serve humanity. 'I will give you', says the Lord, 'as a light to the nations, that my salvation may reach to the end of the earth'.[3] Again, a pluralistic conception is implicit in the statement that 'from the rising of the sun to it setting my name is great among the nations, and in every place incense is offered to my name, and a pure offering'[4] – a pluralism which becomes explicit in the oft-cited Rabbinic dictum that 'The righteous of all nations will have a place in the world to come'.

Christianity, too, has its universal conception that the divine *logos* or thought, that was lived out in human terms in the life of Jesus, was 'the true light that enlightens every man'.[5] According some of the church Fathers regarded the 'righteous of all nations' as in effect Christians without knowing it – in Karl Rahner's contemporary phrase, 'anonymous Christians'. Thus St Augustine said that 'From the beginning of the human race, whosoever believed in [Christ] and lived in a pious and just manner according to his precepts, was undoubtedly saved by him . . . The true religion, although formerly set forth and practiced under other names and with other symbolic rites than it now has . . . is one and the same in both periods'.[6] This was of course by no means the full pluralistic conception. But in our own day a number of Christian theologians have gone on to affirm explicitly the independent reality of salvation within the other great world traditions.

When as a Jew or a Christian or a Muslim one comes to accept that the revelation in response to which one is trying to live is not the only authentic and saving revelation and that the other two faiths are also, and equally with one's own, contexts of salvation, one will naturally emphasise the universal and pluralistic aspects of one's religious inheritance and de-emphasise its exclusivist themes. When such emphasising and de-emphasising occur sufficiently widely, they must gradually affect the 'shape' of the tradition. The exclusivist element will cease to be a dominant influence, though remaining as an important aspect of the history of the tradition. So far as Christianity is concerned, such large morphological changes have occurred more than once in the past – for example in the adoption of neo-Platonism in the early centuries, and in the nineteenth-century acceptance of modern science and the scientific study of the scriptures. I believe that in our own time we are living through an equally major but equally necessary development in the acceptance of religious pluralism. In this development, Christianity is beginning to move from the old perception of itself as the one and only true religion to a new perception of itself, in a global context, as one among several. This enlarged vision will inevitably affect the shape of Christianity's theological self-understanding. And the same holds, though possibly with less extensive theoretical consequences, for Judaism and Islam.

It is not for the adherents of any one of our three faiths to try to tell the adherents of another how to contribute to the development of their own tradition in a pluralistic direction. We each have to work within our own community, though with an interested eye upon parallel developments in the others. I shall therefore confine my recommendations to Christianity, whilst at the same time relating them to relevant aspects of the other two Abrahamic faiths.

I turn then, from this point of view, to the doctrine of the Trinity. The first thing that has to be said is that there is no such thing as *the* Christian doctrine of the Trinity. There is a range of trinitarian theories all interpreting the same traditional language – namely that God is a trinity of Father, Son and Holy Spirit, three in one and one in three. The interpretations fall into two main groups, according to whether or not the 'Persons' of the Trinity are thought of as persons or selves in the sense of distinct centres of consciousness and will. If they are regarded as three persons in this sense, we have what has been called a 'social' conception of the Trinity. This was developed above all by the Cappadocian Fathers of the fourth century, one of whom, Gregory of Nazianzus, proposed the analogy between Adam, Eve and their son Seth, who were three and yet shared the same human nature, with the divine Father, Son and Spirit, who are three whilst sharing the same divine nature. This understanding of the members of the Trinity as persons in a sense analogous to that in which we speak of human persons, has continued down to our own day; so that a contemporary Roman Catholic theologian could write last year that 'the Trinity is a society of interdependent "persons" in the sense of "centres of activity," living a life of absolute love'.[7]

It is this kind of social conception of the Trinity that Jews and Muslims have seen as constituting an incipient, or even an explicit, tritheism. For the doctrine, interpreted socially, points to a family of three divine persons related together in so intimate a community of mutual love that they can be said to be one in three and three in one. A major attraction of this view is that it makes it possible to think of God, 'prior to' and independently of creation, as being love; for the three constituent Persons of the Godhead eternally love one another. But despite its attractions it does indeed seem clear that this is a virtually tritheistic conception. However, Tritheism is not what Christianity has intended; and the social understanding of the Trinity should I think therefore be seen as a picture version, appealing to the anthropomorphising imagination. For it invites visual presentation on canvasses and stained-glass windows, and dramatisation in literature, as for example in some of the medieval mystery plays.

Because it can so readily be assimilated by the imagination it will no doubt persist indefinitely at the popular levels of the Christian tradition. But it does not, I believe, constitute a theologically viable understanding of the trinitarian idea. I am therefore in agreement with Hans Küng when he says that in popular Christian belief 'the Trinity is largely understood in a tritheistic sense. Three "persons" are understood in modern psychological terms as three "self-consciousnesses", three "subjects": that is to say, essentially three God's.[8] I also agree with him when he lays it down as a prerequisite for any new attempts at trinitarian interpretation that 'The mono-theistic faith taken over from Israel and held in common with Islam must never be abandoned in any doctrine of the Trinity. There is no God but God'.[9]

The other kind of trinitarian doctrine – to which we may now turn – understands *persona* in its original sense of a role – deriving from its designation of the mask worn by an actor on the ancient Roman stage, indicating the part that he was playing. For this type of trinitarianism God is unambiguously one, but is known to us in the three roles or relationships of Creator (God the Father), Redeemer (God the Son) and Sanctifier (God the Spirit). Father, Son and Spirit are thus not three distinct but interrelated individuals who could be said to love and communicate with one another, but symbolise three aspects of the divine nature as differentiated from our human standpoint. God is one and undivided in the eternal divine nature, but is humanly experienced, and therefore humanly thought, in these three ways; or again, the doctrine of the Trinity expresses the richness and versatility of the divine reality in relationship to humanity.

Understood in this way the threefold Christian naming of God does not differ in principle from the ninety-ninefold Qur'anic naming of God. For the ninety-nine Beautiful Names also point to aspects of the infinitely rich divine nature as revealed to our creaturely understanding. One could thus group the ninety-nine Names into three columns corresponding approximately to the three trinitarian names. To give just a few examples, the aspect of God as sovereign creator and sustainer of the universe, which in Christian language is symbolised by the name Father, is symbolised in Qur'anic language as, for example, *Al-Malik* (the Sovereign Lord), *Al-Mutakabbir* (the Majestic), *Al-Khāliq* (the Creator), *Al-'Alī* (the Most High), *Al-Muqīt* (the Maintainer); and the aspect of God as gracious love and compassion, symbolised in Christian language by the name Son, is symbolised in Qur'anic language as, for example, *Ar-Raḥīm* (the Merciful), *As-Salām* (The Source of Peace), *Al-Ghaffār* (The Forgiver), *Al-Ḥalīm* (The Forbearing One), *Al-Ghafūr* (The All-Forgiving); whilst the aspect of God as guide, inspirer and life-giver, symbolised in Christian language by the name of the Holy Spirit, is symbolised in Qur'anic language as, for example, *Al-Fattāh* (The Opener), *Al-Latīf* (The Subtle One), *Al-Mujīb* (The Responsive), *Al Hādī* (The Guide), *Al-Muhyī* (The Giver of Life). Without developing this further here, it can I think be shown that the two schemas cover essentially the same ground. They are like two different maps of the world, drawn in different projections but both showing the same seas and continents and islands, and both making possible successful navigation. The many-faceted nature of God as humanly perceived is also acknowledged in the Jewish scriptures and liturgies. God is the Holy one, King of the universe, the Beneficent one, our King, Father, Lord, Deliverer, Refuge, Creator, Shepherd, Protector, Stronghold. He is Lord of wonders, Author of peace, Shield of Abraham, Maker of heaven and earth, Master of all, the

Just, the Mighty . . . This multiplicity of names is not however systematised or built into a doctrine. The divine aspects are not compacted into three, as in Christianity, nor expanded into ninety-nine as in Islam; but nevertheless they are fully reflected in Jewish experience. Clearly, however, these equivalences with Christianity hold only if we interpret trinitarian language as referring not to three divine selves or subjects but to three divine roles in relation to humanity.

We also need to take account of the history of the trinitarian doctrine. It is I think agreed today by virtually all New Testament scholars that it was not part of Jesus's own teaching about God. He himself thought of God in Jewish monotheistic terms, which he developed in the image of God as *abba*, loving father. Those who identified Jesus as the expected Messiah and true king of Israel called him 'son of God' in the sense in which the ancient Hebrew kings had been called 'son of God'. This is (in terms of our modern distinctions) a metaphorical sense. However in later Christian construction, as Hebrew poetry hardened into Latin prose, the metaphorical 'son of God' became the literal 'God the Son', the eternal pre-existent Second Person who is of one substance with God the Father. But if at Caesarea Phillipi, when it was put to Jesus that he was the messiah, it had instead been put to him that he was the Second Person of a divine Trinity, he might well have replied as he did on the same occasion to another seductive misunderstanding.

The trinitarian doctrine took some time to develop. There are a number of uninterpreted triadic formulae in the New Testament referring to the Father and the Son and the Spirit; but the word *trias* was apparently first used by Tertullian in the third century; whilst the doctrine as we now know it was established, as the outcome of intense debates and controversies, in the fourth century. The motivation for its development was not so much to express a claimed metaphysical insight into the inner nature of God as to provide a protective envelope for something else, namely the doctrine of the Incarnation. This doctrine had been implicit in the Fourth Gospel at the end of the first century and was explicitly affirmed, against alternative possibilities, by the Council of Nicea in the fourth century. Jesus, it was held, had in some sense been God living a human life. But it became evident that if one says this, one must say more. For it was also true that God was at the same time 'in heaven' receiving prayer and ruling the universe. And so God must be at least two realities, in heaven and on earth, namely the Father and the Son;

and then the third category of the Spirit acknowledged comprehensively all the other ways in which God is manifested to human beings. Thus a trinitarian – or at least a binitarian – conception was required by the idea of divine incarnation.

We may now move, then, from the Trinity to the incarnational doctrine. This also took some time to develop. The experience of the earliest Christians probably centred upon a transforming awareness of living in the divine presence, and of being the objects of God's limitless love and being confronted by his total claim – this awareness being mediated to them by Jesus out of his own immensely powerful and all-controlling consciousness of God as his heavenly Father. In this new awareness they were at peace with God, forgiven and accepted, filled with the joy of a new spirit within them, and empowered to live as heralds of the coming Kingdom. For in Jesus's presence they were conscious in a fresh way of existing in the presence of God – not that they imagined that he was himself God, but that he was so fully open to God, so fully God's servant and representative (and thus, in the Hebraic sense, God's son) that through him God became challengingly and transformingly real to them. This, or something like this, was, I believe, the experiential reality that became philosophised during the next three hundred years in terms of the hellenic concept of *ousia* to produce the doctrine, which we inherit today, that Jesus had two natures, one human and the other divine, his divine nature being of one *ousia* or substance with God the Father. This was a speculative philosophical construction which no one has in fact professed to understand – indeed every attempt to spell it out intelligibly has had to be rejected as heresy – and which has therefore been revered for centuries as a divine Mystery.

But whilst the theological dogma is an impenetrable mystery its poetic, or mythological, expression has always made a powerful appeal to the Christian imagination, bringing warmth and light to millions of lives. This is the mythic story of God sending his only Son down from heaven to earth to be born as a human baby, to die as a sacrifice for human sin, and then to return to life and ascend back into heaven. This story has gathered around itself the rich artistic and cultural elaborations both of Easter and, more universally, of Christmas. Here the ancient themes (found in the mythology of several other cultures) of an annunciation to the favoured mother, the babe in the manger, angels appearing to shepherds, and wise men from the east following a star, are celebrated in medieval carols and modern oratorios, and now in the nineteenth- and twentieth-century Dickensian Christmas, so fully exploited in our own society as a great commercial opportunity. But despite its secularisation this mythic picture of the divine Son descending to earth at Christmas continues in its many-faceted beauty, and its perennial value as a festival of the family, to fill the imaginations and uplift the spirits of Christian people. As a powerful focus of awareness of God's love, and as a time of mutual caring and family unity, Christmas is a major religious event which should be cherished and if possible rescued from its current commercialisation.

What has to be questioned is not the mythology, with its artistic expressions and its joyous celebration, but the theological theory associated with it since it was elevated in the fourth century to the status of dogma. For although the dogma of an unique divine incarnation in Jesus of Nazareth developed as an internal Christian understanding of the Church's founding event, and did not originally have in view the problem of religious pluralism, yet the dogma does in fact have far-reaching implications for the Christian attitude to the people of other faiths. If God has revealed himself in the person of Jesus, all other revelations are thereby marginalised as inferior and secondary. Indeed their effect can only be to draw people in a different direction, away from God's direct self-disclosure in Christ. For if the Creator has personally come down to earth and founded his own religion, embodied in the Christian Church, he must surely want all human beings to become part of that Church. Indeed it would seem to follow that sooner or later they *must* become part of it if they are to participate in the eternal life of the redeemed. Thus the doctrine that Jesus was none other than God himself – or, more precisely, that he was the Second Person of the divine Trinity living a human life – leads by an inevitable logic to Christian absolutism, a logic that was manifested historically in the development of the dogma *Extra ecclesiam nulla salus* (Outside the Church, no salvation).

Today many Christian theologians are unhappy with this implication and tend in practice to recognise the other great world religions as alternative spheres of salvation. Most of them however do not feel able to change their theological theories to fit their new insight and practice. Instead they indulge in secondary adjustments – such as the suggestion that devout people of other traditions have an 'implicit' Christian faith, or are 'anonymous Christians', or are saved by Christ without knowing the source of their salvation – which are undoubtedly sincerely intended to avoid the traditional Christian exclusivism but which have the effect only of accentuating the dilemma which it creates. We thus exist in a time of tension between traditional formulations and new spiritual and moral perceptions.

I believe that in this situation a way forward is in fact already available. It depends upon recognising that Christian theology does not consist in an unchanging body of divinely guaranteed truths, but is the ongoing human attempt to understand the implications of Christian religious experience, and that this attempt has taken and must continue to take different forms in different regions and phrases of human culture. Within this changing scene, a new form of Christo-logical understanding – though with roots both in the nineteenth century and in the Patristic period – has emerged. It has not been developed to meet the issue of religious pluralism, but has been prompted by the internal Christian critique of the concept of sub-stance, in terms of which the ancient Christologies were cast, and by the results of the modern study of the scriptures and of Christian origins. But although not designed to meet the need for a non-exclusivist understanding of Christ, the new type of Christology does nevertheless in principle make this possible.

I am thinking here of the kind of Christology found in the work of such theologians as, for example, Donald Baillie, in *God Was In Christ* (1948) – described by Rudolf Bultmann as 'the most significant book of our time in the field of Christology' – and Geoffrey Lampe, in *God as Spirit* (1977). Baillie, who was a Presbyterian, was professor of Dogmatics at Aberdeen University, and Lampe, who was an Anglican, was Regius professor of Divinity at Cambridge University, and both were highly respected scholars and churchmen.

Baillie proposed that we should understand incarnation in terms of what he called the paradox of grace. This is the paradoxical fact that when we do God's will it is true both that we are acting freely and responsibly, and also that God, in his supernatural grace, is acting through us. The paradox is summed up in St Paul's words, 'it was not I, but the grace of God which is with me'.[10] As Baillie says, the essence of the paradox

lies in the conviction which a Christian man possesses, that every good thing in him, every good thing he does, is somehow not wrought by himself but by God. This is a highly paradoxical convic-tion, for in ascribing all to God it does not abrogate human person-ality nor disclaim personal responsibility. Never is human action more truly and fully personal, never does the agent feel more perfectly free, than in those moments of which he can say as a Christian that whatever good was in them was not his but God's.[11]

Baillie now uses this paradox of grace as the clue to the yet greater paradox of the incarnation: that the life of Jesus was an authentically human life and yet that in and through that life God was at work on earth. Baillie says:

What I wish to suggest is that this paradox of grace points the way more clearly and makes a better approach than anything else in our experience to the mystery of the Incarnation itself; that this paradox in its fragmentary form in our own Christian lives is a reflection of that perfect union of God and man in the Incarnation on which our whole Christian life depends, and may therefore be our best clue to the understanding of it. In the New Testament we see the man in whom God was incarnate surpassing all other men in refusing to claim anything for Himself independently and ascribing all the goodness to God. We see Him also desiring to take up other men into His own close union with God, that they might be as He was. And if these men, entering in some small measure through Him into that union, experience the paradox of grace for themselves in fragmentary ways, and are constrained to say, 'It was not I but God', may not this be a clue to the understanding of that perfect life in which the paradox is complete and absolute, that life of Jesus which, being the perfection of humanity, is also, and even in a deeper and prior sense, the very life of God Himself? If the paradox is a reality in our poor imperfect lives at all, so far as there is any good in them, does not the same or a similar paradox, taken at the perfect and absolute pitch, appear as the mystery of the Incarnation?[12]

In other words, the union of divine and human action which occurs whenever God's grace works effectively in a man's or a woman's life was operating to a total extent in the life of Jesus.

Now Baillie's suggestion – which has its roots in the thought of St Augustine, and earlier in Origen, and in Theodore of Mopsuestia and others of the later Antiochene school – offers some degree of understanding of what it means to say that the life of Jesus was a divine as well as a human event. But of course in making the idea of incarnation intelligible in this way Baillie has to discard the traditional Chalcedonian language of Jesus having two natures, one human and the other divine, and of his being in his divine nature of one substance with the Father. This language has long since lost its plausibility for the modern mind, and the kind of reinterpretation that Baillie offers is an attempt to bring the doctrine of the Incarnation to life in our time, giving it meaning as a truth which connects with our human experience and which is at least to some extent intelligible in contemporary terms. For whilst few people today use the ancient concept of 'substance', or find the idea of a person with two natures other than grotesque, all Christians have some experience and appreciation of the reality of divine grace operating in human life. Further, they can connect this reality with the extraordinary events of the New Testament.

In an essentially similar way, Lampe uses as his clue or 'model' for the understanding of Christ, the activity within human life of the Holy Spirit, the Spirit of God. And 'the Spirit of God', he says, 'is to be understood, not as referring to a divine hypostasis distinct from God the Father and God the Son or Word, but as indicating God himself as active towards and in his human creation'.[13] The principal activity of God as Spirit in relation to humanity is inspiration; and accordingly, the Christology which Lampe presents is 'a Christology of inspiration'.[14] For

the concept of the inspiration and indwelling of man by God as Spirit is particularly helpful in enabling us to speak of God's continuing creative relationship towards human persons and of his active presence in Jesus as the central and focal point within this relationship.[15]

Again, 'The use of this concept enables us to say that God indwelt and motivated the human spirit of Jesus in such a way that in him, uniquely, the relationship for which man is intended by his Creator was fully realized'.[16] On this view, the Spirit of God has always been active within the human spirit, inspiring men and women to open themselves freely to the divine presence and to respond in their lives to the divine purpose. Indeed, 'God has always been incarnate in his human creatures, forming their spirits from within and revealing himself in and through them'.[17] We must accordingly 'speak of this continuum as a single creative and saving activity of God the Spirit towards, and within, the spirit of man, and of his presence in the person of Jesus as a particular moment within that continuous

creativity'.[18] For 'a union of personal deity with human personality
can only be a perfected form of inspiration'.[19]

Both Baillie and Lampe assumed in traditional Christian fashion
the 'uniqueness' of Christ; for they held that in Jesus the paradox
of grace was 'complete and absolute' or that the working of the Spirit
in Jesus was 'a perfected form of inspiration'. And they accordingly
assumed the centrality and superiority of Christianity within God's
providence. The major new departure which they made (which they
however may not have been conscious of making) is that the dogma
of the unique superiority of Christ and of the Christian religion does
not follow from the idea of divine incarnation as such, but becomes
an historical judgement concerning the degree of grace or of inspiration to be discerned in the life of Jesus in comparison with other
divinely graced and inspired human beings. For if, with Baillie and
Lampe, we see in the life of Jesus a supreme instance of that fusion
of divine grace/inspiration with creaturely freedom that occurs in all
authentic human response and obedience to God, than we are
speaking of a supremacy that could be established only by comparative evidence. We are no longer speaking of an intersection of the
divine and the human which occurs, by definition, only in one unique
case, but of one which occurs, in different ways and degrees, in all
human openness and response to the divine initiative. The primacy
of the Christian revelation thus no longer follows as a logical
corollary from either Baillie's or Lampe's Christology. To see Jesus
as exemplifying in a special degree the paradox of grace, or the
inspiration of God the Spirit, is thus far to leave open the further
question as to how this particular exemplification stands in relation
to other exemplifications, such as those that lie at the basis of some
of the other great religious traditions. Baillie and Lampe both
believed that the reality of grace/inspiration in the life of Jesus was
unique because total and absolute. But the point that I want to stress
is that this belief is no longer, in the light of this type of Christology,
a necessary inference from the concept of incarnation itself, but
must be a judgement based upon historical evidence. And the main
question that arises, for any Christian who is familiar with the
modern scholarly study of the New Testament, is whether we have
a sufficiently complete knowledge of the historical Jesus to be able
to make such absolute statements as that his entire life was a perfect
exemplification of the paradox of grace or of divine inspiration.

In the kind of Christology exemplified in Baillie's and Lampe's
work – the basic ground plan of which is evident in the work of both

the older liberal theologians, such as Harnack, and of such recent and contemporary Protestants as the New Testament scholar John Knox and the systematic theologians Maurice Wiles and Normal Pittenger and also, though much more guardedly and obscurely, in the work of such Roman Catholic thinkers as Karl Rahner, Edward Schillebeeck and Hans Küng – there is, I suggest, the basis for an authentically theocentric development of Christianity which is compatible with genuine religious pluralism.

Let me end by raising a question that is very naturally asked from a traditional Christian point of view. I have been suggesting that we should not insist that Jesus was literally God incarnate, but should see him as a human being who was so startlingly open and responsive to God's presence that God was working through him for the salvation of many; and that whether he was totally and absolutely open to God, or to the divine Reality, and how he compares in this respect with the other founders of great religious traditions, are questions beyond the scope of our very fragmentary historical data. But why then should one be a Christian, rather than a Muslim or a Jew, or indeed a Buddhist or a Hindu? I would say that for one who has been born into Christianity, or into a culture in which Christianity was the only religious option effectively presented to one, and who has been spiritually formed largely by the influences of the Christian tradition, Christianity will normally provide the best framework for one's relationship to God; and that this constitutes a good reason to be a Christian rather than an adherent of some other faith. One will then understand the traditional Christian language, in which Jesus is hailed as the Son of God, Word Incarnate, King of Kings, etc. as a form of the essentially poetic language of love. 'She is the most wonderful girl in the world' expresses a personal response and commitment; it is not intended to report a claim which presupposes an objective comparison with every other girl in the world. Likewise 'Christ is my lord and saviour' expresses a personal response and a commitment to discipleship. It means that, having been born where and when I was, it has been largely through the New Testament memory of Jesus that I have begun to become open to God; that Jesus's life and teaching continue to challenge and inspire me; and that the community of his disciples forms a spiritual home for me. This does not however exclude there being others who have been and are being reached by God in other ways within other religious traditions; nor does it exclude my being also illuminated by light coming through those other streams of religious life. For, in the words of a servant of God who lived within one of our traditions but whose thought has universal validity, 'The lamps are different, but the Light is the same'.

Notes and References

1. *Qur'an*, II, 115.
2. *Qur'an*, XXIV, 35.
3. Isaiah 49:6.
4. Malachi 1:11.
5. John 1:9.
6. Epistles, 102:12.
7. Illtyd Trethowan, *Religious Studies*, vol. 19, (September 1983), p. 322.
8. *On Being a Christian*, Edward Quinn (trans) (London: Collins and New York: Doubleday, 1977) p. 474.
9. *On Being a Christian*, p. 476.
10. I Cor. 15:10.
11. Donald Baillie, *God Was In Christ* (New York: Scribner, 1948) p. 114.
12. Baillie, *God Was In Christ*, pp. 117–8.
13. Geoffrey Lampe, *God as Spirit* (Oxford: Clarendon Press, 1977) p. 11.
14. Lampe, *God as Spirit*, p. 96.
15. Lampe, *God as Spirit*, p. 34.
16. Lampe, *God as Spirit*, p. 11.
17. Lampe, *God as Spirit*, p. 23.
18. Lampe, *God as Spirit*, p. 100.
19. Lampe, *God as Spirit*, p. 12.

A Muslim Response to John Hick: Trinity and Incarnation in the Light of Religious Pluralism

Muzammil H. Siddiqi

John Hick has presented a very clear and thorough pluralistic position and has provided us with important insights for a theology of pluralism. He is unhappy with what he calls 'secondary adjustments' offered by some Christian theologians who in their attempt to accommodate other religions or people of faith in other traditions were willing to call them 'anonymous Christians' or 'saved by Christ without knowing the source of their salvation' or 'implicit Christian faith' (p. 204).

In his attempt to provide a basis for pluralism, Hick sets aside the questions of truth. What is truth? What is its source? Is truth available to human beings? Are all claims to truth of the same value? What is the criterion for judgment? Hick takes the position that all religions are human responses to the One transcendent God. Religious traditions, he holds, constitute 'lenses' by which people have tried to view the Reality, and to be sure these 'lenses' are man-made.

I see this view in its enthusiasm for pluralism as failing to come to terms with two quite important issues that must be dealt with in our religious discourse. Are all religions human responses to God or did God also take any initiative in revealing Himself, self-disclosing, speaking, commanding the human beings? Hick, probably, would say that either God never took such initiative or, for the good cause of peace and pluralism, let us not emphasise this. But I as a Muslim who holds the prophetic tradition seriously find this unsatisfactory to say the least.

The second issue that we should discuss is the issue of value. If all religions were mere 'lenses', to use Hick's metaphor, then are they all of the same value? Can we say that some of them are good, clear while others are foggy, distorted? Some are unifocal, others bifocal or trifocal, etc. We must have some principles for judgement and evaluation. We cannot take everything that goes in the name of religion as being of the same value. Hick has proposed only one criterion for value. He says in the first paragraph of his chapter:

> neither contemporary observation nor historical memory supports the view that one of these streams of religious life and thought constitutes a manifestly more efficacious context of salvation than the others.

One, however, may ask, how can or does one know that 'none of them is a more efficacious context of salvation than the others'? What is salvation? Is history enough to prove that? Are there any other sources of knowledge beside history that can help us in this matter?

I must say that I like the spirit of pluralism. I think it is very gracious and charitable, but it must deal with some of these above-mentioned issues, and they should not be pushed aside as mere obscurantism or fundamentalism.

John Hick's section on Trinity and Incarnation is indeed very interesting and useful. Hick's paralleling of the three Persons of the Trinity with the ninety-nine beautiful Names of God is, however, confusing. He says that a scheme can be worked out whereby you can compact these ninety-nine Names 'into three columns corresponding approximately to the three trinitarian names'. In the twelfth century Paul of Antioch tried the same thing to make the Trinity acceptable to Muslims. Many Christian apologists ever since have suggested that the Trinity of Christianity is compatible or analogous to the doctrine of attributes of God in Islam. Harry Wolfson in his article on this subject pointed out that 'No Greek father has so far been discovered who characterised the three Persons by these properties by which they are characterised in the passages quoted from Arabic (Christian) sources' (*Harvard Theological Review* 49 (1956) p. 9).

One question that immediately comes to mind is, why should one force these attributes into three columns, and not four or five or two? Are we trying to force a Christian pattern on them? Is it helpful for Christians or Muslims to make this analogy? I am reminded of a story that I was told by a Christian evangelist. He said that a man was very doubtful of the Trinity and kept on arguing against it the whole day. At night while asleep he saw in his dream three strings over his head. As he looked upward he saw all of them connected to one rope hanging down from the heaven. He woke up confessing the Trinity. I said to my evangelist friend, 'Suppose he had seen four or five strings over his head what would have been his belief?'

In Islam ninety-nine names do not suggest a limit but the infinity of Allah. The number ninety-nine for Allah's names occurs only in Hadith and is not mentioned in the Qur'an. The Prophet spoke about them in the context of prayer. He said that God has many names and that people should invoke these names when praying to Him.

In Islamic theology it is affirmed that attributes do not exist *apart* from the being attributed. Hence, even in prayer one is not allowed to address the attributes (*sifat*) but the attributed being (*mawṣuf*). Thus it is not allowed in Islam to say in prayer, 'O Life of God! Save me', or 'O Merciful! Help me'. This will show the major difference between Islamic attributes and Christian Trinity.

I like John Hick's discussion on Christology. John knows quite well that his book *The Myth of God Incarnate* is very well received by Muslims. The Christology proposed by John Hick can serve as a good subject for dialogue between Muslims and Christians.

11 Three Faiths and Some Common Problems
John A. Hutchison

I

This chapter will explore some problems of religious experience which, while by no means limited to the three monotheistic faiths Judaism, Islam and Christianity, are nonetheless amply illustrated by them. I shall select my illustrations of these problems largely from Christianity, for the reason that this is my tradition. However I invite adherents of the other two faiths represented in this conference to supply their own illustrations. One reason for this procedure is that it is, in the popular phrase, a cheap shot to confess other people's sins. More substantively I will try to show later in this chapter that the problems I shall discuss actually constitute primary evidence for the transcendence of God, which is a common tenet of Judaism, Islam and Christianity.

All of the religious problems or evils to be discussed may validly be regarded as instances of what Reinhold Niebuhr liked to call 'absolutising the relative' which is to say, taking some finite human concern or interest and according it an absolute significance. Such concerns range from allegiance to one's own philosophical or theological system, or even among religious people, giving an absolute allegiance to one's own religious group or theological system.

All such false absolutes constitute what the monotheistic religions call idolatry or the worship of false gods. This concept or category of idolatry is distinctive to the three monotheistic religions, indeed has no precise parallels in the other religious traditions of the world. It derives from what may be called the principle of discontinuity between God and world as God's creation. This principle contrasts with the principle of continuity (or consubstantiality, as John Wilson expressed it in *Before Philosophy*[1]). The latter asserts the continuity of all things, persons and gods as members together of the cosmic order.

This issue is not only theoretical but also thoroughly practical. The service of false absolutes has been the source of a very great amount of human misery. It is probably true that more human beings have been killed by religious fanatics than by all the criminals or gunmen in history. The ultimate form of such fanaticism is holy war, in which in the putative service of God people seek the annihilation of other people. Holy wars have not been limited to the three monotheistic religions (as sometimes claimed by hostile critics); indeed all wars tend to become holy wars, rationalised by whatever symbols for transcendence are available. However it is profoundly ironical that all three monotheistic religions have, in fact, all at one time or another both taught and practiced holy war. This issue is summarily expressed in Reinhold Niebuhr's aphorism, coined during the years when the totalitarianisms of Hitler and Stalin extended over the world. He declared, 'When man plays God he becomes the devil to his fellow-man'.

In alternative formulation, my chapter is an exploration of what the late Morris R. Cohen called 'the dark side of religion'. I propose the thesis that the concept of religion as such is morally and spiritually an ambiguous category. Wilfred Smith and others have advanced the hypothesis that religion as such is theoretically problematic, often misleading the forms of experience it seeks to express. Here I shall argue that it is also practically and existentially equally problematic. More specifically, religious experience falls victim all too easily to superstition, to sentimentality and otherworldliness, and to involvement in injustice. Let us consider these three problems in order.

II

What Niebuhr called the absolute quality or dimension of religious faith can all too easily be misled into irrational or superstitious formulations. I cite as my first example the Creation Research Society of San Diego and its perversion of natural science. But the list is vastly longer than any single instance. New England Puritans burnt people as witches and executed Quaker dissenters. Dostoevsky's Grand Inquisitor was a devout Christian. So too are the parents of the child cancer victim who seek to withhold medical treatment in the expectation of divine intervention. I rest my case on these few illustrations of the long inglorious line of superstitions inspired and supported by religion.

If superstition is one vice of religion, sentimentality and otherworldliness constitute another – different but equally real – vice. By a 'real vice', I mean one which arises out of the real or actual features of religious experience. By 'sentimentality', I mean sentiment unrelated to the context of reality in which it arises. All the great religions of the world contain precious human values or ideals. However the adherents of these traditions often settle for cherishing the ideals apart from any real application to the world. Equally often these values are then projected into a celestial realism unrelated to the dirt and grime of everyday reality. When this occurs, the vice of sentimental otherworldliness takes place.

This point demands careful exposition, for there is a valid sense in which all religious experience claims a transcendent or transworldly reference. We shall presently defend this Archimedean point in religious experience against those modern people who profess no allegiance or loyalty beyond the finite world.

However, by otherworldliness in the negative sense in which I am now using the term, I mean any preoccupation with this transcendent referent of religion which drains away energies desperately needed for the work of the world. I can recall as a small boy in a Presbyterian Sunday School singing a hymn, one stanza of which begins:

> Heaven is my home
> Earth is but a desert drear
> Heaven is my home.

The hymn made me a hypocrite, for what I really wanted was to be outside playing baseball with my friends.

To cite a more serious illustration, the movement of western history known as the Renaissance was in part at least a critical reaction against medieval otherworldliness, in the direction of affirmative concern with the goods of our present life. Against medieval concern with the 'hereafter', the Renaissance was concerned with the 'herein'.

In general terms, it seems to my psychologically and morally wrong to use the transworldly reference of religious experience as a compensatory mechanism for apparently insoluble problems of present human existence. The distinction between a healthy and an unhealthy or neurotic otherworldliness can be put in pragmatic terms. Does this experience enable a person to return to common experience in this world with new energies and new direction, or is its consequence a weaker, less clearly directed person?

The issue of injustice and its relation to religion overlaps the concern with otherworldliness. It was Karl Marx who called religion the 'opium of the people'. We shall presently argue that while indeed much religion is an opiate, there is religion which is not opiate but stimulant. To consider the third issue, namely injustice, it does seem historically true as Marx alleged that tyrannical rulers have always been able, as it were, to hire a chaplain whose function is to inform the masses of people that the ruler has been divinely selected, and that therefore protest or rebellion against the ruler is really against God. Against this traditional pattern in human history, a secular politics is a recent and largely local achievement.

To this recital of the recurrent evils or 'dark side' of religion, I wish to add just two further brief comments which will serve to distinguish my position from that of traditional anti-clerics and secularist critics of religion. The first comment is that my exposition of the evils of religion in these previous paragraphs constitutes not so much a comment on religion as on human nature or the human condition. If the reader questions this, let him observe the re-emergence of many of these same evils in ideologies such as Marxism and secular Humanism which are professedly non-religious. They too have their superstitions and their false absolutes.

My second comment is that *homo sapiens* is *homo religiosus* or the religious animal. At least so far in human history, human beings are children of the Absolute; and denied a true vision of this Reality, they cleave to false absolutes. The human self demands allegiance to values which are bigger and better than one's empirical self. It was Milton's Satan who said, 'I will not serve', and ended in most abject service. Such apparently is the logic of human finitude.

III

These considerations lead us on to the positive tasks of (1) distinguishing low religion and high religion, and (2) distinguishing three main types of religion in ways which will illuminate our present project.

Writing in 1954 in criticism of the kind of popular American Protestantism illustrated by Norman Vincent Peale, Reinhold Niebuhr acerbically remarked: 'There is nothing in the Bible to support the view that religion is necessarily a good thing. Scripture has no axe to grind for religion; on the contrary it is highly suspicious of much that passes for religion'.[2] A few months later he added with equal acidity, 'Religion per se and faith per se are not virtues or the cause of virtue. The question is always what the object of worship is and whether the worship tends to break the pride of the self so that a truer self may arise, either individually or collectively'.[3]

From these trenchant words concerning a particular situation let us extract a basic distinction between high religion and low religion, which can then be generally applied. Niebuhr observed a difference between those forms of religious experience which serve as a facade for human egotism – individual or collective – and those other forms in which the self is placed under transcendent criticism, its pride broken and the way opened to renewal, or to a 'truer self'.

Such, in a word, is the difference between high religion and low religion, and it has many implications and consequences. The first implication is that this distinction cuts across the lines that separate one religious tradition from another. It is a matter of factual observation that there is high religion and low religion in all the various traditions.

From this a still further implication is that if we define salvation as the fulfilment or realisation of true human selfhood, there is then an observable saving or salvific significance in high religion wherever it occurs.

A different kind of implication is that in terms of this distinction the radical criticism of religion launched by such writers as Marx and Freud actually applies to low religion and not to high religion. In their respective descriptions of religious experience, it is always a function of the self or ego. Egotism is at the root of all religion in either the Marxist or the Freudian description. It follows then that if there exists such a thing as high religion in which the human ego is placed under transcendent criticism, this kind of religion simply eludes the Marxian or Freudian criticism.

Still another implication can be drawn from our distinction. This one relates to the theology of Karl Barth. Barth's theology contains a total disjunction between religion and the Christian revelation. The former is the perennial historical effort, as Barth put it, at human self-justification. In terms of Biblical metaphor, it is the human effort to build a tower up to heaven. As such, religion is inherently sinful – or, in Barth's words, religion as a self-centred egotistical human enterprise is the 'working capital of sin'.[4] The similarity of this view to the radical criticisms of religion of Feuerbach and Marx did not escape Barth's notice.

In polar contrast to religion is the conception of revelation or divine self-disclosure, which in Barth's system occurs solely in Jesus Christ. While I wish to reject out of hand this Barthian discontinuity between Christianity and the other religions, I do wish to extract from Barth's thought his distinction between divine revelation or self-disclosure, on the one hand, and human religion on the other hand, the latter defined as the human response to divine revelation. As a theologian influenced by Barth, John Baillie, remarks in *Our Knowledge of God*, 'When God reveals himself to man a characteristic disturbance known as religion is set up in human life'.[5]

(In passing, this conception of divine revelation in contrast to human religion seems congenial to the monotheistic religion of this trialogue. More work would be required to apply it to religious traditions such as Buddhism, Hinduism, and the Confucian tradition of China. But that is another task for another day!)

A further conclusion for the three monotheistic religions is that the evils of human life – and, indeed, especially of human religious life – constitute by themselves a kind of negative evidence for the image and concept of the transcendent God. To recognise egotism as egotism presupposes an Archimedean point from which this acknowledgement is made. Speaking practically, from the viewpoint of actual religious experience in any of our three traditions, it is the experience of human shortcomings and evils which, in important measure, leads us in our various ways to the one God.

IV

The previous section's distinction between divine revelation, on the one hand, and religion on the other as the human response to revelation, enables us also to focus attention upon religion as, in Nietzsche's words a 'human all-too-human' phenomenon. For some of us, it also carries the still further implication of a radical relativising of human religions. In the face of the absoluteness of God, humankind and all of our works, including our religious works, have properly only a finite or relative significance. The 'confessional relativism' of the late Richard Niebuhr is a congenial vehicle for this important distinction.

But let us turn here to the formulation of a working definition of religion. For the full field of all humanity's religions, a further distinction is necessary. The three monotheistic religions all speak of the one God; but there are many religions which speak only of gods and some which do not use this word at all – which are in fact non-theistic. The Jain tradition of India is strictly non-theistic. So is most of Buddhism. Still again the 'Brahman' of Hinduism's central tradition of Vedanta is badly translated as 'God'. Even less adequate is the translation of the Chinese Confucian tradition's *T'ien* or Heaven as God.

If the term and concept of God or gods are not common to all religious experience, the claim to transcendence or transcendent reality does seem to be so. All religious experience makes a claim to transcendence. In passing, the quasi-religious character of Marxism and secular humanism is apparent in their appeal to Humanity. This indeed is their symbolic form for transcendence, comparable to Brahman, Nirvana, or in the case of the monotheistic religions, the one God. For reasons to be given presently, I for one would limit the symbolic form 'God', (capital 'G' and no 's'!) to the three religions of this trialogue.

In these terms, we can understand Paul Tillich's characterisation of religion in *Systematic Theology III* as 'human culture under the aspect of transcendence'.[6] Religion, in this view, consists of any and all aspects of human culture which claim to be responses to what we have called transcendence. Earlier in *Systematic Theology I*, and in other writings, Tillich had sought the individual psychological quality of religious experience and had found it in what he termed experience of 'ultimate concern'.[7] He also plainly stated that this concept was a secularised formulation of the *Shema* or Great Commandment to love God with *all* of heart, soul and mind. It is the word 'all' which provides the clue to the ultimacy of ultimate concern. The present pertinence of this concept is that ultimate concern (or as I would prefer, the paraphrase 'ultimate valuation') constitutes that aspect of individual or personal experience which claims to be a response to transcendence. A religion may thus in these terms be characterised as a system of symbolic forms for the expression of ultimate concern or valuation.

But if this be the nature of religious experience, how may we order the veritably infinite variety of such forms observable in the wide world and the long course of human history? In answer to this question I propose here a threefold classification based upon the location of the religious object or object of ultimate concern. It may be located (1) within the *cosmos* or common world of nature and society; (2) beyond this common world; or (3) both beyond and within. The three types of religion thus derived may be called (1) cosmic; (2) acosmic; and (3) historical or monotheistic. Elsewhere I have employed this threefold system classification as a device for the classification of the religions of humankind. Here it must suffice to sketch some main features of each of the three types.

In briefest, barest outline, let us note the religious objects – significantly plural – of the cosmic religions. They are more or less personified aspects of nature and/or society, as the gods of Greece, of Rome, of Mesopotamia, of Vedic India and of other ancient civilisations indicate. If one may use the term 'paganism' descriptively and not pejoratively, these are pagan religions. The first (pagan, or cosmic) type is by all odds the most numerous type of religious orientation in human history.

During the period of ancient history sometimes called the 'axis age' there occurred breakthroughs or processes of discontinuous change, from the (1) cosmic orientation to (2) acosmic or (3) historical outlooks. The former took place notably in ancient India in such figures as Mahavira, founder of the Jain tradition, in Buddha, and at least possibly in some of the seers of the Upanishads.

The clearest illustrations of the acosmic type are the Jain tradition, and the Advaita Vedanta tradition of thought and devotion in Hinduism. Speaking generally, this type shows two observable traits, one practical and the other theoretical. First is ascetic practice viewed not as spiritual exercise but as a way of freeing spirit from its prison house in the body. Second is the assertion that the common world of nature and society is 'unreal' – an assertion whose true meaning is a devaluation of the common world.

Again speaking generally, the second or acosmic type of religion is the hardest type for which to find clear instances. This is for the good reason that an acosmic attitude is hard for either an individual or a society to maintain. The common world has a way of reasserting itself in the denials of acosmic religions! Hence we will have to settle for observable *tendencies* of the acosmic kind.

Whatever may be the case with the second or acosmic type of religion, the third type is of all the world the easiest to identify. Indeed I bring up this threefold classification in present context in order to point out the distinguishing features of this third type. Its instances are Judaism, Islam and Christianity. (To this might be added the remainders of Zoroastrianism in the Parsee community of India and the even smaller Gabar Community of Iran.)

We have already noted two distinguishing features of the third type, namely the one God and the clear assertion of false or idolatrous religion. An even clearer distinguishing feature is what may be called a linear–dramatic view of history as extending in a line from creation to judgement day, in contrast to the cyclic views of the first and second types. In this respect, the third type is appropriately called historical religion, though I would add that this historical character is seldom fully realised and developed.

Other distinguishing features of the third type of religion include the concept of revelation, or the asymmetric derivation of truth from God to human selves, and following from this concept of a Book. Still again, these religions find the end or goal of human life not in contemplation but in ethical or social action in the service of God.

The concept of the world as God's creation shows elements of likeness and unlikeness to the first and second types. Unlike the Hindu and Buddhist concepts of the common world as *maya* or *samsara*, the historical or monotheistic religions hold the created world to be both real and 'very good'. In this respect, they resemble the religions of the first or cosmic type. However unlike the first or cosmic type and like the acosmic type, they teach a transcendent reality, in some sense beyond the common world.

In pointing out these distinctive features of the third type of religion let it be clearly added that these are observable factual differences involving no theological judgement about transcendent truth or falsehood, validity or invalidity. In other words, my threefold classification is phenomenological and not theological in character.

V

The last point which I wish to make is that, real and serious as these problems and evils of religion are, there are resources in each of the three monotheistic traditions for coping with the problems and redressing the evils. Let us briefly list some of these resources.

(i) Perhaps first and most basic is a valid perception or understanding of transcendence viewed as the one God. In contrast to all the false absolutisms, an authentic perception of God renders the human condition genuinely open to new truth and compassionate to fellow creatures. Indeed so basic is this assertion that I am inclined to judge the validity of our perception of transcendence by precisely these criteria.

(ii) Correlative with this view of transcendence or God is the human attitude of faith. To be sure, faith is a word of many meanings, some good, some bad, many simply ambiguous. William James once gave a behavioural definition of the root religious meaning, when he called faith a 'tendency to act'. Characterised more fully, it is an attitude of personal trust leading to action. Viewed thus, faith is the basic force making for the inclusive integration of human life, both individual and social. Its fruits are social action to foster justice and ethical love.

(iii) A third (and often overlooked) resource of all three monotheistic faiths is what I shall call their universalism. One of the remarkable aspects of the great prophets of ancient Israel was their argument from one God to one humanity or humankind. We read this revolutionary perception in the biblical prophets from Amos to Deutero-Isaiah. There is a lineal relation, long and at times circuitous but nonetheless continuous, from these ancient writers to the United Nations in our time. One of the significant features of the thought of Jesus of Nazareth, in a time of strong nationalism, was to reach back and reclaim this prophetic heritage of a universal kingdom of God. Similarly too in his time and place, the prophet Mohammad bade his fellow humans to rise above tribalisms to a universal humanity. 'Every Muslim a brother to every other Muslim', declared the Prophet. In our age when we humans have been thrust together as never before in history we need to repeat this ancient argument: 'One God therefore one humanity'. And we need to mean it as never before, for today it is one humanity or none'.

Notes and References

1. H. Frankfort *et al.* *Before Philosophy: The Intellectual Adventure* of *Ancient Man* (Baltimore: Penguin Books, 1971), ch. II, pp. 39ff, see especially pp. 71–2.
2. *Christianity and Crisis*, XIV, (1) (8 February 1954).
3. *Christianity and Crisis* XIX (22) (24 January 1955).
4. Karl Barth, *Church Dogmatics*, I, 2 (Edinburgh: T. & T. Clark, 1956) ch. 17, pp. 280ff.
5. John Baillie, *Our Knowledge of God* (New York: Scribners, 1939) p. 3.
6. Paul Tillich, *Systematic Theology*, III (Chicago: University of Chicago Press, 1963) ch. III, see especially III b, pp. 245ff.
7. See, *inter alia, Systematic Theology*, I, p. 10 *et seq., Systematic Theology*, III, p. 102 *et seq.*

Conclusion: Three Reflections

'Conventional theology assumes that the different religions must necessarily oppose each other . . . But on reaching full maturity the human spirit aspires to rise above every manner of conflict and opposition, and a person then recognises all expressions of the spiritual life as an organic whole . . . There will remain a decided difference in the qualities of the different faiths and in the values of one as compared with another. From the entire ensemble there will automatically become manifest the central essence which is at the heart of all faiths.'

Abraham Isaac Kook, *Talelei Orot* pp. 17ff (*apud* Ben Zion Bokser, *The Jewish Mystical Tradition* (New York: The Pilgrim Press, 1981) p. 266).

'There is but one and the same God who, from the beginning to the end and by various dispensations, comes to the rescue of mankind.'

St Irenaeus, *Adversus Haereses*, III, 12, 13.

'The lamps are different, but the Light is the same: it comes from Beyond.'

Jalālu'l-Din Rūmī, 'The One True Light' (*Math.* III, 1259).

Appendix[1]
Rolf P. Knierim

Our focus on the Old Testament in its own right is, while not exclusive, legitimate. Its legitimacy does not depend on whether the Old Testament should be read together with the New Testament, or whether it should be read by itself before being read with the New Testament. This question should not be determined by an either/or. As long as both testaments are read together eventually, the question of where to start the process of reading is of secondary importance.

However, the claim that the Old Testament is theologically significant only when it is read in light of the New Testament, or of Christ, has imperialistic implications and is theologically counterproductive: it is imperialistic because it censures the Old Testament's theological validity by external criteria; and it is counterproductive because the theological significance of Christ or the New Testament – in as much as the Old Testament has something to do with them – cannot be substantiated with reference to the Old Testament's theological insignificance.

The legitimate focus on the Old Testament in its own right depends on some mutually supportive reasons. *First*, this corpus is claimed by the Jewish as well as by the Christian tradition. The two claims conflict, and an arbitrating third party is not around. It should be clear, at least for the Christians, that an interpretation of their Old Testament must be mindful of that dissensus and therefore rest on the Old Testament itself, and not on their New Testament or an *a priori* combination of both. Such a combination of both testaments on the well-meant assumption by some Christians that Christianity is essentially Jewish because Jesus was a Jew does not stand the test. Jews will recognise no Jewishness of Christianity on the ground of Jesus's Jewishness, rightly so. And for Christians, the condition and ground for the election of all humans into God's kingdom and salvation are not based on the Jewishness of Jesus. Salvation may have come from or through a Jew, but it is not Jewish in nature. Christians owe Jews a great debt indeed, for more than one reason. But Christianity is not essentially Jewish.

The recognition that Jews are no Christians, and by far most of the Christians are no Jews, has nothing to do with racism. It amounts to a mutual recognition of difference. However, the denotation by Christians of the Jewish Bible as their Old Testament must not mean 'passed away, inferior, invalidated, abolished'. It can mean only antecedent to the New Testament historically, even as this antecedence is not the basis for determining the relationship of the two testaments.

Secondly, the Christian tradition has distinguished, in essence, between two testaments in its Bible. Their relationship has been subject to varying and often controversial interpretation. However, each interpretation has always claimed to be legitimate, and not a usurpation or imperialisation of one testament by the other. This claim must be taken seriously. The proper way for the Christian tradition to submit to its standards is to recognise the Old Testament in its own right before its relationship with the New Testament is determined.

Thirdly, there are, in a substantive sense, not only continuity and congruency connecting both testaments but also discontinuity and incongruency separating them. The question is open – and, indeed, undecided – as to which of the testaments interprets which, and what the role of continuity or discontinuity is in such interpretation, or whether any of the two testaments should be at all the basis for the interpretation of the other. This open situation suggests that the case not be prejudged in advance, and that each testament be understood as a whole in its distinctiveness before both are compared.

It is true that the title 'Old Testament' presupposes the 'New Testament' and, hence, the Christian Bible. This fact does not mean, however, that the Old Testament cannot be interpreted in its own right. It means only that the relationship of the two testaments must also be determined. Under discussion is whether this relationship is to be determined prior to and as the basis for, or after and on the basis of, their independent interpretation.

Likewise, nothing is said against the need for a biblical theology. What is emphasised is only that the approach to it must be based on a genuine comparison of the ideologies of the two testaments, for which the independent interpretation of each is at least as viable a starting point as their correlated interpretation from the outset.

Reference

1. From 'The Task of Old Testament Theology', *Horizons in Biblical Theology*, 6 (1) (June 1984) pp. 52–3, n. 1.

Index of Authors

Index of Foreign Language Terms

ARABIC

GREEK

arché 52–3

diabolos 33

logos 198

ousia 203

telos 150

trias 202

HEBREW AND ARAMAIC

Abba 47, 50, 202
Adam 107, 108–9
Adama 108–9
afar 108
aliya 149, 153
'al tiqrē 32
Amida 139
'amîdat ha-zāqēn 32

Baavorecha 110
bal tashchit 131
Bar Mitzvah 12
Bat Mitzvah 12
Benai Adam 107
bikkurim 151
b'rith 182

chadash 151
challah 151
chazakah 149–50
chovot haguf 144
diratam 160
dorotam 160

elohim 8
Eretz Yisrael 138–9, 141, 143–4,
   147–9, 162
even shetiyyah 145

galut 160
geulah 160

haggadah 30–1
halachah 30–1, 77, 83, 141, 182

kedoshim 181
kedushah 149–51
kedushah rishonah 148
kedushah shniyah 148
kibbush 142–3, 148
kilayim 151

le-dorotam 160
leket 151

ma'or 29
maserot 151
Medinat Yisrael 147
mezuzot 144
midrash 20, 135, 141, 144
mishnah 151
mitzvah 142–4, 163
mitzvot 18, 61, 130, 144, 163, 182–3
mitzvot hatluyot ba'aretz 151

ohel 160
Ohel Moed 146
omer 151
orlah 151
ot hi l'olam 160

peah 151

Satan 33
se'or 29
shechinah 149, 159
shelilat hagolah 163
Shema 221
sheviit 151
shikchah 151
sod 144
sod 'adonai 185
sod 'elohîm 185

terfillin 144
terumah 151
Teshuva 109
tikkun olam 182
tiqqun sopherim 32
T'nak 138, 158
tochachah 153
Torah 31
Torah she bĕ 'al peh 31

yhwh 9
Yigdal 29
yishuv 143, 148

Zoreh Gavoha 80

LATIN

OTHER

Index of Textual Citations

TANAKH

NEW TESTAMENT

QUR'AN

RABBINIC TEXTS